GREENWOOD
GUIDES

THE GREENWOOD GUIDE TO
NEW ZEALAND

Fifth Edition 2008/9

hand-picked accommodation
things to do and places to eat

www.greenwoodguides.com

Series Editor Simon Greenwood
Writing collaboration and inspections
Mary Malyon, Anna Stopes
and Simon Greenwood
Maps © Collins Bartholomew Ltd 2008. Reproduced
by permission of HarperCollins
www.collinsbartholomew.com.
Design and layout Tory Gordon-Harris
Printing, Colorcraft, Hong Kong
UK Distribution, Portfolio, London
NZ Distribution, Addenda Publishing Ltd., Auckland

The cover image is courtesy of Balloon Adventures -
Up Up and Away Up, page 205.
Other picture credits are to be found
on the last page of the book.

First published in 2001 by Greenwood Guides,
12 Avalon Rd, London SW6 2EX, UK.

Fifth edition

ISBN 978-0-9551160-5-6

Printed in China through Colorcraft Ltd., Hong Kong.

THE TEAM

Simon Greenwood

Anna Stopes

Mary Malyon

CONTENTS

accommodation

accommodation

SOUTH ISLAND

CONTENTS NORTH ISLAND
things to do and places to eat

CONTENTS NORTH ISLAND

things to do and places to eat

CONTENTS NORTH ISLAND

things to do and places to eat

SOUTH ISLAND

CONTENTS SOUTH ISLAND

things to do and places to eat

CONTENTS SOUTH ISLAND

things to do and places to eat

introduction

Whatever you think of the look of this guide (and we hope that you like it, of course) we know that in the end we will not be judged by the book's cover but by its content. In other words we need to be a major reason why you enjoyed your holiday.

To this end we are particularly fussy about whom we accept into the guide, relying only on our own experience and the recommendations of our trusted accommodation owners. I hope this will become apparent to first-time users of the guide once you hit the road.

Hand-picked Things to do and Places to Eat

The first thing I would like to say is... read the whole book right through (if you've the stomach for it) before setting off on your travels. The guide will throw up all sorts of ideas you might not have considered. It will also introduce you to the best people to do a particular activity with.

We've been driving about in New Zealand for 7 years now, truffling for the best (by which I mean the most friendly and fun) lodges, B&Bs, farm stays, guest-houses and self-catering cottages for our accommodation guide. In the course of these years I have been buttonholed many a time by travellers who complained that if we could provide them with the most interesting places to stay, why could we not stump up the Greenwood Guides take on where to eat and what to do? Well, this is now the second edition that attempts to do just that. Our selection of hand-picked restaurants, wineries and activities starts on page 94.

What we wanted at the outset was a new kind of guide-book that showcased genuinely exciting things to do and places to eat, rather than exhaustively listing a bewildering series of possibilities accounting for all ages and tastes... and leaving you to take pot luck.

The common denominator for all entries has always been the positive attitude of the owners or staff. We are looking for people who enjoy what they do, but who also take genuine pleasure in looking after their customers. This is our approach with the accommodation section, and we have applied exactly the same philosophy (a grand word I know!) to restaurants, cafés, wineries, tour guides, jet-boat operators, caving experts, bird-watching enthusiasts etc. The lists of Things we Like and Things we Don't Like on the back cover sums up our prejudices as neatly as we know how.

What do the Things to do and Places to Eat Sections Contain?
We have researched and divided the book up into the following main categories:
Food and Drink:
Restaurants, cafés, bars, delis and wineries. All are atmospheric, with genuinely friendly waiting staff. We have leant towards small, family-run places in interesting or sensational settings... but always making sure that good food is a given. If you are ever disappointed we would like to be told.
Nature and Activities:
This includes hiking, bird-watching, dolphin-watching, gardens, nature reserves etc. These include many fun things to do with the kids, and exciting things to do for the young at heart, such as micro-lighting, helicopter and small aircraft trips, bungy

jumps, horse-riding, quad-biking, river trips (both tranquil and not so tranquil), caving, diving... the list goes on.

Guides, Tours and Experts:

There are also many guides throughout the book who can take you on tours, treks or excursions. They are usually very small outfits, often just one-man bands. They are all people who mix high levels of expertise in their various fields (birds, walks, flora and fauna, wine, history, yacht trips, fishing etc) with great charisma.

Culture and History:

Museums, architecture, heritage houses, history tours, etc.

The key to enjoying these activities successfully is the person that organises them for you. We have only included highly recommended outfits, which have been tried and tested many times with reliably good reports.

Who is the Guide Aimed at?

Anyone looking for a unique personal experience from their holiday, who is prepared to leave the beaten track... but would rather not at the same time sacrifice too much on creature comfort. We put a great deal of emphasis on the charm of the people that are behind each entry, whether it be a restaurant or a walking guide. You can find both cheap and expensive restaurants run by relaxed and amusing people. So long as a place sees hospitality as its real goal then our radar starts to bleep.

If this approach appeals then the book is for you. The guide is not really aimed at backpackers for whom cheapness is paramount... or at 'high-rollers' for whom expensiveness is paramount!

We have taken the view that you are better served by a limited number of great options, than by an exhaustive list of ALL the options. We have done the hard work for you, and as with our accommodation, pared down the range of possibilities to just those that you can rely on.

Kids

Any activity that we feel is child-friendly we have given the following symbol ![kids symbol]. You will see from the index at the back of the book that children are pretty well catered for in the guide, although we have tried to include only activities and restaurants that will appeal to both parents and their offspring. I would welcome any reports on this issue from parents (or kids I suppose!). The index lists all the entries suitable for kids under their relevant area.

Doubling up

Places that appear in both sections of the guide, for example they run both a restaurant and also a lodge, have been given the following symbol ![symbol].

Golf

New Zealand is apparently the country with the most golf courses per capita... although it is not a country with a very large population one has to concede! But every area has great courses to play on and overseas visitors are always delighted with the excellent value for money. Green fees on rural courses average $25 - $35 but can be as low as $15... while even top courses are only around $65. Even the properly expensive ones like Kauri Cliffs ($300 - $400 for overseas player) are so amazing that they are well worth the money.

introduction

New Zealand and The Greenwood Guide to Hand-picked Accommodation

The Creator seems to have had a soft spot for New Zealand. It doesn't matter where in the country you go. All His (or Her!) state-of-the-art, top-of-the-range showpiece scenery items are on display: bays sprinkled with islands, snow-capped volcanoes, bright blue mountain lakes, sea cliffs and rocky coves, rivers and waterfalls in semi-tropical rainforest, white-sand beaches, ancient and giant trees, green grassy hills that suddenly plummet into river gorges. And so it goes on. The landscape is relentlessly awe-inspiring.

And yet the place isn't crawling with tourists like you'd think it would be. It's too far away for most Europeans. If these islands were found in the Mediterranean, you can be sure they would not be the Utopian travel destination that they are today. If you want to share some of the world's most varied and beautiful scenery with just a handful of film crews... and at the same time enjoy highly sophisticated levels of comfort and hospitality... AND, most vitally of all, be looked after by genuinely friendly, well-travelled, humorous, down-to-earth hosts, then you're going to have to travel further than most people can be bothered. New Zealand's remoteness is precisely what keeps it precious.

It's simplicity itself to hire a car and drive around under your own steam. All you really need is someone to tell you the most exciting and friendly places to stay. Enter triumphantly the Greenwood Guide to New Zealand....

This is now the fifth edition so we are really pretty clued up about places to stay in New Zealand. We have made several hundred visits over the years and have whittled down the final entries to 93, evenly spread across both islands (actually three islands including Kawau).

We have found extraordinary places to stay at all levels of the price spectrum, except the extravagantly expensive (which you can certainly find in NZ) and the suspiciously cheap. Great accommodation is not defined by how much you pay and what you get for your money. It is a complex compound of atmosphere, location, creature comfort and human interaction. We gravitate towards places that have something I'm going to call 'soul', like it or not.

Our natural biases often lean towards the lived-in feel, artistic inclination, creative design, historical interest... but only if these qualities are backed up by owners who have a real liking for other people and take a real pleasure in looking after them. Only the character and humanity of each place determine its acceptability.

At its simplest the Greenwood Guides approach is to recommend places that we have been to ourselves and particularly liked.

This is not a full-blown directory of accommodation therefore. You will often be disappointed if you expect to find a Greenwood place in a particular town. Not every town has great places to stay. The book is designed to be followed as a guide book. Stay in our places as destinations in themselves and meet lovely, warm, friendly, humorous New Zealanders.

This is not just for self-propelling overseas travellers looking for something a bit magical and different from their holiday. Kiwis will love these places just as much.

Expensive does not Mean Good

There are essentially three types of place to stay. There are those that fulfil their obligations in a commercial way and leave you feeling throughout your stay like the paying customer that you are. And there are those few great places where you are welcomed in and treated as a friend, cliché though this may now have become, and where paying at the end of your visit is a pleasurable surprise. And, of course, there are those places where paying is a disagreeable inevitability!

It is a particular irony of the accommodation world that no price is ever put on the essential qualities of a place – people, atmosphere, charm. These terms are too woolly, perhaps, to quantify, but this is where one's real enjoyment of a place to stay stems from. You are asked to pay instead for tangible facilities like marble bathrooms and en-suite showers.

This is a fallacy that we try to dismantle in all our guides, which is why you will find places at all reasonable price levels. Expensive does not mean good. And nor does cheap, however appealing the word may sound! If a place costs plenty then it will probably offer facilities in keeping with the price. But that does not mean that you will have any fun. Some very expensive places forget that they are providing a service and look down their noses at their own guests. At the other end of the scale, the very cheapest places are often cheap for good reasons. Sometimes for spectacular reasons!

Character and genuine hospitality, the extra qualities we search for, are found spaced evenly across the price spectrum. Nowhere in this guide cuts corners at the risk of your displeasure. We give equal billing to each place we choose, no matter if it is a gorgeous lodge or a home-spun B&B.

At the top end, the most jewel-encrusted, nay 'boutique' places may drip with luxurious trimmings, but have retained their sense of atmosphere and humour, are friendly and informal and are still owned and managed by the same people.

Equally, there are places in the book that do not have much in the way of luxury, but easily compensate with unique settings, wonderful views and charming hosts.

It is the quality of experience that draws us in and this is not determined by how much you pay. In the end I know that you will really like the owners in this book, many of whom we now count as friends. And you will certainly make friends yourselves if you stick to the Greenwood trail.

Driving

One point worth making is that, although this is not the largest country in the world, you can easily underestimate how long it takes to get from A to B (and on to C). This is because: a) many NZ roads twist and wind their way around hills, volcanoes and other mountainous terrain and there's not much anyone can do about that; b) there is a culture of slow driving in NZ, a practice encouraged by conscientious traffic cops; and c) it seems impossible to overtake anyone, despite the small number of cars on the roads. So I recommend you leave lots of time to get where you're going, relax into it and enjoy the impossibly lovely scenery that seems to line every road in the country.

introduction

Car Hire in New Zealand

The best way to see New Zealand is by car. Most of our epic research period in New Zealand was spent behind the wheel of one of About New Zealand's rental cars. We always found them helpful, friendly and great value. They also have bases throughout the country, which is always handy when travelling from point A to point B. About New Zealand Head Office: 33 Iversen Terrace, Christchurch, freephone: 0800-45-55-65, phone: +64 3 3666 094, fax: +64 3 3666 069, email: aboutnz@rentalcar.co.nz.

It is a good idea to book your car hire and accommodation in advance. In peak season both can get booked up very quickly.

Inter-island Ferries

You can fly or ferry between the two islands; both methods are scenic treats. From Picton, Bluebridge and Interlander Ferries take their cargo of cars and passengers out into the Cook Strait, a bright strip of dolphin-filled sea, fringed by the intermittent islands and lush hilly fingers of The Marlborough Sounds. You'll be received at the other end by winking lights and the lively sweeping embrace of Wellington Harbour.
Bluebridge Cook Strait Ferry www.bluebridge.co.nz 04-471-6188.
Interislander Ferry www.interislander.co.nz 04-498-3302.

Directions

We have provided directions, unless a 30-word spiel was unlikely to clarify matters, i.e. if a place is in the middle of a town or city. Most owners can fax detailed maps/ directions or they will have a web site that can help.

Pay for Entry

We could not afford to research and publish this guide in the way we do without the financial support of those we feature. Each place to stay that we have chosen has paid an entry fee for which we make no apology. It has not influenced our decision-making about who is right or wrong for the guide and we turn down many more than we accept. The proof of this is in the proverbial pudding. Use the book and see for yourself. It is also very hard for us to write up a place that we are not enthusiastic about.

Prices and Payment

Prices are quoted in New Zealand dollars per couple sharing per night, unless specifically stated otherwise. Single rates are also given. We have provided a range to allow for expected price increases over two years. There might be unexpected increases if the property changes radically or exchange rates alter, in which case we would ask you to be understanding.

Quite a few places do not accept payment with credit cards – these have a symbol in the book – but may take travellers' cheques or other forms of payment. Again, ask when booking.

Maps

The maps in this book are not road maps, but merely general indicators of where the properties are. You should get a detailed road map when you arrive.

Cancellation

Cancellation policies vary as much as the wallpaper and should be clarified on booking. Many establishments will ask for a credit card number when you book so that they are not wholly compromised if you fail to turn up.

Smoking

It is most unlikely that anyone will want you to smoke indoors.

Telephones

Calling New Zealand from abroad: the international dialling code is 64. So to call New Zealand from Britain, you key 00 64, then the eight-digit phone number.

Disclaimer

We make no claims to god-like objectivity in assessing what is or is not special about the places we feature. They are there because we like them. Our opinions and tastes are mortal and ours alone. We have done our utmost to get the facts right, but apologise for any mistakes that may have slipped through the net. Some things change which are outside our control: people sell up, prices increase, exchange rates fluctuate, unfortunate extensions are added, marriages break up and even acts of God can rain down destruction. We would be grateful to be told about any errors or changes, however great or small. We can always make these edits on the web version of this book.

Please write to us

My email address is **simon@greenwoodguides.com** for all comments. We are always grateful to hear how much/little you enjoyed the places in the book.

We also have guides to Australia, Canada, South African Accommodation (with Mozambique, Namibia, Botswana, Zambia and Zimbabwe) and South African Highlights (Things to Do and Places to Eat). These books are available in bookshops or by emailing us direct.

Our web site address is **www.greenwoodguides.com.**

Finally a big thank-you to Mary (Malyon) and Anna (Stopes). They drove tirelessly all over New Zealand during the four-month research period and it is with a sigh of relief and satisfaction that we finally send the tome off to be printed. You are the happy inheritor of the fruit of their efforts. I am sure you will enjoy your trip.

Simon.

SYMBOLS

and What They Mean

  No credit cards accepted

  There is a restaurant on the premises or meals can be provided

  Rooms all have TV

  Children are welcome without conditions

  Working farm

  Off-street car parking

  Full wheelchair facilities

  Access only for wheelchairs

  Swimming available in pool, sea or river

  No smoking anywhere inside the buildings

  Good walking from the house

  Fishing organised here

Great Walks of New Zealand

The Great Walks are the Department of Conservation's finest walking tracks, through areas of some of the best scenery in the country. With a limit to the number of huts available to trampers, many have booking systems that fill up surprisingly quickly – so book as far ahead as possible to avoid being disappointed! For further information visit www.doc.govt.nz.

Lake Waikaremoana Great Walk, EAST COAST
Magnificent forested scenery and plenty of opportunity for swimming and fishing are great features of this walk.

Tongariro Northern Circuit, CENTRAL PLATEAU
The Tongariro Northern Circuit is a terrific one-day walk. It makes its way over Mt Tongariro and around Mt Ngauruhoe. This track passes through unique and incredible landforms including volcanic craters and stunning glacial valleys.

Whanganui Journey, WANGANUI
The Whanganui River winds its way from the mountains to the Tasman Sea through countless hills and valleys. Lowland forest surrounds the river in its middle and lower reaches - the heart of beautiful Whanganui National Park.

Abel Tasman Coast Track, NELSON
This is a 51km, easy to moderate walk that passes through a gorgeous landscape of coastal forests and golden sandy beaches. All streams are bridged and most people can walk it in 3 - 5 days with plenty of time to explore.

Heaphy Track, NELSON
Crosses a range of landscapes in Kahurangi National Park, from the junction of the Brown and Aorere Rivers, over expansive tussock downs to the lush forests and roaring sea of the West Coast.

Routeburn Track, OTAGO/SOUTHLAND
This famous 32km, 2 - 3 day, moderate tramping track links Mount Aspiring and Fiordland National Parks via the Harris Saddle (1,277m). Waterfalls, forested valleys, rich birdlife, lakes and spectacular mountain scenery make this a real feast of a track.

Milford Track, SOUTHLAND
Described as 'the finest walk in the world', the track extends for 54km from the northern end of Lake Te Anau, to Sandfly Point near Milford Sound. It is renowned for its glacially carved valleys, alpine flowers and waterfalls.

Kepler Track, SOUTHLAND
A 60km, moderate walk that takes 3 - 4 days to complete. It traverses lake edges, beech forest, alpine mountaintops and a splendidly U-shaped glacial valley.

Rakiura Track, SOUTHLAND
This 29km, 3-day tramping track is suitable for anyone with moderate fitness. It's positioned in a remote part of the already remote wilderness of Stewart Island. It can be walked year round.

And finally, a handful of fantastic tracks that may not be 'Great...' in official DOC-speak, but that we think are great enough for this page:

Distances chart

The maximum speed limit on New Zealand's roads is 100km/hr. Due to its hilly and mountainous terrain, average speeds are lower and it always takes slightly longer than expected to arrive at your destination. All the more reason to relax into your drive and really enjoy the spectacular scenery out of the window.

Distances in kilometres per hour

NORTH ISLAND

From	Gisborne	Hamilton	Kaitaia	Napier	N. Plym	Paihia	Rotorua	Taupo	Tauranga	Waitomo	Wangonui	Well'ton
Auckland	449	127	325	423	357	241	234	280	206	202	457	658
Gisborne		394	823	216	585	739	287	332	298	445	468	538
Hamilton			452	296	231	368	107	153	107	75	331	532
Kaitaia				748	681	108	558	602	531	524	779	983
Napier					412	661	225	143	299	307	252	323
N. Plym						597	299	296	308	173	160	355
Paihia							474	518	445	440	697	898
Rotorua								80	86	166	309	460
Taupo									156	163	229	380
Tauranga										151	439	545
Waitomo											273	473
Wangonui												195

SOUTH ISLAND

From	Christ'ch	Dunedin	Fr Josef	Grey'th	Inv'gill	M. Cook	Nelson	Picton	Q'town	Te Anau	Wanaka	Westport
Blenheim	321	683	520	331	899	651	117	29	808	971	749	265
Christ'ch		361	408	255	578	330	417	350	487	650	428	336
Dunedin			570	565	217	319	799	711	281	289	276	670
Fr Josef				189	542	506	485	549	365	539	294	294
Grey'th					731	524	296	360	554	728	483	105
Inv'gill						445	1016	928	189	159	248	836
M. Cook							747	680	271	426	212	629
Nelson								113	850	1024	779	230
Picton									837	1000	778	294
Q'town										166	71	659
Te Anau											245	823
Wanaka												588

To an English ear it sounds as if the Kiwi vowels have been shuffled: 'a' becomes 'e', 'e' becomes 'i', 'i' becomes 'u' and u seemingly disappears. If you're after a pen, ask for a pin; if you actually needed a pin ask for a pun.

Although we generally speak the same language I came across plenty of Kiwi-isms. Here's a quick translation of just a few.

Bach – a small holiday home.
Dairy – A corner shop that stocks most essential supplies
Kia ora – hello.
Going bush – Taking yourself off into the wilderness and getting away from it all.
Gummies – Wellington boots.
Lux – a vacuum cleaner.
Pakeha – a non-Maori.
Sammie – a sandwich.
She'll be right – It'll work out fine.
Tiki tour - a scenic route or tour.
Tramping – hiking.

And some food items...

Anzac biscuits - a wartime biscuit that has stuck. They're made out of oats, coconut and treacle and contain no egg.
Chocolate fish – choc-covered fish-shaped marshmallows. These tasty treats are often given as a reward hence the saying, "you've earned a chocolate fish."
Hangi - a Maori meal of meat and root vegetables that's cooked underground over hot stones.
Hokey pokey – honeycomb. You'll often see 'hokey pokey ice cream' and 'hokey pokey chocolate.'
Kumera – sweet potato.
Pav – or '**Pavlova**', which you're probably familiar with. The Kiwis have made this pudding of meringue, fresh fruit and cream their own and you will come across it everywhere. They like to serve it with kiwi fruit.
Pies – Okay, so you know what a pie is, but New Zealand really do excel when it comes to pies and fillings. Chicken satay and possum were my favourite.
Pipis and **pipi fritters** – these are small clam-like shellfish that are dug up on the Northland beaches at low tide. The meat is often made into fritters.
Whitebait fritters – a battered ball of whitebait.
Vegemite – A milder version of marmite, you're likely to enjoy one or the other. I hate both.

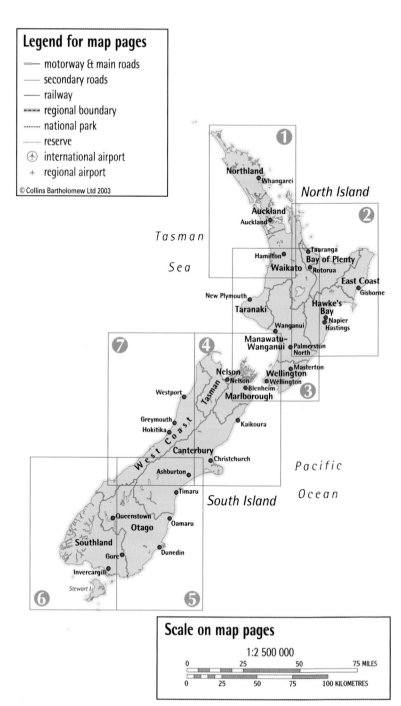

Legend for map pages

- motorway & main roads
- secondary roads
- railway
- regional boundary
- national park
- reserve
- ⊕ international airport
- ✈ regional airport

© Collins Bartholomew Ltd 2003

North Island

1

Northland
● Whangarei

Tasman

Auckland
● Auckland

Sea

❷

Hamilton ●
● Tauranga
Bay of Plenty
Waikato ● Rotorua

East Coast
● Gisborne

New Plymouth ●
Taranaki
Hawke's Bay
● Napier
Wanganui ● ● Hastings

Manawatu-Wanganui
● Palmerston North

❼

❹

Masterton ●

Nelson
● Nelson
Wellington
● Wellington

Westport ●
Tasman
● Blenheim
Marlborough

❸

Greymouth ●
Hokitika ●
West Coast
● Kaikoura

Canterbury
● Christchurch

Pacific

Ashburton ●

Ocean

● Timaru

South Island

Queenstown ●
Otago
● Oamaru

Southland
Gore ●
● Dunedin

Invercargill ●

Stewart I.

❻

❺

Scale on map pages

1:2 500 000

| 0 | 25 | 50 | 75 MILES |

| 0 | 25 | 50 | 75 | 100 KILOMETRES |

Accommodation entry numbers are flagged in red.

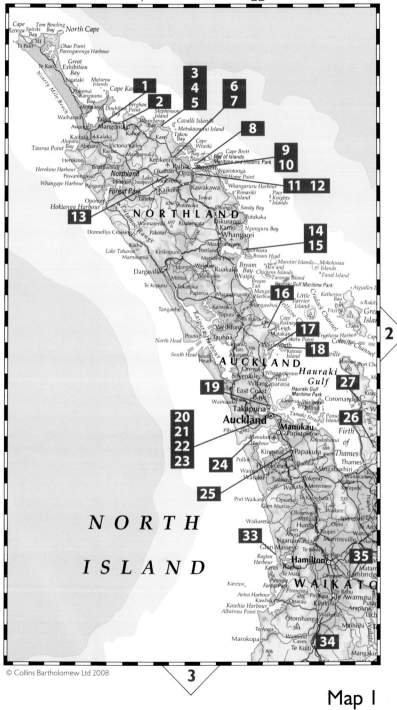

Map 1

© Collins Bartholomew Ltd 2008

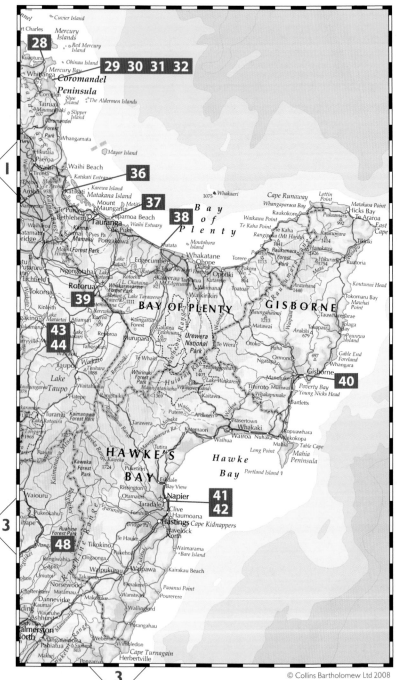

Map 2

© Collins Bartholomew Ltd 2008

© Collins Bartholomew Ltd 2008

Map 3

Map 4

© Collins Bartholomew Ltd 2008

Map 5

Map 6

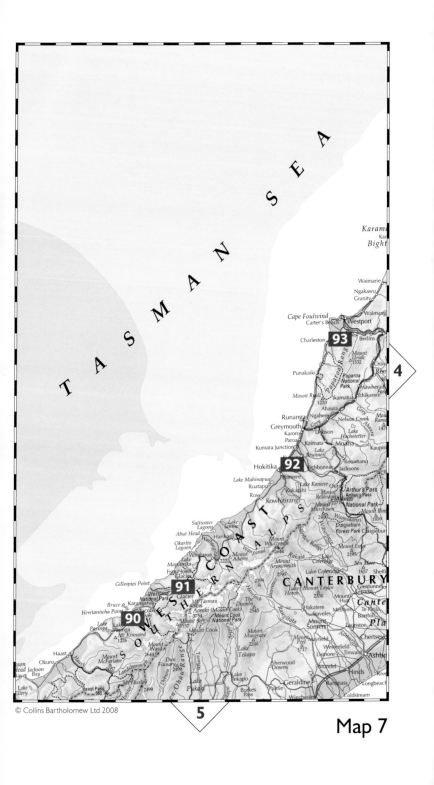

TASMAN SEA

Karame
Kar
Bight

Waimarie
Ngakawu
Granity
Waimang

Cape Foulwind Westport
Carter's Beach
Charleston **93** Berlins

Mount
Uriah
1532 Cron
Ree

4

Punakaiki Paparoa
National
Park Mawhera
For

Mount Ryall Ikamatua Hukarere
1220
Ahaura

Runanga Ngahere Nelson Creek Mou
Greymouth Grey Rame
Karoro Dobson Lake
Paroa Hochstetter
Kaimata Moana
Kumara Junction Lake
Brunner Kapuni
Rotomanu
Jacksons
Hokitika **92** chbonnie
Kaniere

Lake Mahinapua Lake Kaniere Otira Arthur's Pass
Ruatapu Kokatahi Mount Arthur's Pass
Ross Rolleston *2920* National Park
Kowhitirangi Mount
Murchison Mount Bins
Saltwater Lake *2400* *1859*
Lagoon Ianthe
Abut Head Harihari Craigieburn
Okarito Forest Park Craigieburn
Lagoon Mount
Whataroa Whitcombe Lake
Whataroa Mount *2644* Rakaia *2195*
Mapourika Adams Mount
Franz Josef Arrowsmith Lake
Glacier *2795* Coleridge Ben More
Gillespies Point **91** *2399* **CANTERBURY** *1657* Sheff
Westland Glacier Lake Coleridge Gleni
National Park Mt Tasman The Mount *2330*
Bruce Bay Karangarua *222* Mount Cook Thumbs Hakatere
Heretaniwha Point Jacobs Aoraki (Mount Cook) *2545* Methven Te Kite
Lake **90** *3754* Mount Staveley Barrhill
Paringa Mapaura Mount Sefton Harper Mount Lauriston Pla
Mt Kinnard Mount Cook Somers
National Park Mayfield
Okuru Mount Mount Cook Mount Westerfield Chertsey
Haast Ward Musgrave Peel Tinwald
McFarlane *2246* *1717* Lismore Ashb
Jackson *4444* Dun Lake Sherwood Winchmore
Head Haast Fianau Tekapo Downs Arundel
Bay Jackson *2499* Lake Hinds
Bay Landsborow's Tekapo Geraldine Coldstream
Lake Haast Pass Mt Huxley Pukaki Burkes Rangitata Longbeach
Ellery *563* Hunter *2499* Pass Fairlie Winchester

SOUTHERN ALPS

SOUTHER N COAST

Ben Ohau Range

Tasman

5

© Collins Bartholomew Ltd 2008

Map 7

Macrocarpa Cottage

Jamie and Sara Rogers
2 Bush Point Road, Taipa, Mangonui
Tel: 09-406-1245
Email: maccotage@xtra.co.nz
Web: www.holidayhouses.co.nz/properties/1515.asp

The best place to laze around inside is on the window-seat in the corner - you can watch the fish swim by below. Macrocarpa is heavenly. Jamie built it from scratch and the deck hangs out over the Taipa River as it turns left past the sand spit and spills into Doubtless Bay. The view stretches up to Tokerau beach on the Karikari Peninsula about ten kilometres away and a wall of glass in the downstairs bedroom means you don't have to get out of bed for it. If you do make it to a vertical position, roll ten metres down to the shore and swim in crystal clear water when the tide is in. The cottage is spic and span, simply furnished and flooded with light. It's all open-plan, with a good queen-size bed, a sitting area, a kitchen downstairs and a twin-bedded room in the loft. Jamie and Sara are young, mellow and know all the best spots in the area, including deserted beaches of silica sand – probably the best in New Zealand - and mangrove swamps. Jamie not only managed to talk to me, but he also got dinner ready for his in-laws and entertained his children, all at the same time and with no apparent effort. This relaxed attitude has spread to the cottage and I challenge you not to feel supremely zoned-out by the time you leave.

Rooms: 1 cottage with 1 double and 1 twin sharing a shower room.
Price: $120 - $150. Extra adults $20, kids $10.
Meals: Self-catering.
Directions: West through Cable Bay on SH10. Up hill to Taipa, then down hill with estuary on right. Cottage on right and signed, but turning impossible, so pass and do a U-turn.

Beach Lodge

Margaret Morrison
Mangonui Far North
Tel: 09-406-0068 Fax: 09-406-0068
Email: margaret@beachlodge.co.nz Web: www.beachlodge.co.nz

One of Margaret's guests, an ambassador to New Zealand, was overjoyed to have foun 'paradise' here at Beach Lodge. This is not faint praise considering that he was sent from Braz Approaching in my car it took only a fleeting glimpse to see exactly what he meant. Fringed by th crimson trail of blossoming pohutukawa trees, with soft waves gently licking the shore, the lodg presides over the most exquisitely golden and deserted sands I had come across in NZ. Set ju above the trees each apartment has a large deck from which to gaze to the shore and you ar just a few steps away from making the beach your own. In true pioneering spirit, Margare returned from her travels some years ago to find her plot and build her bach. Bright and oper plan with high ceilings and big french windows that encourage the sea breeze in and swirl around, the apartments are places for easy holiday living. One minute you'll be on the kitche barstools dangling your legs and eating lunch and the next you'll have jumped back in your kaya and be paddling offshore. I loved the recent addition with its rustic whitewashed finishes ar kaleidoscope of bathroom mirrors for those 'are there really seven of me or did I have one to many gins at sundown?' moments. Best of all is Margaret herself, a spirited lady and a no-nonsens *bon viveur.* She knows all the special spots in this largely - and thankfully - undiscovered part of th North Island. *Golf, boats and personalised trips to Cape Reinga can be organised from here. W broadband.*

Rooms: 5 self-contained apartments: 4 with I quee and I twin and a shared shower; I with I queen and en-suite shower.
Price: $195 - $450 per lodge per night.
Meals: Fully self-catering.
Directions: From Auckland take SH1 north to Whangarei. Continue along SH1 to Kawakawa, then turn L keeping on same highway. Turn R onto SH 10 towards Bay of Islands and Doubtless Bay. Go past turn-off to Mangonui. Beach Lodge is on beachfront 1km from the Coopers Beach sign.

Waiwurrie

Vickie and Rodger Corbin

Mahinepua Bay, Whangaroa
Tel: 09-405-0840 Fax: 09-405-0854
Email: info@coastalfarm-lodge.co.nz Web: www.coastalfarm-lodge.co.nz
Cell: 021-186-7900

Firstly, because I know you want to know, Waiwurrie is not a real Maori word. It reflects Rodger and Vickie's philosophy and once you get there you will see what they mean. From the lawn in front of the house we surveyed the stupendous view, which looks down to the horseshoe of Mahinepua Bay just below. The hills of the Mahinepua Peninsula that curl round its far shore beg to be explored so backpack a picnic (which can be provided by Vickie) and take a full day over it. The whole area is a natural playground. Waiwurrie itself is a 1200-acre farm with fantastic walks across the hills from the house to its own private beach. Yachting and sea-kayaking can be arranged, while boat and game fishing is available on site. So once you've done all that, flop back at Waiwurrie where you will shortly feel like part of the furniture. Both bedrooms have great showers and beds; upstairs has the best view, downstairs its own direct access to the garden. And there are always fresh flowers. You should choose Waiwurrie for an informal New Zealand experience, where chatty, fun dinners or barbecues are taken with a complimentary bottle of wine. The area is a golfing Mecca by the way. *Kauri Cliffs is 10km away.*

Rooms: 2: 1 king with en-suite shower; 1 superking/twin with private shower.
Price: $425 - $520 for dinner, bed and breakfast.
Meals: Full breakfast and dinner (and complimentary bottle of wine) included. Lunches and packed lunches can be arranged.
Directions: SH10 from Kerikeri north for 18.8km to Matauri Bay Tourist Route. Right here, 14.4km, L at Matauri Bay intersection. Follow 7km, turn R at Mahinepua Rd. Down hill, R before bridge. At Ronaki electric gates, ask for code when booking. House 2nd drive on R.

Crab Cove

Dave Crabb

Mahinepua Rd, Mahinepua Peninsula
Tel: 09-405-0075 Fax: 09-405-1176
Email: crabcove@xtra.co.nz Web: www.waterfrontretreat.co.nz
Cell: 021-804-889

Dave has created this cave-cottage mainly, I think, because he wanted to see the look on your face when you arrive. The cottage is literally woven into the hillside, the roof covered with grass. The 'cave mouth' opens onto a deck where two chairs have been placed as if with tweezers. Another few yards and you'd be plummeting down the cliff to your own rocky cove below. There is a path that descends more gently, if more slowly. The cove, leaned over by old pohutukawa trees clutching the cliff-face with talon-like roots, has kayaks for exploring the nearby sea-caves. Or one of Dave's great pleasures is to take guests out diving or crayfish-hunting. Dave's many hats of expertise include that of master-builder/architect…but he was also no less than NZ skateboard champion. If a thing's worth doing….The cottage is a single open-plan room with a low bed looking straight out to sea. There is a blue-glass shower behind the scenes, a sauna and up in the hills a private spa pool. Small bottles of champagne sit in the fridge alongside the excellent breakfast provisions. If you can book Crab Cove stay as long as you can. No wife/husband/partner will be able to repay you elsewhere without spending their life savings. Simple yet sensational. (The instinct to call it The Crabb Cave of Crab Cove must have been hard to resist!)

Rooms: 1 cottage with king, en-suite shower and sauna.
Price: $350.
Meals: Breakfast basket provided.
Directions: From Kerikeri 40 mins. 18.8km north of Keri' turn R, Matauri Bay. After 14.4km L signed Te Ngaere Bay – follow for 7km. R at Mahinepua Rd, over bridge and then immediately L. Electric gates, ask for code when booking. 300m turn R past Privat Property sign.

Huntaway Lodge

Diane and David Lennan

1692 Wainui Rd, Te Ngaere Bay, Kaeo
Tel: 09-405-1611 Fax: 09-405-1612
Email: info@huntawaylodge.com Web: www.huntawaylodge.com

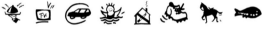

Huntaway Lodge is small and superb, perched on a hillside with a wide balcony-deck overlooking two pristine wine-glass bays and the Cavalli Islands beyond. There is, in fact, an even better beach out of view below the house. Recently designed, modern comforts are in plentiful supply: hidden TVs, personal CD players and a companion library of CDs, ceiling fans, heated floors and towel rails et al. There are as many extras as you can think up without being ridiculous: chocolates and port in bedrooms, boogie-boards, kayaks, towels for the beach, shampoos, soaps in the fantastic green bathrooms. The rooms have french doors out to tables on private areas of the deck where you will linger under parasols with a bottle of wine before dinner… or perhaps all day. Dinners are taken round one huge table and served from the kitchen behind the bar, a giant slab of macrocarpa with corks resin-sealed into its natural knotholes. Cuisine is tailored to suit guests' tastes and dietary requirements. The central guest area is a high, breezy space with comfy sofas, games to play….The aim is to allow you the feeling that this is your private house, but to provide excellent personal service with it.

Rooms: 5: 3 queens, 2 kings all with en-suite shower.
Price: $495 - $695. Room rates only.
Meals: Full breakfast included. Dinners $90 p.p. (3 courses and pre-dinner nibbles). There is a wine list.
Directions: SH10 from Kerikeri north for 18.8km to Matauri Bay Tourist Rte. R here, 14.4km, L at Matauri Bay intersection. Follow Wainui Rd 5km, thro' Te Ngaere Bay, 600m after 100 kmph sign turn L thro' gates behind Huntaway Lodge sign.

Stone Store Lodge

Richard Miller
201 Kerikeri Road, Kerikeri
Tel: 09-407-6693 Fax: 09-407-6693
Email: richard@stonestorelodge.co.nz Web: www.stonestorelodge.co.nz
Cell: 027-233-0602

Though many guesthouses like to promote themselves as 'a home away from home', very few actually are. And so it was with no little delight that while rootling around in Kerikeri for GG gems I unearthed Stone Store Lodge, a clear exception to the rule. Clearly not a man to shy away from a challenge, Richard sold his farm to spend a couple of years sailing the high seas in the South Pacific, and then when the time was right, he returned to shore, trading water for a patch of land on which to build himself a lodge. And here it is, teetering on the hillside behind town looking out over sub-tropical native bush to Kerikeri's famed historic Stone Store by the watery inlet below. Glimpses of Richard's former life are framed on the walls in daughter Lucy's fantastic photographs, an exotic mix of colour and cultures and endless points of conversation. Purposefully designed for privacy and utmost comfort, the rooms, like the rest of the house, are beautifully presented and elegantly ethno-chic, with huge walk-in showers, flowers by the bed and floor-to-ceiling windows to soak up the early morning sunshine that pours down the leafy valley. You'll have the run of the house with its many spots inside and out to sit and linger and there's even an old piano in the corner. This is a happy, family-run place where you'll be fed (Lucy's breakfasts are divine) and entertained by hosts so charming that packing to leave is a dire business performed with reluctant step and a heavy heart! *Wireless broadband*.

Rooms: 3: all kings with en-suite showers.
Price: $175 - $230.
Meals: Full breakfast included. Home wood-fired pizzas for dinner by prior arrangement $35pp.
Directions: From SH10, pass through Kerikeri. Just before St James's Church and the Historic Stone Store, the lodge is sign-posted on the right.

North Island - Northland

Bed of Roses

Louisa and Cliff Hobson-Corry

165 Kerikeri Road, Kerikeri
Tel: 09-407-4666
Email: bedofroses@xtra.co.nz Web: www.bedofroses.co.nz
Cell: 0274-949-062

Freshly-brewed coffee and a home-baked chocolatey delight in hand, I squidged into the comfy cream sofa and listened to Louisa as she reeled off their legendary breakfast menu. As delicious as it is elaborate, everything is home-made from the bread and the blueberry muffins to the pancakes with berries and passion fruit curd, all served out on the terrace with panoramic views to the hills and woods just outside town. As the name suggests, everything here is designed for your sheer comfort and delight. Great beds, crisp white linens and fluffy towels are the guest stars in elegant rooms full of country-style French antiques, gorgeous old oak chests, Liberty prints and flowers. Kerikeri is a charming little town, the historic 'cradle of the nation' and full of bountiful orchards and greenery, evident in their tropical-flavoured garden, which yes, does have a bed or two of roses that are set among other flowery treasures brought over by early settlers. It's only a short walk to the shops and cafés or to the picturesque river basin with its yachts, historic buildings and Maori heritage. Enjoy this place for as long as you can - a stay away from home will not find you in safer, more hospitable hands than these. The Hobson-Corrys are consummate hosts and it is a pleasure to welcome them back both to the North Island and to this guide.

Rooms: 3: 1 king and 1 queen both with en-suite showers. The Monet Suite has 1 queen with en-suite bathroom, living room and cooking facilities.
Price: $275 - $295 for rooms in house. Monet Suite is $325 for 2 pp and $50 per head above 2, not exceeding 4 in total.
Meals: Full breakfast included.
Directions: From Whangarei take SH1 north to Pakaraka. Turn right onto SH10 and travel 18km. Then turn right onto the Kerikeri Road. Bed of Roses is at the end of the village on the right past the Northland Technical Institute.

Map Number 1

Entry Number 7

Hardings' Aotearoa Lodge

Dulcie, Kate and Lindsay Hyland

39 Aucks Rd, Russell
Tel: 09-403-7277 Fax: 09-403-7277
Email: info@the-lodge.co.nz Web: www.the-lodge.co.nz
Cell: 0274-738-170

The lodge is known locally as the English House, largely I suspect, because it is a lot easier pronounce than Hardings' Aotearoa. I certainly felt very *chez moi* coming up the drive - althou one is reminded, by the call of a kiwi breaking the nocturnal silence, and by those olive tre fringing the slopes above the driveway, that this is certainly not Kent. Gardens and 220 acres farmland surround the house, which is sandwiched between sea and hills. I would have se Suffolk sheep in the paddock, but unfortunately they were away for shearing. I stayed in t house, in a huge bedroom tucked up under the eaves, fittingly furnished with country-style line antique furniture, large wardrobes and personal fridges. A guest lounge with armchairs, stereo a large balcony offers private space and sea views. At the bottom of the drive Brook Barn has be converted into two luxurious suites beneath ancient-looking gnarled trees dripping with liche Dulcie is an artist and a potter (her studio is out in the yard) and the main house and Brook Ba are both filled with lovely local artwork (some of it Dulcie's) and other objects. I loved the brig aquatic scenes in the suites and Dulcie's butterfly vases in the main house. Breakfast was a gre spread. I tucked into Kate's eggs Benedict - eggs and spinach "grown" themselves - with relis For a guaranteed purple moment sink into the hot tub, which sits with a sauna at the foot of t hills that back onto the property, and accompanied by the baa of the sheep become either vaca or pensive. *No dogs or cats - kiwis in residence!*

Rooms: 3: 1 queen room with en-suite shower an access to guest lounge; 2 superking/twin singles with en/s shower in Brook Barn.
Price: $195 - $285. Singles $185 - $250.
Meals: Full breakfast included.
Directions: Ferry across from Opua ($19 return, 7am - 10pm, every 10 minutes, no booking required). Follow road to Russell, and lodge is 4km along on the right, signposted.

Chalet Romantica

Inge and Ed Amsler
6 Bedggood Close, Paihia, Bay of Islands
Tel: 09-402-8270 Fax: 09-402-8278 Email: info-chalet@xtra.co.nz
www.chaletromantica.homestead.com/accom1.html
Cell: 027-226-6400

I don't think I can remember a place that offers so much for so little and I'm going to have to hurry along to mention everything. Chalet Romantica marches into this book simply for Ed and Inge whose warm natures and dedication to their guests mean the battle is won before the warships set sail. Bedrooms all have sea-facing balconies, firm beds, crisp linen, strong massage showers with adjustable heads, fridge, music-player, microwave, dial-out phone, TV, VCR, bathrobes, small bottle of bubbly, fresh flowers. Breakfast is Swiss-style which means soft-boiled eggs, muesli, cheese, yoghurt, different types of bread… but less Swissish dishes like eggs Benedict or bacon and eggs are also on the cards. There is a small swimming pool inside the house with an exerjet system that drives a current against which you can swim for fitness. They have "a bit of a farm" with goats and two acres of land and you can walk from the house into the bush. They have a restaurant in town. And, best till last, Ed runs a beautiful 42-ft yacht as a private charter for guests to explore the Bay of Islands, a highlight of many people's trips to New Zealand. No corners are cut here, proper meals provided, so too bottles of good New Zealand wine. One of the most impressive B&Bs I've ever visited and extraordinary good value. More is more.

Rooms: 3: 2 king suites with kitchen-lounge and en/s shower; 1 queen with private shower.
Price: $145 - $285. Singles on application. You can book the rooms without breakfast for $15 less per person.
Meals: Swiss-style breakfast included. They also have their own restaurant, The Swiss Café in town, but you are under no pressure to eat there!
Directions: From Opua 5km towards Paihia down hill, turn L into McMurray Rd, then 1st L into Bedggood Close, opposite the tennis courts.

Decks of Paihia B&B

Phillip and Wendy Hopkinson

69 School Road, Paihia,
Bay of Islands
Tel: 09-402-6146
Fax: 09-402-6147
Email: info@decksofpaihia.co
Web: www.decksofpaihia.cor
Cell: 021-278-7558

Phil, gregarious and cheerful even after an epic series of flight misadventures the previous nig
escorted me into the upstairs lounge area, and the question at the back of my mind was instar
settled: yes, Decks of Paihia does have a lot of decking. The front of the house is bordered b
long deck that appears to float over the wooded valley stretching down to the sea-shore benea
and ushers into the room a tidal wave of sunlight. On the bottom storey are the guest roor
with their own private decks beside the lawn and swimming pool. Hosts of ceaselessly busy bir
including the striking crimson rosella parrots, live in the surrounding trees. The rooms are bri
and airy, with local artwork and sumptuous bed linen providing splashes of colour. The gu
rooms all have TVs, DVDs, and fridges and in the lounge a collection of elephant-themed ima
and artefacts rather caught my eye. There is also a treadmill in the office space, along wit
computer for guest use, but apparently nobody ever uses it - and why would they? Wendy a
Phil love travelling, swapping stories and relaxing, and they've created a great space for you to
all three in, with no more effort than a gentle stroll… and perhaps the occasional bend of t
drinking elbow.

Rooms: 3: all superkings with en/s bathroom with shower.
Price: $145 - $220.
Meals: Full breakfast included.
Directions: From Opua 5km towards Paihia dowr
hill, turn L onto School Road. Decks of Paihia is
number 69.

Crow's Nest Villas

Marj Browning (Manager)
20 Sir George Back Street, Opua, Bay of Islands
Tel: 09-402-7783   Fax: 09-402-7783
Email: marj@vivid.net.nz   Web: www.crowsnest.co.nz
Cell: 027-210-5242

With the Bay of Islands spread out beneath me, I counted the twinkling lights of the boats bobbing on the waters below the verandah at Crow's Nest Villas, and couldn't imagine a nicer place to loiter as the twilight deepened. High on the hill above Opua harbour, the villas have spectacular views of the whole bay area. Both are immaculately presented with a nautical theme throughout that leaves you feeling refreshed rather than slightly queasy. There are ropes at the entrance, portholes for windows and even a 'welcome aboard' sign by the front door. The bedrooms are wrapped around with huge, unfolding French windows that face out into the blue and each has a glass wall to separate the en-suite bathrooms so that you can gaze out to the ocean as you wash. I could happily picture myself here padding around barefoot on the smooth qwilla-wood floors, flitting somewhere between the huge, comfy decks, open-planned living spaces and the beach down below. Added to all this, Marj is a delightful and naturally caring person and is always at the ready to help with any queries. This is a great holiday pad that has all the necessaries, including TV, internet, breakfast provisions and a complimentary bottle of wine, to make you feel right at home... but on holiday.

Rooms: 2 villas: Sails Villa has 1 queen and 1 twin both with en/s shower; Bridge Deck has 2 queens both with en/s shower.
Price: $225 - $575. Maximum 5 guests per villa.
Meals: Complimentary Continental breakfast provisions on 1st morning. Other mornings by arrangement.
Directions: Ask when booking.

The Boathouse

Angie Kyriak
5 Beechy St, Opua
Tel: 09-402-6800; freephone in NZ 0800-683-722
Email: info@theboathouseopua.com Web: www.theboathouseopua.com

This building has had a checkered career, but today it is the coolest of wharf conversions, mo boat than house, water constantly lapping beneath its prow. The Boathouse is supported on pol in the Opua Harbour, next to the Russell ferry jetty so you can watch the boats come and from your huge deck with its glass and metal rail (last boat at 10 p.m.). You can even fish from t deck of the lower apartment, The Landing. The two apartments sit one above the other, simi in style, although there seemed to be even more space in the topmost living area, The Bridg perhaps because the entire front wall slides away making the deck an extension of the room itse The interiors are state-of-the-art, chic, shiny-new, lots of blue and glass, the nautical theme sub and atmospheric (rather than obvious and annoying). And the kitchens have everything, includi ice-makers. Basics like milk, tea and coffee, olive oil, washing powder etc are all provided, so you need are the main food items and away you go. Right next door, by the way, are the Op General Store which has a great bakery, and a restaurant. Other mod cons are a full entertainme system, washing-machines, air-conditioning and wireless broadband. You will live luxuriously w at The Boathouse and all the boat and bird activity make its unique position in the heart of t harbour fascinating.

Rooms: 2 flats: The Landing has two double rooms The Bridge above has one double room with en-su shower and one office with fold-out bed.
Price: $550 (1st Oct – 1st April) for either apartment. $385 off-season. $100 surcharge from 1 December to 15th January.
Meals: Self-catering. Meals can be provided by pric arrangement.
Directions: Right next to the car ferry in Opua. C from Kawakawa to alert the owners of your arrival.

Ludbrook House

Sam and Christine Ludbrook
7491 SH1, Ohaeawai, Bay of Islands
Tel: 09-405-9846 Fax: 09-405-9845
Email: ludbrook@xtra.co.nz Web: www.ludbrook.co.nz

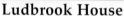

Ludbrook is in Sam's blood. His great-great-grandfather first came here in 1823 (having fought alongside Nelson at Trafalgar) and for over 140 years the Ludbrooks of Ludbrook House have run cattle and sheep on their 1000 acres. It is 'back-of-the-hand' country to them and they will lead interested guests to its many secrets: *pa* sites (fortified dwellings), archaeological remains, burial mounds, then deep into the native bush itself. Roger (Sam and Christine's son) now runs the farm and he will guide you along old Maori tracks to waterfalls, rock pools and wetlands, where birdlife flourishes. Back at the homestead you'll find rimu panelling and a grandfather clock in the hall, kauri in the sitting-room and exceptional art hanging on the walls (the house doubles as an art gallery). Christine cooks professionally. She stocks delis throughout NZ and her new home-produce shop is a popular stop-off on the region's food and wine trail - so expect supper to be divine. And bedrooms have a pretty country feel in soft pastels with old wood furniture, the odd chest, comfy beds, big baths, all flooded with light. A grand, but very lived-in country manor-house, fab food, fascinating surroundings, a lovely garden with swimming pool... but most importantly some very charming Ludbrooks to make you feel at home. *Ideal base for the Bay of Islands, Waipoua and Puketi forests, Waiomio glowworm caves and flights to Cape Reinga. Tours can be taken around the farm, a registered historic site.*

Rooms: 4: 2 twins and 2 doubles all with private bath and shower.
Price: $380 p.p for dinner, bed and breakfast.
Meals: Full breakfast and 3-course dinner with drinks included in the price. Picnic hampers also available.
Directions: North on SH1 from Whangarei, through Kawakawa, and past turn-off to SH10. House on left of SH1, 1km south of Ohaeawai and signed.

Breakaway Retreat

Mark and Sheelagh Prosser

1856 Whangarei Heads Road, McLeod Bay, Whangarei
Tel: 09-434-0711
Email: breakaway@breakawayretreat.co.nz
Web: www.breakawayretreat.co.nz Cell: 027-331-8009

Stepping into Breakaway Retreat is like clambering into a tree-trunk hideaway. Tucked away ju above the seashore, surrounded by native bush and singing with birds, this self-catering cottage a sylvan idyll, newly built by Mark and Sheelagh entirely out of pinewood. The walls have bee left simple and bare - the view and the trees are your three-dimensional works of art here. Th cottage windows open onto the trees and to the seashore below and, lying on the bed in th main bedroom, I was comforted by the sounds of birds plashing in the water. You can stroll acro the lawn to the shore and perch yourself on moeraki boulders (unusual to find them outside th South Island), or take the kayaks out for a splash. Alternatively, one could always watch DVDs o the huge TV in your living room; or I quite fancied the idea of indulging myself in the enormo two-person spa bath. Mark and Sheelagh lived in the cottage themselves last winter to see f themselves what would be needed to create a perfect home from home; so I doubt you will b at a loss for anything during your stay. Despite the feeling of rural seclusion, Breakaway is perfec situated for further exploration of the Whangarei Heads area if you are feeling adventurou Otherwise the Prossers' secluded beach (safe for children) offers endless opportunities f swimming, beach-combing, fishing and general pottering.

Rooms: 2: 1 king, 1 twin, sharing bathroom with sp bath and shower. Open-plan living area and kitchen.
Price: $250 - $290. $45 per additional person.
Meals: Fully self-catering. Complimentary breakfast basket supplied on first day.
Directions: Follow signs from Whangarei to Town Basin and then to Onerahi. By Hammer Hardware turn L onto Whangarei Heads Road. Follow this roa until you reach the McLeod Bay 50km speed sign. 2nd entrance on R after the sign.

Ara Roa

Paul and Susanne Olsen

Harambee Road, Taiharuru
Tel: 09-436-5028 Fax: 09-436-5028
Email: pvista@xtra.co.nz Web: www.araroa.co.nz
Cell: 021-293-5981

Susanne and Paul add a surcharge for one-night stays at Ara Roa and you'll kick yourself all the way back down the mountain if you have to pay it! The cottage is at the very top of a kilometre of exciting driveway… next stop heaven. Time to wheel out some of the big-gun adjectives: magnificent, awe-inspiring, breath-taking. That sort of thing. From the deck the world is laid out below you, miles of grassy hills and fields, until the mountains finally drop into the sea. The muffled roar of distant surf wafts up the mountain and envelops you. I sat staring until darkness forced me to evaluate my living quarters. Given the token price put upon it I suggest you try and book in for a year. Everything is hard to get out of… the bed, the bath, the shower, the beanbag in front of the telly. Walls are enlivened with colourful pieces of art you want to walk off with (like the blue fish sculpture in the main bedroom). Mod cons include a complex series of spotlights, phone (mobile coverage is perfect), very functioning kitchen, hi-fi, video, board games. Kayaking in the estuary sounds great, sting rays commonly seen. Or cockle-fossicking. Or next-door's farm is a big hit with kids. This is a fantastic find and may well be difficult to get into. You will thank me (and the wonderful Olsen family of course!) if you do.

Rooms: 1 guest house: 2 bedrooms sharing 1 double bath and separate shower.
Price: $250 per couple. $50 per extra person. Surcharge for one night only $80.
Meals: Fully self-catering so bring your own breakfast etc. Dinners can be arranged with a bit of notice: $45 - $60.
Directions: Ask when booking.

Sandspit Retreat

Dennis and Sue Anderson
18 Beach Street, Sandspit, Warkworth
Tel: 09-425-7128 Fax: 09-425-7128
Email: sandspitretreat@value.net.nz Web: www.sandspitretreat.co.nz
Cell: 021-782-979

Sandspit Retreat, perched on a leafy cliff-top overlooking the spit below, is reached up a secluded path with fresh lemons growing freely all about. The house itself has been built as environmentally friendly as possible – heated either by solar panel or a wood-burner (although there is electricity for an emergency), and quite modern in design with a huge open-plan kitchen and living room with massive sofas and open doors onto decking and hot tub. Fresh flowers and home touches abound, and the bathroom has one-way glass affording a great view into a bush- and shrub-filled garden. Dennis and Sue are two of the most charming people I have met in New Zealand and are full of suggestions of places to go and things to do. Plus Dennis makes a truly exceptional English 'cuppa'! Although they live in the house next door they are aware that people sometimes just need to 'get away', and to this end they've put their heart and soul into creating the perfect retreat. Well, they've succeeded admirably and it is not easy picking your way back down the secluded path. *House kayaks, dinghy, table tennis, pool, archery and even an indoor rock-climbing wall and gym available.*

Rooms: 1 self-contained guesthouse with 1 superking/twin and double sofa-beds sharing shower.
Price: $300 for 1 night, $550 for 2 nights, $750 for 3 nights etc. Cheaper rates for longer stays.
Meals: Full breakfast provisions provided for first morning.
Directions: Ask when booking or see website. 50 mins north of Auckland.

The Shanty

Peter Sullivan

Cowan Bay Farm, 592 Cowan Bay Rd, Warkworth
Tel: 09-425-9550 Fax: 09-425-9553
Email: info.shanty@xtra.co.nz Web: www.cowanbayfarm.com
Cell: 021-045-1383

On a flat tidal rock bed, flanked by native bush, in a tiny private bay complete with a short sweep of sandy beach you will find an idyllic cottage, raised on stilts to allow high tide to lap beneath the deck. When I first laid eyes on it, all I could manage was a sigh and some goose pimples. The 'Shanty' was once genuinely a shanty, but it is a bit of a joke name now for this highly styly beachside retreat. Inside, polished kahikatea-wood floors are strewn with rugs, walls are white, russet timbers smell of wood wax. Deep couches flank a beautiful antique table scarred with age and French windows open wide onto a long deck built around ancient pohutukawa trees. The pantry is chock-full of provisions (herbal teas, spices, flour, sauces etc) and mod cons include a dishwasher, stainless-steel oven, microwave, outdoor BBQ, outdoor heaters… but no TV or phone here, although there are DVDs and a stereo for rainy days. The only sounds are the mud that pops or the herons that fish for snapper, like you can, five metres from the door. You can hunt for rock oysters, too, or build beach bonfires. Two kayaks, life-vests and fishing gear are all provided. This place is so special that friends wonder why Megan and Peter don't live there themselves. *Warkworth is 12 mins away. Children are welcome.*

Rooms: 2: 1 king, 1 queen and a queen pull-out sofa in the lounge, all sharing 1 shower room.
Price: $295 for two. $50 for each extra person. Minimum two-night stay.
Meals: Self-catering only.
Directions: 50 mins north of Auckland. SH1 through Orewa, past Puhoi, up hill, along ridge, past Moir Hill Road on L. Right down Cowan Bay Rd (just past teddy bear sign on R). Go 6km and through farm gates. Pass barn and stock yards, L at T-junction to waterfront.

Kawau Lodge

Helen and Dave Jeffery
North Cove, Kawau Island
Tel: 09-422-8831 Fax: 09-422-8832
Email: mail@kawaulodge.co.nz Web: www.kawaulodge.co.nz
Cell: 021-951-038

One of the great joys of staying on Kawau derives from being forced to leave certain things behind. With sheer delight I turned my back on the car park, the street-lights, my mobile and my car and made my way towards Dave, a boat, a welcoming grin and an ice-cold beer. The trade was good and my satisfaction ran high as daylight turned to dusk and we sped off into open sea. Set in a colourful garden and flanked by native ponga ferns and the odd kauri tree, Kawau Lodge is situated in the most sheltered inlet in the Hauraki Gulf. Here, all houses that dot the shore have floating jetties that branch out into the harbour like driveways in a watery cul-de-sac. At the end of Kawau Lodge's, I couldn't have hoped for a more relaxed and friendly welcome or to be treated more like one of the family. Conversation flowed merrily over pre-dinner nibbles and wine, a delicious supper of freshly-caught (by Dave) and cumin-baked (by Helen) snapper, pausing only later during brief and decisive moments in the rugby game and finally for bed. Below the main house the rooms are a delight with cosy beds, great big showers and French windows onto the palm-fringed deck they share that wraps around the house. Explore the waters in kayaks, read in the hammock by the shore or let Dave take you out on his sailing boat to nearby islands or to historic Mansion House in the next bay. Whatever you choose to do, expect Kiwi hospitality in its truest form, informal, genuine and fun, an NZ experience not to be missed.

Rooms: 2 queens with en-suite shower.
Price: $150 - $175 for B&B. 2-night packages that include all meals, transfers to and from the main land from $635 per couple. Transfers to Auckland city or airport can be arranged for an additional cost.
Meals: Special breakfast included in B&B rate. 3-course dinner $60, casual dinners $25 - $30 and lunches/picnics from $12.
Directions: Meet at Sandspit Harbour, 10 mins from Warkworth, for pick up. Directions emailed or faxed on booking.

Peace and Plenty

Judith Machin

6 Flagstaff Terrace, Devonport, Auckland
Tel: 09-445-2925 Fax: 09-445-2901
Email: peaceandplenty@xtra.co.nz Web: www.peaceandplenty.co.nz
Cell: 021-665-661

Peace and Plenty faces the harbour, guarded by Old Albert, the giant Moreton Bay fig, and his attendant pohutukawa trees that make the green of this seaside village so impressive. The house is an elegant Victorian villa, built in 1888, a grand old residence in NZ terms. You approach up the garden path beside tiers of lavender hedge and roses. Once inside, one's natural inclination is to follow the high-ceilinged central passage through to the breakfast room with its dresser of blue china. The breakfast table was elegantly laid out when I visited and laden with home-made muesli, lemon and poppy seed cake and warm plum crumble. If it's not grown in Judith's garden, incidentally, most of the produce is local to Devonport. And then out onto the flower-laden back veranda, which overlooks a small but very well designed tropical garden, a honey-pot for tuis, wax-eyes and wagtails. The house is made of original kauri with Marseilles roof tiles and corbelled chimneys. The rooms are very different and I liked them all, particularly those upstairs with their brass beds, shuttered doors, little balconies overlooking Mt Victoria and Tuscan-tiled bathrooms housing deep, slipper baths. Peace and Plenty is rightly held up as a high-water mark for accommodation in Auckland. *'Uncle' is on hand for airport pick-ups and drop-offs. Stanley the dog will accompany guests on walks with extreme willingness. Cheltenham Beach 15 mins walk. Ferry to City Centre and islands 2 mins' walk. Wireless internet access.*

Rooms: 7: 1 king en/s bath & shower; 1 king en/s shower; 1 king en/s bath and separate shower; 2 queens en/s shower; 2 superking/twin en/s shower.
Price: $230 - $325. Singles $200 - $265. Winter specials available.
Meals: Full breakfast including smoked salmon, scrambled eggs, waffles with warm berries or smoked bacon & maple syrup. In the evening, Devonport groans with eateries.
Directions: Ask when booking or see web site.

Ascot Parnell

Bart and Thérèse Blommaert

St Stephens Avenue, Parnell, Auckland
Tel: 09-309-9012 Fax: 09-309-3729
Email: info@ascotparnell.com Web: www.ascotparnell.com

In following Thérèse and Bart around their ultra-modern, newly-built apartment I managed to all the white space I allow myself for notes and I cannot read the tiny scrawl that followed! This a measure of how much there was to enthuse over. In a couple of broad statements I will say th your hosts could not care more enthusiastically about their guests. And that every practical det of their B&B has been minutely considered from your point of view… and only the highest qual has been sought in all things. All is super-modern, with the large, open living space drawing yo eye - and your entire body - out to the balcony for the city view. There is much solid woo pebbles in pot plants, marble in bathrooms, thick glass showers, mirrors, modern art, war simple colours, perfect white linen on new beds. Mod cons include an open-plan kitchen with coffee-maker and free juice, there's a Mac for guest use (Airport available throughout th apartment for those that understand) and guests have access to a heated swimming pool, securit swiper for the lift, underground parking, CD player, laundry… I mean, the list is endless. It is beautifully decorated, slick, well-organised but always homely flat. Thérèse and Bart, who we once Belgians (French, German, Flemish/Dutch spoken), live in the adjacent apartment wi Khalifa, their aristocratic and well-mannered saluki, and will make absolutely certain you are w looked after.

Rooms: 3: 2 garden-view queens with en-suite shower; 1 king suite with harbour view, en/s showe and separate bath.
Price: $225 - $385. Singles $195 - $295.
Meals: Full breakfast included. On occasion if raining hard, suppers can be arranged, but Parnell is restaurant heaven.
Directions: See the web site or ask when booking

Braemar on Parliament Street

Susan and John Sweetman

7 Parliament Street,
Auckland
Tel: 09-377-5463
Fax: 09-377-3056
Email:
braemar@aucklandbedandbre
akfast.com
Web:
www.aucklandbedandbreakfast
.com Cell: 021-640-688

Living history pervades Braemar on Parliament Street. Positioned next to the site of a sacred Maori spring, this 1901 townhouse shares its space with some of the oldest colonial parliamentary buildings in town. In 1994 Sue and John pooled everything they had to buy the house and save it from circling developers and demolition. Now, to walk through its doors is to step back in time to a house dressed in Edwardian elegance and filled with bygone charm. A grand old kauri staircase leads to high-ceilinged rooms set with antiques and refined bathrooms with check-tiled floors and claw-footed baths. Old photographs line the walls upstairs while downstairs in the rose dining room you'll use silver cutlery to eat your delicious breakfast off fine bone china on white damask tablecloths. I spent the night in the Batten Suite, its rooms often visited by the 1930's aviation star Jean Batten during the years her father lived there. With even more character than their home, your hosts are as incredibly helpful as they are charming and will match your interest in the city and the house with as much information as they can. Sue loves to sing. You'll no doubt hear her hum to the sounds of the new day as she prepares breakfast, and John, who does voice-overs for TV and radio, is a natural-born raconteur. Braemar is as much a place to curl up on the sofa and read as it is a base from which to explore the city and you'll be sure to find both equally rewarding.

Rooms: 4: Batten Suite has 1 queen with en-s bath and shower and private living area; 1 queen and 1 double share bath and shower; 1 queen with private bath and shower.
Price: $180 - $295. Singles $150 - $270.
Meals: Great choice of full breakfasts included in price. Picnic lunches can be ordered on booking. Prices vary accordingly.
Directions: Emailed or faxed on booking.

Viaduct Landing

Jennifer McBrearty

Apartment 32, Shed 24, Prince's Wharf, 147 Quay Street, Auckland CBD
Tel: 0800-377-362 (in NZ only) Fax: 09-358-2214
Email: stay@essencenz.com Web: www.essencenz.com
Cell: 027-542-4202

Viaduct Landing, cantilevered over the water on a disused wharf, is the kind of place where I take swipes, items of furniture are pieces and where the art isn't there just to look pretty but initiate conversation. You've probably seen it in a video on MTV. Floor-to-ceiling French window wrap around enormous rooms where quirky furnishings, original works of art and pristine sha lines in neutral shades vie for your attention. Geek-chic rules here with an über-smart AV sou system that lets you flick tracks and channels from your bed (!) and Pixar-animated lights t literally bend over backwards to satisfy your lighting preference. And then there's the deck. 200m of it! If it were not there for your sheer amazement it could quite feasibly have had successful career as a runway for small planes. From here the city felt my very own. It only seem fitting to have a glass of champagne in hand as I let my eyes wander over my domain. The loom Sky Tower, the thrumming bustle of downtown, the sailboats jostling into lines in the viad below and finally the evening sun, glowing in the suspended frame of the harbour brid Whether you're pouting from the verandah, cart-wheeling across the deck or bubbling away the hot spa, foot in the air and tracing the Auckland skyline with your toes, it will always be h not to feel very, very smug that you're occupying one of the smoothest pads on the block a that it's completely, utterly and exclusively yours.

Rooms: Self-catering apartment sleeping 6: 1 super king/twin with en-suite bath and shower; 1 super king/twin and 1 queen sharing a shower. Gourmet kitchen, BBQ, dining, living, self-ser laundry.
Price: $890 +GST - $1090 +GST for up to 4 persons. Additional Guests $150 +GST pp. Personal chef and wine selection available at additional cost.
Meals: Full breakfast provisions provided on arrival. Chef servic on site and pre-prepared gourmet meals can be arranged.
Directions: Inner city on Prince's Wharf in the Viaduct Basin. Available on website, emailed or faxed on booking.

Omahu Lodge

Robyn and Ken Booth
33 Omahu Road, Remuera, Auckland
Tel: 09-524-5648 Fax: 09-524-5108
Email: info@omahulodge.co.nz Web: www.omahulodge.co.nz
Cell: 021-954-333

We stumbled into Robyn and Ken's breakfast room at an unseasonably early hour on our way to the airport, and were greeted by just the kind of breakfast to set you up for a day – or two – and the sort of welcoming hosts that we love. Robyn and Ken have been pretty much everywhere (although the Great Wall of China is still on the to-do list) and have amassed a whole host of *objets d'art* and travellers' tales. Their best collection, though, is Kiwi through-and-through: an assembly of mottled kauri-wood furniture that the museums are dying to get their hands on. Upstairs, the Omahu Room has the kind of window-seat I dream of snuggling up on with a book. The Mt Hobson and One Tree Hill rooms give views of, you guessed it, Mt Hobson and One Tree Hill, with white walls and bright paintings. The glass brick wall of the bathroom makes the space seem even brighter. My favourite, however, was the Pool Suite downstairs, with its separate lounge with cream walls, tapa cloth and en-suite bathroom (I'm always one for a luxurious bathroom) which has a glass wall looking through to some enclosed fernery, almost evoking the feel of a bush bath in the middle of the city. All the little things have been taken care of here, with a thousand thread count sheets, rattan furniture for relaxing by the courtyard pool, and four hot water cylinders so that they *never* run out of hot water!

Rooms: 4: 1 king with en/s shower; 1 king/twin with en/s shower; 2 queen with en/s shower.
Price: $160 - $275.
Meals: Full breakfast included. Meals by arrangement, $60 p.p. for a 3-course dinner, inclusive of wine.
Directions: Traveling either north or south on the Southern Motorway (State Highway 1), take the Market Road exit. Travel east and continue to Remuera Road. Turn R, then R again into Omahu Road. Omahu Lodge is on the R.

Titirangi Coastal Cottage

Fiona Jeaffreson and Mike Reynolds
12 Opou Road, Titirangi
Tel: 09-817-8323
Fax: 09-817-6896
Email: info@coastal-cottages.co.nz
Web: www.coastal-cottages.co.nz
Cell: 021-897-731

Just moments from my car and I found myself deep in native bush. A glorious green canopy bending nikau palms and ferns shaded me from the sun as I trotted down the boardwalk ste towards the sea and the cottage below. Not that I'd have known it was there without Fio guiding the way. The dark wooden structure blends skilfully into its surrounding environmer Being an air steward, Fiona knows a thing or two about staying away from home and has design the cottage according to what she likes best when in the air. She is a fun and vibrant type; so to the décor inside. The walls are white, windows big, sofas suede and furnishings funky ar contemporary. I particularly liked the 70's-print chairs in the reading corner by the wood-burne the wood-stain varnished flooring, and the fabulous artwork (and plasma TV) on the walls. In th kitchen, sunlight twinkles on the chrome fittings and the bright orange cupboards are filled to th brim with organic breakfast goodies. Downstairs, the finest of linens adorn the fairest of beds. Th bedrooms are whiter than white except for the odd splash of colour in rugs and paintings ar both open onto the huge lower deck. With the secluded Wood Bay just there, a hot spa po (specially helicoptered to your verandah!), sauna and fabulous Italian-style bathroom with a ser al-fresco claw-footed bath, you should find a way to make yourself comfortable! Comple seclusion and tranquillity rarely come as accessible as this.

Rooms: 1 cottage with 1 superking/twin and 1 king sharing a bath and shower.
Price: $450 for two pp. $30 per extra person.
Meals: Very substantial provisions (organic where possible) for continental and cooked breakfast on arrival.
Directions: 30 minutes from Auckland, directions emailed or faxed on booking.

Hunua Gorge Country House

Ben and Brandi and Joy Calway
482 Hunua Road, Papakura
Tel: 09-299-9922 Fax: 09-299-9922
Email: hunuagorge@xtra.co.nz Web: www.hunuagorge.co.nz
Cell: 021-669-9922

A steep, gorge-traversing, gravel drive took me off the beaten track and into another dimension, instantly restoring my va-va-voom. Joy met me at the door and her house won me over from the moment I walked in. The bedrooms are all very different, and all filled with Joy's finds. Downstairs there is a black-and-white golf-themed room while upstairs takes you to Africa complete with ebony statues of Mama and Mototo and zebra throws. There is also a nautical room that pays tribute to Sir Peter Blake with an exotic teak bathroom and loads of sea-shells. Everywhere you look there are amazing touches to surprise you from duck-shaped baskets holding cutlery in the kitchen to a red phone-box in the garden, surrounded by red impatients, a red geranium and a vintage bicycle. There is a comfortable sitting room which Joy shares with her guests and a verandah from which to view the countryside. The house is set on a hill, with views through wild bush across to Auckland harbour. Guests often (if they're wise) take advantage of Joy's great culinary skills and eat *al fresco* beneath the Southern Cross. Ben and Brandi (Joy's son and his new wife) are returning to Hunua to join her in running the B&B, so by the time you arrive there will be some fifth-generation Kiwis to show you the local ropes. And like them, you'll probably end up coming back.

Rooms: 4: 1 suite with king (and an extra room with bunk beds if needed for children) with en/s shower, 1 queen with private bath, 1 twin, 1 double with private bath and wheelchair access.
Price: $125 - $250. Singles $75 - $90.
Meals: Full breakfast included, lunch and dinner available from $25 - $35.
Directions: From SH1 take the Papakura off-ramp. Turn east into Beach Road, across three sets of traffic lights and into Settlement Road. Turn right into Hunua Road. The house is 5km along on the left.

Rapaura Water Gardens

Sacha and Sally Sank

586 Tapu-Coroglen Rd, RD5 Thames
Tel: 07-868-4821 Fax: 07-868-4821
Email: info@rapaura.com Web: www.rapaura.com

Seven waterfalls cascading over black granite boulders through dense rainforest into deep cl
pools – aka 'The Seven Stairs to Heaven'. Here are 64 acres of private paradise for you to explc
at your leisure. Further down, the creek weaves and gurgles through rambling gardens, past nat
trees, exotic flora and Monet-esque lily ponds. "The best garden is a well-kept wilderness," is c
of the sayings at Rapaura. This is especially true as the gardens have been restored to their form
glory after being devastated by a 'weather bomb' in 2002. Semi-camouflaged by native tree-fe
the lodge combines antiques, bright colours and *objets d'art* from the owner's time in Hong Ko
I loved the bold Chinese calligraphy that greets you when you enter and cooed over the porce
elephants bearing potted ferns in the soothing setting of the breakfast room. I stayed in the cotta
where I found every creature comfort had been taken care of, from extremely comfortable sc
and bed to top-quality linens and fresh coffee in the kitchen. We ate a delicious dinner in the lod
eating in the dining room with its full-length sliding doors looking out onto the wilderness belc
Simply put, an amazing place. Sally and Sacha have also opened Koru at Rapaura, an inviting pla
serving all their home-cooked favourites and selling local art on the premises.

Rooms: Lodge: 2 queens with shared bath and shower. Cottage: 1 queen with bath, shower and toilet.
Price: Lodge: $275 for two and $65 per extra person. Cottage: $165 for two, $45 per extra person.
Meals: Continental breakfast provisions included. Dinner available by prior arrangement.
Directions: From Thames take the road toward Coromandel. At Tapu turn right toward Coroglen a Whitianga. Follow signs to Rapaura, 6.5km on the right.

Driving Creek Villas

David Foreman

21a Colville Road, Coromandel Town
Tel: 07-866-7755 Fax: 07-866-7753
Email: reservations@drivingcreekvillas.com
Web: www.drivingcreekvillas.com Cell: 021-116-6393

It was on these very banks of the Coromandel stream that gold was first discovered in New Zealand. Some 150 years later, I struck gold myself... in the form of the Driving Creek Villas, two little retreats tucked away amongst the trees and native bush. David has designed everything to pull you into a state so hypnotically tranquil that no matter how long you spend here, it will never quite seem enough. Once you step inside, the villas are so fresh, airy and naturally uplifting that you'll seemingly float within their light wooden structures. With polished wooden floors, sprightly orange and purple furnishings, chrome fitted kitchens and French windows that bi-fold onto the deck, they ooze from all the right places that understated style of laid-back modern living. And you'll not want for comfort with the finest Egyptian cotton linen on beds and all the gadgets you could dream of elsewhere. But I'd forfeit them all simply to wallow in the Japanese hot tub and listen to tui birds sing over the sound of the stream. Kids and opportunists alike will love exploring the creek to feed the eels (!) and search for gold. There's also the famous Driving Creek Railways, a gold stamper battery and two beautiful gardens right at your door and with stunning beaches and walks all around you can happily idle your way through a lazy weekend or more. *Wireless broadband. Renowned for its artsy community, the village and its fab restaurants are 5 minutes away.*

Rooms: 2 villas: both have 1 queen and 1 twin sharing a bathroom; both have Japanese hot tubs.
Price: $245 - $295. Extra person $25.
Meals: Fully self-catering. Meals are available on request though.
Directions: Drive 2km north of Coromandel township, where the road forks take the left-hand Colville Road turning. Driving Creek Villas are 200m past here on your left over the one-lane bridge.

Kuaotunu Bay Lodge

Lorraine and Bill Muir

8 State Highway 25, Kuaotunu/Wharekaho, Whitianga
Tel: 07-866-4396 Fax: 07-866-4396
Email: muir@kuaotunubay.co.nz Web: www.kuaotunubay.co.nz
Cell: 027-601-3665

Turning your back on the views at Kuaotunu might well be the hardest thing you have to do
your holiday. I longed to stay to watch the sun set and the moon rise, but needs must when
devil drives, and I had to press on. The house is perched above the beach among ten acres
garden, its wrap-around decking offering up a panoramic spread of sparkling sea, white sand a
open expanse of sky for your delight. Think of a picture postcard and, unlikely as it sounds, y
are probably there. No wonder Fitz the dog is so lazy he once allowed quails to walk over
back - no need to move when such a view is available right where you are sitting. It's worth try
out the rest of the house, though, because Lorraine and Bill have built it especially for guests, v
an open-plan layout that cleverly allows you to be just as sociable as you choose. I was fascina
by the collection of *objets trouvés* scattered throughout the house, such as the child's rainc
made from woven reeds, or the collection of model Pacific Island boats from Bill's childhood. T
guest rooms, each with private decking, are similarly appealing spaces, with the strong colours
local artists' work competing for attention with the bright sunlight and the sea views. If one sho
want to venture further afield than the beach below, then the hot spot (literally) of Hot Wa
Beach is within easy driving distance, and the artistic community of Coromondel offers a great
trip.

Rooms: 3: 1 twin with shower/bath across hall, 2
queen with en/s shower.
Price: $200 - $275.
Meals: Full breakfast included. Light meals by
arrangement.
Directions: From Whitianga take the SH25 north
Kuaotunu. Kuaotunu Bay Lodge is clearly signed on
the road.

Flaxhaven Lodge

John and Lee Hughes
995 Purangi Road, Flaxmill Bay, Whitianga
Tel: 07-866-2676   Fax: 07-866-2396
Email: welcome@flaxhavenlodge.co.nz   Web: www.flaxhavenlodge.co.nz
Cell: 027-286-1088

It was a tough day taking the GG road around the Coromandel Peninsula (searing sunshine, white beaches, verdant vegetation - oh, how I suffer), and it was with glee that I arrived at Flaxhaven, dropped my bags and collapsed onto my bed. The natural tones of the room, echoing the colours outside, do a marvellous job of soothing any jangling nerves. John and Lee, two of the most charming hosts I have yet to meet in New Zealand, built the lodge here a few years ago, "retiring" from their award-winning café near Cambridge - and yes, the breakfasts are excellent! They're full of enthusiasm for the area... after all, they first met, rather romantically, on nearby Hot Water Beach. They designed the lodge themselves, with an open-plan lounge and kitchen (complete with huge sofas to curl up on) for sociability, and a secluded guest wing and separate cottage, if you would rather tuck yourself away under the pergola with a paperback. The lodge has extensive gardens, and just across the road from Cooks Beach, where our eponymous hero anchored his HMS Endeavour in 1769 - and apparently from Cook's offshore vantage point, the image of Shakespeare could be spotted in the cliffs now named after him. These days they are a native bush reserve, with a short walking track up to a viewing point for all of Mercury Bay. With this, and four beaches within walking distance, pray for some of my sunshine, and bring your tramping shoes and your swimming togs.

Rooms: 2 suites: 1 superking with en/s bathroom and shower, separate toilet and private sitting room; one semi-self-contained cottage with 1 queen and bathroom with shower.
Price: $180 - $250. $75 for each additional person.
Meals: Full breakfast included.
Directions: 20 mins north of Tairua on SH25 turn R into Hot Water Beach Road. Follow for 2km then bear L into Purangi Road signed Cooks Beach. Flaxhaven is 1km after the turn-off to Cooks Beach on the L.

Hahei Oceanfront

Raewyn and Joe Whitham

23 Wigmore Crescent, Hahei
Tel: 07-866-3199 Fax: 07-866-3198
Email: info@haheioceanfront.co.nz Web: www.haheioceanfront.co.nz
Cell: 0274-753-301

I arrived early and made my usual bumbling English apologies, but Raewyn and Joe were tota unperturbed. Within minutes we were settling down with good coffee and Raewyn's hom made and wickedly moreish shortbread. We sat in the centrepiece of this minimalist home, a hu lounge with white sofas and day-beds, lined on most sides with local art and with a huge de with views down to the beach only yards away. It really is the most stunning setting and the hou an architect's delight, even more picture-perfect than its photograph suggests. My room w simply but skilfully turned out with beautiful framed photos of nearby Cathedral Cove on the w and a multitude of pillows and cushions piled on the bed. The en-suite bathroom caught my e too, with its border of paua shells set into the tiles and the ocean-green sink raised above t counter. Even swankier than this, the Whithams are particularly, and rightly, proud of the sui with its living room and deck and 180-degree views. New this year is a courtyard perfectly plac to catch every last ray of the setting sun, if you should happen to want a change from sundowne on the deck. Raewyn and Joe are perfect hosts and will gladly fill you in on the best spots to di boat and bathe on the peninsula. Back at the house later that night, I stepped outside to mar at the clearest of night skies, full of stars, before falling into bed and being lulled to sleep by the s crumping of ocean waves.

Rooms: 3: 1 suite with king and en/s bath and shower; 1 superking/twin with en/s shower; 1 king with en/s shower.
Price: $250 - $350 (high season Mahurangi room) for rooms, $700 for the suite. Singles $20 less. Min. 2-night stay in rooms between 20/12 and 31/03. For the suite there is a 2-night min year round.
Meals: Full breakfast included.
Directions: From Tairua follow SH25 and turn right into Hot Water Beach Road. Follow signs to Hahei. First right into Pa Roa then first left into Wigmore Crescent. House at end of crescent on right.

Hot Water Beach B&B

Gail and Trevor Knight

48 Pye Place, Hot Water Beach, Whitianga
Tel: 07-866-3991; freephone in NZ: 0800-146-889 Fax: 07-866-3291
Email: tknight@xtra.co.nz Web: www.hotwaterbedandbreakfast.co.nz
Cell: 0274-799-620

The draw cards for the tiny beach-village itself are a spring-fed lagoon and the rare hot-water springs that bubble up beneath the sands of the tidal zone. At low tide you go out, dig a hole in the sand and wallow in your own home-made hot bath. This is even more extraordinary at night and Trevor and Gail know about the tides and will provide spades and wine. Not many B&Bs provide spades and wine. You will be hard-pressed to find fault with this place. I tried, but failed. The vital elements of bedrooms and bathrooms are immaculate with any trimmings you might dream up (shower-caps, PC plugs, extra blankets) already thought of and covered. Downstairs: a full-size snooker table with an (honesty) bar and telly for blokesy sports occasions. For the beach: boogie boards, beach towels and, of course, spades to dig your bath. Breakfasts are enjoyed together in the open-plan sitting-room-kitchen-deck with a full wall that opens towards the beach. The house is fresh, modern, beachy with loads of space, neat tubs of aloes on gravel paths, wooden decks, one bearing an outside hot tub which looks out to sea. And to top it all Gail and Trevor are just incredibly nice and natural, committed to your happiness. AND the rates make very pleasing reading. The 4-night *maximum* stay in operation here gives others a turn! Tazz, a boxer dog, and Pipi, a tabby cat, are the animals in situ.

Rooms: 2 queens with en-suite shower.
Price: Doubles $200 - $320.
Meals: Full breakfast included.
Directions: From Tairua follow the SH25 north. Turn R into Hot Water Beach Rd. Follow for 8km, bearing R at intersections & following signs. After 2nd single-lane bdge, bear L into Pye Place. House on R but go past & U-turn to make it up steep drive.

The Mussel Bed B&B and Cottage

Chris and Paul Hopkins
892 Purangi Road, Cooks Beach, RD1 Whitianga
Tel: 07-866-5786 Fax: 07-866-5706
Email: welcome@musselbed.co.nz Web: www.musselbed.co.nz

The newly-built Mussel Bed is just a short walk from the white sands of Cooks Beach and its 3k crescent of safe swimming. And there can be no better place to wash off the salt than at Ch and Paul's B&B. The three guest rooms, in a separate wing of the main house, have be decorated in distinctive themes and blessed with many little extra touches, such as fresh browni jars of sweets, coloured scarves in the wardrobes and bonsai plants. The Victorian room with fine floral china tea set was influenced by a stint in the UK, while the Pacifica is awash with regio paintings and wall hangings and a Koru symbol in the bathroom. The Beach Hut is ideal for fc friends travelling together, with a queen downstairs and a loft room with twins. Each room ha large window-seat and a deck overlooking the rock garden, and this is where Chris will bring yc breakfast (assuming you don't want it in bed), complete with fresh coffee, home-baked bread a her sumptuous home-made, honey-drizzled muesli. Paul is equally 'hands-on'. A tiler by trac he's responsible for the glories of the bathrooms, while much of the furniture was made by neighbour using recycled kauri from an old homestead. Coromandel adventuring starts he *Diving, fishing and shellfish all 5 mins' walk away. Cathedral Cove & Hot Water Beach 10 mins by c*

Rooms: 3 rooms in B&B guest wing: 2 queens with en/s showers, & 1 queen & 2 singles sharing sh'r; se contained cottage: 1 queen & 2 singles sharing sh'r.
Price: B&B Guest Wing $175 - $250 per couple. $50 per extra person. Singles $150 - $200. Self-co cottage $150 - $250 per couple with 5-night min st during peak periods. $25 per extra person.
Meals: Continental breakfast included. Breakfast provisions are provided in Cottage for the first night only. Meals can be provided with prior arrangement
Directions: 20 mins north of Tairua on SH25 turn into Hot Water Beach Rd. Follow for 2km then bea left into Purangi Rd signed Cooks Beach/Ferry Landing. Follow 9km & The Mussel Bed is 200m or R past Cooks Beach Hall.

Matawha

Jenny Thomson
61 Matawha Rd, Ruapuke, nr Raglan
Tel: 07-825-6709 Fax: 07-825-6715
Email: jennyt@wave.co.nz

My directions told me to go straight across the road into Matawha. This confused me somewhat as all I could see in front of me was a field. Which appeared to be full of cows. Showing the great pioneering spirit of my British ancestors I ventured forward and at the end of the field, Matawha suddenly loomed in front of me with beautiful wild gardens and flowers abounding. The house does not disappoint. From the infamous double room complete with piano and binoculars to the studio with spa and obligatory candles for atmosphere everything is welcoming and homely. At sunset you can sit in the spa, roll back the windows and gaze out to the sea or the mountain – whichever takes your fancy. You have the run of Jenny's 900-acre cattle and sheep station and you can tramp down past her horses, over the paddocks to five kilometres of possibly the best surf beach in the Southern Hemisphere. Jenny is an extremely well-travelled and knowledgeable lady, having spent time in Jordan, Europe and South America, often as a boffin on bovines (cattle expert). She'll also spoil you rotten with a groaning table of wonderful food, much of it from the Matawha organic vegetable garden. You'll not find anywhere else like this in New Zealand. *Raglan, Bridal Veil Falls, Waitomo Caves, horse-riding, hot water beaches and gardens are all nearby.*

Rooms: 3: 1 double with private shower; 1 twin room and 1 king studio sharing a bathroom.
Price: Doubles $130 - $150. Singles $60. Spa use extra. N.B. cash only!
Meals: Full breakfast included. Dinner $20 p.p. for 2 courses, lunch $15, BYO wine.
Directions: From Hamilton, west on SH23 for 28km, then L for Te Mata. R into Ruapuke Rd. 9.5km of road and track, keeping L. At Y-junction, L into Tuturimu Rd. Straight ahead 2km to T-jct. Straight across into Matawha.

Tapanui Country Home

Sue and Mark Perry
1714 Oparure Rd, Te Kuiti
Tel: 07-877-8549 Fax: 07-877-8541
Email: info@tapanui.co.nz Web: www.tapanui.co.nz
Cell: 027-494-9873

Negotiate a natural buttress that crosses the driveway at Tapanui and you will reach a cleft blast from a daunting, crenellated limestone ridge… and here you'll find a welcome in true K country style. This is a working farm with 1900 acres of sheep and cattle. Sue and Mark's peace home is set on a small hill overlooking a limestone ha-ha, which protects the flower garden fro ever-optimistic sheep. Food is simple, delicious and fresh: roasts of lamb and beef are favourit There are tall stone fireplaces, a piano, binoculars to spot wildlife hopping across the landsca and big couches and rugs to snooze on. Down the road, an even more peaceful - if that's possi - self-catering cottage is tucked away amongst the Middle Earth hillocks. Sleep in comforting be under navy mohair throws, and eat at the stately mahogany table, that has been in Sue's fam for years. If you're all travelled out, you can slump in front of the roaring log fire and watch a D\ with a glass of red in hand before venturing to the amazing Waitomo Caves and the Blackwa River for (underground) rafting; or perhaps go on a more gentle tour of the farm if they and y have time. This less-travelled and wildly beautiful region was charted 'King Country' after Ma 'King' Tawahiao dropped his white top hat on a map and declared all beneath it his! A rece arrival, Boots the cat, is now in residence but spends most of his time exploring. *Hiking a Marokopa Falls nearby.*

Rooms: 2: Huntaway Suite, 1 king with en/s. 1 cottage, sleeps 4.
Price: $195 - $250. Singles $185 - $200.
Meals: Full breakfast included at homestead. Continental breakfast provisions supplied for cottage Dinner available by prior arrangement.
Directions: From Te Kuiti, take SH3 north for 3km Turn left into Oparure Road and continue for 17km. Homestead is on the right through a limestone entrance.

Church on Church Road

Steve and Kim Grounds
2 Church Rd, Cambridge
Tel: 07-827-5440 Fax: 07-827-5509
Email: info@churchonchurchrd.co.nz Web: www.churchonchurchrd.co.nz

After a century of Sunday services, the much-loved – and much-used – Cambridge Methodist Chapel building was beginning to look decidedly worse for wear and itself in urgent need of saving. The cavalry arrived in the form of Kim and Steve. They transformed the cavernous space into a light-drenched temple dedicated to the gods of relaxation: soaring, red-flecked, stained-glass windows opening onto green fields full of grazing Fresians; original tongue-and-groove ceilings; native matai wood flooring; and an open wood fire. I loved The Chapel room. Once filled with God-fearing farmers and their bonneted wives and children, it is now a huge, clutter-free space filled with an equally huge bed and Kim's oft-played piano. Thankfully, sofas and an extensive NZ film library have replaced the pulpit and bum-numbing pews so you can swot up on the country's culture without changing out of your PJ's. Through the French windows, a walled garden opens onto the road so there's no creeping guiltily through the family home at one in the morning. Outside, we caught a rare sighting of Vienna the cat, her teeth gleaming through the primordial ponga ferns like some fantastical Rousseau creation. Incidentally, Kim once lived in the Austrian capital hence the name. If you want the outdoors proper, try nearby Maungatautari. It's a world-renowned nature reserve, but you'll find no wild cats here. After all this is predator-free NZ.

Rooms: 2: 'The Chapel' I queen with en/s shower; 'The Vestry' I queen, I single, en/s shower and kitchenette.
Price: $155 - $210.
Meals: Full cooked or continental breakfast included; a huge choice including eggs Benedict and omelette with different fillings. Many good restaurants nearby.
Directions: Drive north from Cambridge on Victoria Rd for 7km. Turn left into Church Rd and then immediately right. See website for a map.

North Island - Bay of Plenty

Malvern Mudhouse

Vern and Wendy Meyer

185 Matahui Rd, Katikati
Tel: 07-552-0616 Fax: 07-552-0167
Email: vernwendy@hotmail.com
Cell: 027-498-5431

Banish all childhood prejudice against mud right now. Here it is sublime... or shouldn't I s
glorious. Wendy and Vern's mud-brick house puts wood and stone to shame. A monumen
effort has gone into creating this environment and, as the three guest rooms are let out to or
group at a time, you can hog it all for yourself. The rooms are enticingly decorated with Australi
silk bed linen (the most beautiful I can remember seeing), big beds and soft velours bathrobe
Kauri-wood furniture abounds and there are wall hangings and wooden gifts (for sale) made t
Wendy's father and a table made by Vern's. One room even has a bed dating from 1906. Th
sitting-room at the end of the hall is stuffed with red velvet Edwardian-style sofas and a leath
armchair. The apartment links up with the main house at the kitchen where Wendy whistled u
some memorable muffins during my visit. Just returned from Patagonia when I met them, Wend
and Vern have been everywhere and run trekking tours around Nepal as well as New Zealan
Outside the house is a tempting swimming pool where you can gaze down the hill all the way t
the sea. For further endorsements, consult the local heron. He is clearly happy here and spen
hours up at the house, staring at his own reflection in the glass windows.

Rooms: 1 apartment attached to house with 3
rooms: 1 double and 2 queens sharing shower.
Price: $200 - $250.
Meals: Full breakfast included.
Directions: SH2 to Katikati and head south toward
Tauranga. 9km after Katikati turn left into Matahui
Road.

Number Eight

Heather and John Gillies
8 River Oaks Drive, Woodford Park, Tauranga
Tel: 07-543-4550 Fax: 07-543-4551
Email: info@noeight.co.nz Web: www.noeight.co.nz
Cell: 021-618-806

What initially struck me about Number Eight - and no doubt strikes anyone sighted who goes there - were the terraces of the landscaped garden that stride down the hill in flat steps of green and floral patchwork; this is an oasis in the town. Its semi-rural position means you enter through a townhouse front door and step out through the gleaming homely kitchen into a country back yard. With your pick of golf courses, world-class fishing, beaches, wineries, Mt. Maunganui and shop-filled Tauranga all within a 10 - 15 minute radius you can virtually feel the Bay of Plenty action pulsing beneath your feet. If those feet are a bit weary though, you'd do just as well to prop them up in the garden-gazing, sun-drenched lounge and retreat into a book selected from one of the laden shelves. Bedrooms are quaint, sporting fine-quality linen on comfortable beds that are turned down to greet you in the evenings. The mysterious appearance of night-time chocolates are just one of the small personal touches that Heather and John provide unobtrusively. Help yourself to seemingly inexhaustible quantities of yummy home baking, tea and top-quality coffee. Heather's passion for cooking is reflected in the wide range of fresh and seasonal home-made creations that appear at breakfast and you should certainly indulge in dinner judging from the menu. This modern property has been designed as a B&B, yet exudes the character and warmth of a home creating the perfect balance between privacy, independence and good old-fashioned Kiwi hospitality. *Wireless broadband available.*

Rooms: 2: both queens with en-suite showers.
Price: $200 per night. Rates negotiable dependent on length of stay and time of year.
Meals: Full breakfast included. 3-course dinner available with prior arrangement $50 a head.
Directions: Emailed on request.

Fothergills on Mimiha

Bev Fothergill

84 Mimiha Rd, Matata, Whakatane
Tel: 07-322-2224 Fax: 07-322-2224
Email: bev@fothergills.co.nz Web: www.fothergills.co.nz
Cell: 027-460-5958

Bev Fothergill is the nurturing type. An ex-teacher with three children and four grandchildren, h
sprawling garden - which was once part of the family farm - is testament to her abilities: crimso
liquid-amber trees, flowering cherries, crab apples, orange persimmon, passion fruit, three typ
of apple, piles of pumpkins and that Brazilian/NZ staple, feijoas. If you like freshly-grown foo
you'll be as happy as a pig in mud. And incidentally, there actually is a pig living here. Fotherg
have farmed this spot for 42 years, hidden away in "this special, lovely little valley" (Bev's word
but I'm inclined to agree) with the Mimiha stream meandering through the garden. It was a balm
autumnal afternoon when I visited, perfect weather for an outdoor Mediterranean feast
mozzarella and heirloom tomato salad, all freshly picked from the garden. My only regret was th
I didn't come on a summer's evening. With the patio lit by fairy-lights and flares, Bev's husba
often plays his ukulele for guests and neighbours and parties can go on into the wee hours. Whe
guests retire, they can look forward to cosy rooms. The queen has marine-blue walls and
perfectly-made bed. Next door is a good-sized single, with a stripy duvet cover and views acro
the valley. In between, the kitchenette is well stocked with fresh and dried fruit, home-ma
cookies and jelly beans, and the bathroom is downstairs. You can also stay in the self-cateri
cottage at the bottom of the garden. This is real rural NZ.

Rooms: 2: 1 B&B suite with 1 queen bedroom & 1
king single with kitchenette & shared bathroom with
shower downstairs;1 s/c cottage sleeps 6 (1 queen,
bunk room and 1 sofa bed). Spa pool available.
Price: B&B from $140 pp for 2 pax sharing, $25 pe
extra. Mimiha Cottage: min 2-night stay, $320 for 2.
reduced tariff for weekly stay of $750. $10 per extra
Meals: Breakfast of seasonal fruits, muesli, yoghurt
plus bagels with avocado, tomato, smoked salmon
and preserves. Evening meals by arrangement.
Directions: From Whakatane, take Thornton Rd
past airport, then on thro' Matata. 5km past Matata,
on to Mimiha Rd. From Tauranga/TePuke, follow SH
turn into Mimiha Rd. Fothergills 840m further on.

Pukeko Landing

Jennifer McBrearty

6 Ronald Road, Lake Tarawera, Rotorua
Tel: 0800-377-362 (in NZ only) Fax: 09-358-2214
Email: stay@essencenz.com Web: www.essencenz.com
Cell: 0275-424-202

A brief 20-minute drive from the razzmatazz of Rotorua's thermal parks, Maori cultural experience, cafés, bars and shops you will discover Pukeko Landing, snoozing serenely by the lake. It was as if someone had stopped the clock when I arrived at this leafy haven. In fact, an equally serene and cheerful Geoff (the manager of Pukeko Landing and an open book on local advice) hardly seemed to notice that I was late as I needlessly rattled off my series of navigational errors. Views over the Otumutu Lake are interrupted only by giant ferns that rise from the terraced garden (specifically planted with native species to lure in the birdlife). I took the sculpture-dotted bush-walk down to the jetty and found a private lawn for picnics and pétanque waiting alongside a rowing-boat. With only the swans for company you could fish with borrowed rods to your heart's content then take a cooling dip. The property has the highest quality of everything from the sleek, wine-stocked kitchen to the lounge with its entertainment system, DVD and music library and wood-burning fire. Underfloor heating runs throughout to cosy up those cooler nights. Pristine bedrooms are accompanied by lavish-mirrored bathrooms where, and this is my favourite bit, I found the bath. Not just any old bath but a mammoth partly al-fresco spa-bath where waterfalls can be created without flooding the place (you'll see). You may be there for some time but that doesn't seem to be a problem at Pukeko.

Rooms: 1 self-catering house sleeping 6 containing 1 super-king/twin en/s spa bath & sep' shower; 1 super-king/twin & 1 twin that share private bathr'm; kitchen, BBQ, dining, living, self-serve laundry.
Price: $790 - $990 +GST for up to 4 pax. Additional Guests $150 +GST pp. Personal chef and wine selection available at additional cost.
Meals: Full breakfast provisions provided on arrival. Chef service available on site and pre-prepared gourmet meals can be arranged.
Directions: From Rotorua go N on SH33 towards Whakatane, turn R at roundabout into Tarawera Rd signed Blue Lake & Lake Tarawera. After 13km continue into Spencer Rd. 7km to Ronald Rd on R.

Map Number 2 & 3   Entry Number 39

Knapdale Eco Lodge

Kees and Kay Weytmans
114 Snowsill Rd, Waihirere, Gisborne
Tel: 06-862-5444 Fax: 06-862-5006
Email: relax@knapdale.co.nz Web: www.knapdale.co.nz
Cell: 0274-465-658

When I arrived Kay and Kees were sprucing up an already stunning Knapdale for the New Zealand 'House of the Year' assessment. (Incidentally they went on to win gold, just another acknowledgment to add to a long list of awards for accommodation and environmental achievements). Needless to say this 32ha sustainable farm is an absolute cracker. The Weytmans are aiming for complete self-sufficiency. This means that freshly-harvested veggies are served alongside home-grown beef, venison or lamb for dinner (you must experience one of Kay's four course wonders); while orchard fruits, fresh eggs and home-made muesli make their entrance at breakfast. All the animals, the eels in the lake, the roaming deer and the penned porkers for example, are up for a bit of personal interaction so feel free to join Kees on a farm-feeding spree. Kees, a forestry man by trade, is utterly entranced by nature: "I'm in love with my trees!" he enthused, directing a flow of aborial information my way. Things to do here are as numerous as the thriving community of woody perennials. Knapdale is home to unique geological phenomena, is steeped in Maori history and supports a wide array of NZ wildlife. A multitude of shade-dappled strolls suitable for the lazy poets among us and endless trails suitable for the hardier hiker extend through the farm into the wild lands beyond, taking in caves, waterfalls and magical Maori spots. With Gisborne just 8km away this beautifully tranquil place could keep you entertained for weeks... or the rest of your life in the case of Kay and Kees.

Rooms: 2: 1 king with en-suite bath and shower; 1 king with private bath and shower.
Price: $250 - $330.
Meals: Full breakfast included. 4-course gourmet dinner by arrangement including pre-dinner drinks $75 per head.
Directions: From Hawkes Bay on SH2, turn L at Makaraka, direction Opotiki/Auckland. Turn R 5km past Makaraka at green sign saying: "Gisborne, via Mangapapa". Snowsill Rd is 1st L & Knapdale Eco Lodge is signed. From Gisborne: Snowsill Rd is last road on R before reaching SH2 on Back Ormond Rd.

Apartment 4

Robyn White

4 Waghorne St, Ahuriri, Napier
Tel: 06-835-5017 Fax: 06-835-5019
Email: apartment4@xtra.co.nz Web: www.apartment4.co.nz
Cell: 027-249-0543

As soon as I reached the bright blue steps and Mediterranean patio of Apartment 4 I knew it was going to be different. The original triangular-peaked structure of an old wool store has been segmented into a number of apartments that share Ahuriri, the new Napier hotspot with its funky cafés, cobbled streets and busy art galleries. Right at the heart of it all, cosseted by art deco buildings, lies Apartment 4. Letting myself in through patio doors fringed by aquamarine waves of curtain I dropped my bags and flumped onto a hugely comfortable bed. My only dilemma... what to choose for breakfast? An amazing array of goodies is delivered to your door in the morning and, although I did spend a few moments admiring my beautifully presented bacon, pesto, avocado and cream cheese bagel, I confess that its destruction was not long coming. Here you can be as independent or as pampered as you wish, but I would certainly recommend meeting your host. Robyn is a fascinating character who has travelled extensively and sailed at least six of the seven seas. Her credentials for running this sort of operation are also impeccable having headed up hotels and restaurants in the past, as well as being Napier born and bred. We chatted and giggled all night and I don't think I have ever felt quite so *chez moi* this far from home.

Rooms: 1 queen en/s with shower.
Price: $155 - $185. Singles $135 - $165.
Meals: Full breakfast included: croissants with bacon, tomato and cheese and poached eggs with wilted spinach and hollandaise. Excellent restaurants nearby.
Directions: Drive along Napier's Marine Parade, the sea to your right. Keep going past the port, turn right into Hardinge Rd along the waterfront. Keep going until near the end you turn left at The Crown Hotel into Bridge St. Take first right into Waghorne St. Apartment 4 is opposite The Union Hotel.

Mornington Private Lodge

Diana Swayn
20a Sealy Road, Bluff Hill, Napier
Tel: 06-835-4450 Fax: 06-835-4452
Email: diana.swayn@paradise.net.nz Web: www.mornington.co.nz

Mornington perches on rock buttresses on the seaward side of Bluff Hill and gazes out at th
sweep of the bay. Diana and I sat out for cocktails on the balcony and chatted about her time
a fashion designer. Later, after a brief wander past rows of tall-stemmed roses, I joined paths wi
a cat just leaving the vine-covered courtyard and followed him through the house to lounge wi
him and his astute buddy by the fire in the sitting-room. We all knew we were onto a good thin
A high-ceilinged central corridor leads the way to bold and beautiful guest rooms. Mary Wesley
characters would have been happy to contemplate their suitors from the balcony. I wou
normally have been tempted by the enormous claw-foot bath, but the shower here won ou
It's in an unusual alcove, tiled dark red and the inside halogens make the steam visible. I opene
nearly all the tempting bottles and stepped out and engulfed myself in masses of soft burgund
towels, before diving into the deep bed and revelling in the joys of electric blankets. Breakfast w
a simply outstanding honey porridge with buttered apples, croissants and fresh OJ. Lucky cats.
Napier, Cape Kidnapper's gannet colony, massage, hot pools.

Rooms: 2: I queen and I twin room, sharing I private
bathroom. Only one group of guests at a time.
Price: $300 for the double. $270 for a single.
Meals: Full breakfast included. Dinners by arrangement $75 per
person (3 courses including wine).
Directions: From the north, turn L at Pandora roundabout, the
R into Battery Road, R into Shakespeare Road and R into Sealy
Rd. From south, take Marine Parade; turn L into Coote Rd, L int
Shakespeare, then R into Sealy.

Entry Number 42   Map Number

Te Kowhai Landing

Jennifer McBrearty
325 Lake Terrace, Lake Taupo,
Taupo
Tel: 0800-377-362 (in NZ
only) Fax: 09-358-2214
Email: stay@essencenz.com
Web: www.essencenz.com
Cell: 027-542-4202

"Absolute lake edge," says the brochure and there's no exaggeration. You can virtually paddle your toes in Taupo's famous water-feature from the back door at Te Kowhai Landing. Such a setting means that every room claims a wedge of mountain-lined lake scenery and you can take your pick from a range of watery activities: row the on-site boat, soak in the outdoor spa, try your hand at a bit of fly-fishing or simply take a swim. Te Kowhai is a gadget-master's dream. With state-of-the-art smart wiring (I assure you it's as cool as it sounds), everything can be adjusted with the merest twitch of the little finger. The roaring open fire, key-less door, underfloor heating and inter-house DVD and stereo all jump to it running off this system. The full gourmet kitchen with sleek modern lines also holds its own in the hi-tech stakes. Nicky, Te Kowhai's vivacious manager and fully-trained chef, was confidently putting together a 5-course meal for a group of 20 when I stopped in. I'd certainly recommend investing in her expertise for dinner with a bottle of wine selected from the under-stairs cellar. Both bedrooms and bathrooms, like the rest of the house, have slatted wooden shutters that open up completely making your bath virtually open-air and letting you drink in the breeze at sunset. Coolly decorated in sharp greys and whites and softened by contemporary Kiwi art, Te Kowhai Landing is truly chic.

Rooms: Self-catering house sleeping 6: two superking/twin suites, 1 with en-suite bath and shower 1 with en-suite shower. Extra share-twin available if required. Gourmet kitchen, BBQ, dining, living, self-serve laundry.
Price: $890 +GST - $1090 +GST for up to 4 persons. Additional Guests $150 +GST pp. Personal chef and wine selection available at additional cost.
Meals: Full breakfast provisions provided on arrival. Chef service available on site and pre-prepared gourmet meals can be arranged.
Directions: Heading south of Taupo on SH1 continue past the Napier Highway (SH5) turn-off. The property is on the right-hand side just before Hawai Street on the left and the 'Sail Centre' on the right. Available on website, emailed or faxed on booking.

Map Number 2 & 3

Taupo Garden Lodge

William and Suzanne Hindmarsh

70 Hindmarsh Drive, Taupo
Tel: 07-378-9847; freephone 0800 HAMLET, 0800-426-538
Fax: 07-378-5799 Email: wehindmarsh@xtra.co.nz Web:
www.taupogardenlodge.co.nz Cell: 0275-531-253

This is a beautiful small fishing Lodge. William and Suzanne have lived at Taupo Garden Lodge for 43 years and in the process they've designed the garden, the furniture and even the house itself. Walking through three acres of mature and tranquil gardens - which include towering native trees, irises, camellias, rhododendrons, lily ponds, waterfall and an olympic-sized grass tennis court – easy to forget that you're close to the centre of town. The lawn slopes right down to the inviting clear, blue/green waters of the Waikato River where guests can fish (if you catch one Suzanne will cook it up for breakfast), swim or simply admire the view. The famous Huka Falls are also only a twenty-minute walk from the house. The lodge is packed with oil paintings, Persian rugs and dark native wood-panelling and in winter guests like to warm their feet by a vast stone-surround fireplace, cradling a glass of good wine in one hand (William knows a thing or two about wine) and enjoying the view out to the snow-capped mountains of the Central Plateau. Both bedrooms have views over the gardens and wooden beams in the ceiling. The Garden Suite has a double bay window and fridge complete with complimentary wine, and even a spare bedroom 'for the chauffeur'… I knew I'd forgotten something. Meals are usually taken with William and Suzanne but for those who really want to feel they're on holiday, breakfast in bed is always an option.

Rooms: 2: 1 queen + single en-suite (Heron Suite), 1 super-king en-s + small single/dressing room (Garden Suite).
Price: $400 for one night, $650 for two nights and $975 for 3 nights. Includes complimentary pre-dinner drinks. Rates negotiable for stays of more than 3 nights. Singles on request.
Meals: Breakfast included. Dinner by arrangement if staying 2 or more nights: $65 - $85 pp. Selected wines for additonal cost of $10 - $15.
Directions: Just north of Taupo on State Highway turn into Huka Falls Rd (Taupo Lookout entrance). Turn into Rangatira Park (Kahurangi Drive), then Hindmarsh Drive. Number 70 on lower terrace with wrought-iron gate.

Whare Ora

Diana and Tiri Sotiri

1 Kaha Street, Rangataua, Ohakune
Tel: 06-385-9385 Fax: 06-385-9385
Email: office@whareoralodge.co.nz Web: www.whareoralodge.co.nz
Cell: 027-481-5667

You are in the middle of the Tongariro National Park here, one of the first World Heritage sites ever to be declared. It is home to the Tongariro crossing, New Zealand's finest one-day trek. It's a magical world of lush rainforest, emerald lakes, purple desert, with an active volcano thrown in for good measure. No surprise, then, to discover they filmed Lord of the Rings here. Hundreds of walks, from 15 minutes to a week in length, and you can also canoe, mountain-bike, ski, horse-trek, fish, ride or read your book. At the lodge: huge rooms, peace and quiet, and piping hot baths to bring your feet back to life. The upstairs suite is enormous and has a vast triangle of glass through which Mt. Ruapehu provides a magnificent and ever-changing view. There's a wall of books, an open-plan sitting-room and a bed from which you can gaze out at the mountain. The downstairs suite is smaller but still has a bed with a view and the most luxurious bathroom. I slept blissfully in crisp linen and awoke to the sound of birdsong. The house, originally built in 1910, is warm with lots of wood lending it a smart mountain-hideaway chalet feel. Log fires in winter and wine with Diana and Tiri before supper. They have a wide range of music and Tiri knows his jazz, too. *Scenic flights over the mountains available.*

Rooms: 2 suites; 1 with en/s spa bath and separate shower and 1 with en/s shower over the bath.
Price: $225 - $295 (seasonal rates may apply). No single rates. Extra people $70 pp.
Meals: Full breakfast included. Dinner by prior arrangement only: $50 - $80 per person, dependent on the number of courses. includes wine.
Directions: East from Ohakune for about 5km, then left, signed Rangataua. Straight ahead for 0.5km, then left into Kaha Street. House on right at end of road.
Closed: Christmas.

Te Popo Gardens

Bruce and Lorri Ellis
636 Stanley Road, Stratford
Tel: 06-762-8775 Fax: 06-762-8775
Email: tepopo@clear.net.nz Web: www.tepopo.co.nz

At Te Popo, it seemed like the clocks had turned back to an older, more primitive time. On tw sides the near-vertical walls of a moss-carpeted ravine stretched upwards for some 50 feet wh verdant curtains of strange fern draped down, sun-shafts slashing through the moth-eaten velv Wading along the stream, I half-expected to meet a grazing diplodocus. The stream meanders a full kilometre through the 34-acre property. Crossing the soaring suspension bridge, wh hovers above the river gorge, I climbed back through ancient forest giants into the splendour the 6-acre woodland garden crammed with perennial borders, shrubs and trees. Te Popo is o of only two Gardens of National Significance where you can stay. The rooms are spacious a well equipped: fridges, TVs, stereos and wood-burning stoves, not to mention great views of t garden itself. It also provides a base from which to explore one of New Zealand's more interest and less visited areas, the Egmont National Park, dominated by the majestic cone of Mt. Taran I, though, was happy to do very little on my sadly brief stay. That night I followed a path lined w flickering candles and flares to an outdoor bath of clear river water. Perched on the gorge a shaded by trees laced with fairy lights, I took in the immense backdrop and relaxed. N morning, I awoke to the roaring of stags and the melodious sound of birdsong – Te Po incidentally, translates as lullaby.

Rooms: 4: 1 queen, 1 king and 1 superking/twin (king singles); 1 king plus 2 singles. All with en-suite shower.
Price: $145 - $180. Singles $120 - $150.
Meals: Full breakfast included.
Directions: In Stratford turn into Regan Street and SH43 (The Forgotten World Highway) from the northern roundabout. Travel 4km, cross one-way bridge, turn L into Beaconsfield Rd. 4km R at schoo into Stanley Rd, follow for 6.36 km down into valle Te Popo on your right.

River Valley

Brian and Nicola Megaw

Taihape
Tel: 06-388-1444 Fax: 06-388-1859
Email: thelodge@rivervalley.co.nz
Web: www.rivervalley.co.nz

Long ago, when giant Moa birds stalked New Zealand's shores, a Maori adventurer named Hau went in search of his errant wife. The journey was long with many arduous river crossings. But most challenging of all was a torrent of water, which rose in the volcanic country of Ruapehu; Hau named the river Rangitikei, the day of the long walk. Fast forward to the late 20th century when in the spirit of Hau, Kiwi adventurers discovered that a lot of fun could be had hurtling down the Rangitikei in a rubber dinghy. These white-water rafting fanatics needed somewhere to stay, so River Valley was born. On the evening I stayed, damp-haired twenty-somethings drank with their rafting guide in the cavernous bar and restaurant, whilst the week-long art-course students discussed life drawing's finer points. After a meal of local chicken and warm chocolate and raspberry muffin, I walked back to my clutter-free room, with its rough-hewn furniture and neutral walls the colour of river pebbles. I climbed into my huge bed and dozed off with the gushing Rangitikei only metres away. Next morning was riding time. My pony was a feisty Arab... and it could go! Galloping up an escarpment overlooking the eternity of wild, volcanic country I felt a bit like Arwen from Lord of the Rings... except without the unearthly beauty or the fluent Elvish. After my GG visits I hope to return; after one night at River Valley I am determined. *Golf, fly-fishing, Maori cultural walks and spa complex also available.*

Rooms: 8: 2 triples, 5 twins/doubles, 1 family with 2 bunks and 1 double. All with en-suite shower.
Price: $149 for whole room.
Meals: Buffet Continental and cooked breakfasts. Cooked breakfast $11. Evening meals cost $35 for 3 courses, and $25 for 2.
Directions: See website.

Mairenui Rural Retreat

Sue and David Sweet

1019 Ruahine Road, Mangaweka, Kimbolton
Tel: 06-382-5564 Fax: 06-382-5564
Email: mairenui@xtra.co.nz Web: www.mairenui.co.nz
Cell: 027-451-7545

Sweet land, indeed… a real hideaway in wild country, where a 200-foot gorge crumbles into the river below and cars pass by at the rate of one an hour. The Sweets farm the land as far as you can see on their side of the river and when David's father returned from Palestine in 1921, built a rope-bridge across the gorge that still survives today. The views are inspiring, and exploring the Rangitikei River, the green sheep-mown hills, gorges and white cliffs of the area is irresistible. Mairenui is a way of life for Sue and David, not a slick business, and every crumbling outbuilding, painting or antique car has a story and a reason to be here. The land has not been over manicured, just allowed to follow its nose. I saw a huge bush of never-pruned wild lavender, willow bathing its branches in the lily pond, orchids growing from the tops of trees, wild turkey strutting in the fields. You can stay in various places: the house, for traditional farmhouse B&B; an extraordinary architect-designed retreat with its awesome views of ridge and peak; or a cottage across the road surrounded by a ha-ha to keep the horses at bay. You're free to help on the farm, chop the wood, take to the hills. David and Sue are fabulous, well-travelled, humorous hosts, and dinners at the homestead are great fun. This is one of the great places to stay in New Zealand. *French and German spoken, golf and world-class fly fishing nearby.*

Rooms: The retreat sleeps 6 with bath and shower. 1 cottage (sleeps 10) with bath and shower. In house: 1 double with bath and shower; 1 twin/king with en/s shower.
Price: B&B in house $130 - $300 B&B per double; Retreat from $150 per double, $50 for each additional person; Villa $80 (accommodation only).
Meals: Full breakfast included if staying in the house. Breakfast provided at homestead for others $10 - $15 pp. 3-course dinner by arrangement $40 - $60 pp.
Directions: South for Mangaweka on SH1. Just before town sign, left for Rangiwahia on Ruahine Road. Down hill, over bridge, straight on along side of gorge for 9km and signed half way up hill on L.

The Schoolhouse

The Melling Family
91 Rua Ave, Waitarere Beach,
Levin
Tel: 021-530-549
Fax: 04-385-8685
Email:
david@architecturecentral.co.nz
Web: www.schoolhouse.co.nz

If this had been my school I know I wouldn't have got an awful lot of work done. With the beach beckoning a short stroll away through tufty sand-dunes, the temptation to whip a swimming costume on and sling a surfboard under my arm would have been too much. (Incidentally a surf-board is stowed in the rafters if you want to do just that.) Two original school prefabs have been merged and lovingly fleshed out under the watchful architectural eye of David (whose craftsman's hands have also played a considerable part). Salvaged matai floors now run throughout the open-plan kitchen and large lounge, where you'll find a pool table, TV and a wealth of videos, DVDs, games and books. Meanwhile a brand-new contemporary kitchen is nicely offset by the satisfying curves of a matai worktop (originally joists from a Wellington office block). This poised-for-a-party house breathes laughter and fun with an expansive sunbathing, sundowning, barbecue deck. Bedrooms are neat and simple with two bunk rooms for kids or friends and a great double that can be opened up entirely on a hot night to catch the fresh sea breeze. This is a fantastic family spot, but if it's space and tranquillity you're after you'll do just as well to leave the kids at home. *Kapiti Island bird sanctuary is nearby, while, on a good day, Mt. Taranaki can be seen on the horizon. Rambling, horse-riding, biking and fishing in the Tararua ranges and Wellington is an easy one and a half hours' drive. Linen and towels are taken care of.*

Rooms: 1 fully self-contained cottage sleeping 6. 1 double and 2 bunkrooms sharing 1 bathroom with shower.
Price: $120 - $180 per night - for the whole cottage!
Meals: Fully self-catering. Initial breakfast supplies can be provided by arrangement at an additional cost.
Directions: Heading north from Wellington on SH1 pass through Levin and take Waitarere Beach turn-off to the L. Follow road to far T-junction and turn L into Rua Ave. The Schoolhouse is number 91 on R.

Map Number 3 & 4

Entry Number 49

The Ranch

Jennifer Clark
Maungakotukutuku Road, Maungakotukutuku, Paraparaumu
Tel: 04-384-7713 Fax: 04-384-7731
Email: info@theclarkcollection.com Web: www.theclarkcollection.com
Cell: 021-472-406

Gazing across glassy waters to the velvet green hills of the Kapiti Island bird sanctuary, The Ranch would effortlessly win any most-beautiful-view competitions the North Island might wish to host. I am sure that the rather splendid sculpted figure beside me would agree. With spectacular coastal views that stretch from the top of the South Island to the slopes of Mt Taranaki in the north, it feels like you have the whole of New Zealand in your pocket, or in this case at the bottom of your huge and rolling garden. Excelling equally as both a viewfinder and a cosy family-holiday home, obligatory cinematic widescreen windows girdle both storeys of The Ranch's wooden frame. Inside locally-crafted furniture, plumped up sofas, high cedar-wood ceilings and a great stone fireplace created that instant warm-on-the-inside glow. There are enough bedrooms to sleep eight, two big living areas and a dining area where family, friends, and even a few friends of friends could all happily sit together at the 18th-century French provincial dining table. Activities galore will keep everyone at leisure and include a golf green, a spa pool, a tennis court and a games room. Best of all is the fabulously jungle-like swimming pool that's fringed with ferns and all lit up at night for pool-side BBQs. You are also seconds away from native bush walks and mountain biking tracks and just a few minutes from golf courses, beaches and national parks. However, like the surreal, gorgeous, come-hither landscape outside, there is a make-believe quality about this place that will keep you from roaming too far from home.

Rooms: One house with 4 bedrooms: 2 kings with en-suite bathrooms on upper level; 1 room with double bed, 1 room with twin beds on lower level, with a shared bath and shower room.
Price: $590 - $790 + gst for 6 persons. $50 pp per night for extras, up to 8 people. Two-night minimum stay.
Meals: A first-morning breakfast basket is provided. private gourmet chef and/or catering for functions is available by prior arrangement at an additional charge.
Directions: Faxed or emailed on booking.

Number 11

Virginia Barton-Chapple

11 Hay Street, Oriental Bay, Wellington
Tel: 04-801-9290 Fax: 04-801-9295
Email: v.barton-chapple@xtra.co.nz
Cell: 021-130-9544

Hay Street is a thriving little community in the heart of the city and it climbs uphill, thereby allowing views of Oriental Bay and Wellington harbour. From this vantage point, big windows look onto the water and you can watch sailing boats, ferries and cargo ships chug back and forth… the binoculars are close at hand. Turn around and look inwards and the view is just as good. Virginia is a sculptor (she may kill me for letting this particular cat out of the bag) and her work, and the work of her friends, is everywhere. I counted 30 pieces on her terrace, which seems to double as a gallery. Her home is delightful and she runs it without too much ceremony, just as you would if you had friends coming to stay. The bedroom downstairs is big, with cool interiors and a very comfy bed, and I didn't hear a sound all night. The heart of Wellington is a ten-minute walk along the waterfront. You can swim in Oriental Bay, where a fountain bursts ten metres into the air. Alternatively, a 30-minute walk to the summit of Mount Victoria brings fine views. Virginia will give the best advice on all matters artistic, travelistic, foody. Great fun and excellent value in all departments.

Rooms: 1 twin/double sharing a shower room.
Price: $140 - $150. Singles $120 - $130.
Meals: Full breakfast included. Lots of restaurants locally.
Directions: SH1 into Wellington. Take 'Aotea Quay' exit. Keep left on main road for about 3km. At T-junction, left along waterfront, signed 'Oriental Bay'. Road bends right, then hugs the bay. Hay Street is on the right and signed.

Palliser House

Jennifer Clark
Roseneath, Wellington
Tel: 04-384-7713 Fax: 04-384-7731
Email: info@theclarkcollection.com Web: www.theclarkcollection.com
Cell: 021-472-406

This historic 1904 villa is a great launch pad from which to explore the capital: it is city without the slick, central without being cocooned, and beautifully mapped out. Arranged on one level, super native timber and original period features give clues to the restored villa's Victorian past. Moder New Zealand sculpture and paintings jostle for space with historic NZ art works. An antiqu dresser-cum-writing table, Victorian fireplaces, Persian rugs and a fantastic wood-carved bed an mirrored wardrobe are just a few remnants from Palliser's past. From its height above Wellingto Harbour the city is laid out beneath you. After days spent exploring the city, sit on the enclose balcony and watch the lights twinkle in Oriental Bay before heading down into town again. O find some friends (there's room enough for ten at the table) and make use of the fab open-pla modern kitchen. At the end of the walkway and up the steps, you're just minutes from Orient Bay's lovely swimming pool as well as Wellington's theatre, arts and restaurant district and th famed Te Papa Museum. Despite this, from inside the grounds, you could be in another worl The villa is set in its own acre of native garden where birds chatter away as a collection o sculptures look quietly on, in keeping with the tranquility, privacy and calm. *Palliser House is ju 10 minutes from the airport.*

Rooms: One house with 3 bedrooms: 1 superking, 2 queen. They share 2 character bathrooms with showers.
Price: $490 - $690 + gst for 4 persons. $50 pp per night for extras, up to 6 people. Two-night minimum stay.
Meals: A first-morning breakfast basket is provided.
Directions: Emailed or faxed on booking.

Grace Cottage

Ross Stevenson

112 Abel Smith St, Wellington
Tel: 021-938-096
Email: reservations@gracecottage.co.nz Web: www.gracecottage.co.nz
Cell: 021-938-096

Firstly a confession... I didn't actually make it to Grace Cottage, but I love romantic stories. This cosy dwelling is one of the oldest buildings in Wellington. A seaman built it in 1865 for his beloved wife, Grace, so that she would be comfortable whilst he rode the seven seas. This historic cottage has been carefully restored and blended with 21st-century urban chic under the watchful eye of trusted GG owner and architect David Melling... so all things considered, we couldn't resist putting it in. The exterior is typical of Wellington's settler cottages; a white-washed, one-storey dwelling with a tin roof and shaded verandah framed by ornamental columns and punctuated by a cabbage tree. Once inside the design edge is revealed with an open living/dining area with views beyond the ultra-modern galley kitchen through to a flat lawn bordered by native New Zealand ferns and grasses. A strip of skylights further enhances the connection to the outside and filters light deep into the house. All furnishings and artwork are by local designers and artists. The bedrooms are original with coal-range fireplaces and natural wood flooring. Two have double beds and the third has two fold-away bunks so it can also be used as an office space. This place is ideal for garden lovers. A glass door leads onto the garden deck where guests eat, gossip, sunbathe on the lawn, barbeque and generally do whatever takes their fancy. At sundown they retreat indoors to cosy up to the open fireplace with a Sky and DVD controller in hand. If a night out is on the cards, Cuba Street - one of the capital's buzziest locales - is a mere hop skip and a jump away. *Full linen service available.*

Rooms: 3: 2 doubles, 1 with 2 bunks. Separate bathroom with bath/shower.
Price: $400 per night. $2400 per week.
Meals: Self catered. Meals can be provided by arrangement.
Directions: Head south on Victoria St and turn right into Abel Smith Street – the property is the third house on the right.

City Bach

David Melling

230 Victoria Street, Wellington
Tel: 04-385-8685
Email: david@architecturecentral.co.nz Web: www.citybach.co.nz
Cell: 021-530-549

For the uninitiated, a bach is the Kiwi equivalent of a holiday home. A generation ago they we
simple affairs; my cousins, for example, loaded a wooden shed onto a trailer and transported th
'bach' from Northland to Taupo. Over the years, bits and bobs have been added and remov
but the simple, honest character is still retained. While 'City Bach', exudes the feel-good factor
a Kiwi bach in its simplicity and setting – within the branches of a rare northern rata tree –
comparison ends there. This brand-new, designer, stand-alone apartment has all the elements
luxury city living. There is a glass-fronted double bedroom ideal for one couple, while a seco
couple could use the sofa-bed in the living area. It's perfect for urban types, who conversely cra
space. High up on the rooftop entertaining-deck with only native tuis for company, you can surv
New Zealand's capital city from all angles, sunbathing in the 360-degree, all-day sun (unless
raining, of course). Come evening you can pour yourself a sundowner and BBQ some fresh
before descending into the maelstrom for a night of fun and frolics on Wellington's buzzing Cu
St, literally on your doorstep. *Sky TV, full linen service and garage parking available for up to 2 ca*

Rooms: 1 queen and a wet-room with shower.
Price: $250 per night, $1,500 per week.
Meals: Self-catering. Refreshments can be provide
by arrangement.
Directions: Head south on Victoria Street past
Vivian Street, turn right half-way down the block
before Abel Smith Street and head to the end of th
slip road - City Bach is in front of you.

Parehua Country Estate

Mike and Lois Kunac

New York St, Martinborough
Tel: 06-306-8405 Fax: 06-306-8409
Email: info@parehua.co.nz Web: www.parehua.co.nz
Cell: Freephone within NZ 0800 4 PAREHUA (727 348)

Tucked away below Hawke's Bay and bursting with micro-vineyards and delis stocking such exotic delicacies as chilli chocolate and basil brie, the Wairarapa is the mini-break destination *du jour* for Wellington's creative types and wine enthusiasts. Martinborough in particular is the jewel in the region's crown. Set in a vineyard with the snow-capped Tararua Mountains glowering in the distance, Parehua is an easy ten-minutes' walk from the town centre. It's owned by Mike and Lois, a self-confessed "hands-on" couple who arrange in-house beauty treatments for guests, as well as courtesy vans – so no need to worry about Mr Plod after an afternoon sampling the local pinot. Rooms are self-contained – you won't see a soul during your stay, if you so desire - with the kind of urban interiors that keep all those city-dwellers coming back for more, notebook in hand. My favourites are the lakeside cottages, with their outdoor hot tubs. Even on the dull autumn day of my visit, the taupe walls glowed with natural light flowing through the French windows that open onto the garden where pukekos poke for worms. Inside the space is divided into a sitting room complete with gas-fire; a white-tiled kitchen; a bathroom with spa bath; and of course the bedroom with its huge chocolate-coloured bed, a fluffy sheepskin rug and a window-seat ergonomically designed for the reading of tattered paperbacks. Most importantly though, the mini-bar comes stocked with Pringles: heaven.

Rooms: 28: 22 suites, 4 cottages, 2 two-bedroom villas. All with bath and shower en/s. Cottages and villas also have outdoor hot baths.

Price: Doubles are $320 - $450, for 4 pp $590 until end Sept 2008. Then from $350 - $475 for doubles, $650 for 4 pp until end April 2009.

Meals: Full cooked & continental breakfast included.

Directions: From Wellington, take SH2 through the Hutt Valley, to Featherston. Take main turn right to Martinborough and follow signs. In Martinborough township, take left at Princess St, then left into New York Street – Parehua is at the end of the road on R.

South Island - Accommodation

Adrift Beachfront Accommodation

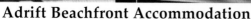

Gordon and Bess Hampson and Emily and John Lolani
52 Tukurua Road, Golden Bay, Takaka
Tel: 03-525-8353 Fax: 03-525-8353
Email: stay@adrift.co.nz Web: www.adrift.co.nz
Cell: 027-301-5832

The spectacular mountains that surround Golden Bay create quite a backdrop to this beach-set property. Gordon's beaming face was the first to greet me on arrival followed swiftly by the soothing tones of the sea. Here you are literally a pebble's throw away from Tukurua Beach, the Hampsons' own private slice of shell-peppered sands and gentle surf. Whales and blue penguins are known to frequent the tranquil waters while Einstein and Gracie (the family's two silver-haired cats) are more likely to be found hunting in the bushes. Adrift is the perfect launch pad to vibey Golden Bay's brimming culture of artists, Maori history and its multitude of walks and hikes. The brand-new self-catering cottages are elegantly finished in greens and dark woods with fully kitted-out kitchens, chic bathrooms (including all-singing-and-tap-dancing spa baths) and lavish beds that overlook the beach. Green-fingered and knowledgeable hosts Gordon and Bess have now turned their attentions to maintaining the natural wetlands, shoreline and gardens, filling them with native species, encouraging the birdlife and ensuring that each cottage has its own pretty trail to the shore. A morning breakfast basket brims with everything local, fresh and home-made reinforcing the wonderfully wholesome family-run atmosphere of Adrift. *Kayaks and BBQ available.*

Rooms: 5 cottages: all king/twins with full kitchen, lounge, bedroom and bathrooms with double spa bath and shower. Additional pull-out bed available. 1 studio room: king/twin with en/s bathroom with shower.
Price: $100 - $360. $40 for each additional person.
Meals: Hamper of breakfast provisions included. There are over twenty restaurants in Golden Bay.
Directions: 18km north of Takaka on SH60. Adrift is signed on the right (Tukurua Rd), 2km past the Mussel Inn.

Stafford Place

Bob and Sally Livingston
61 Redwood Rd, Appleby, Richmond
Tel: 03-544-6103 Fax: 03-544-6103
Email: staffordplace@xtra.co.nz Web: www.staffordplace.co.nz
Cell: 027-232-5121

Gracious among flowers, lawn and bird-filled agéd oaks, Stafford Place flaunts her auther
Victorian beauty. Built in 1866 as a replacement to the Redwoods' 1842 family home t
originally fell prey to an earthquake, this house is steeped in history and stories - both of wh
your hosts will happily tell if you are interested. Surveyor Bob and wife Sally have inadverter
won an award for their restoration of the property since they moved here in 2000. The stat
guest lounge, flushed with light from towering windows and filled with intriguing antiques, focu
on its skilfully-restored fireplace. With deep red walls and classic complimentary hues this is a roc
that warms in winter and cools in summer. I loved the bathroom, a whole suite in itself, with gi
clear-sided shower, delicately-flowered walls and polished matai floor. It was also the cause c
good two-hour extension to my bedtime when I fell into a bubbly sleep in the claw-footed ba
Staying true to the traditional nature of the property Sally pulls out all the stops at breakfast w
her home-made muesli and scrumptious kedgeree that will set you up, as it did me, for the wh
day. You are free to roam the 10-12 acres of olive groves and farmland with welcoming golc
lab Katie. And, with only the one suite, the peace and space are exclusively yours. *Rabbit Islar
secluded beaches are only a moment away.*

Rooms: 1 king with full en-suite bathroom. 1 single
room suitable for additional person.
Price: Double $250. Single $150.
Meals: Full breakfast included.
Directions: Guest pick-up service from Nelson
airport. From SH6 heading west from Nelson turn
right onto SH60 heading for Collingwood. Take a le
from the main highway onto Redwood Rd opposite
the turn-off to Rabbit Island (also Redwood Rd).
Stafford Place is 900m on the right, then 500m dov
a tree-lined drive.

39 Russell

Owner Jane Evans; Managers, James Taylor and Richard Hewetson

c/o 41 Russell Street, Nelson Tel: 03-548-7621 Fax: 03-548-7645
Email: 39Russell@NelsonLuxuryAccommodation.co.nz
Web: www.nelsonluxuryaccommodation.co.nz Cell: 021-679-795

Jane Evans is an icon in New Zealand, a painter whose works feature in prints or even originals - you wish! The waiting list for a JE is 130 and counting - in nearly every house I visited. And her own house (next door, try and get a look) and guest cottage are further testament to her creative powers and eye for detail. Studio visits are available. You, the guest, need do no more than rock up and be royally spoiled. The raked gravel garden is lined with citrus trees and feijoa vine with a deck for barbecues and sunbathing. This is where most evenings are spent, a surprisingly private place with high views down to the docks, gorgeous at night. And inside? Well, I can hardly improve on the photo, but I will take you round the corner to the bathrooms where a large slipper-bath is filled from a space-age laser tap and the showers have half-inch-thick glass doors and walls. Colours are stunning, furniture comfortable, paintings original, mod cons (TV, video, washer/dryer, under-floor heating) state of art; there are magazines, CDs, books and lots of delicious things to eat and drink in the fridge… and film crews are quite reasonably lining up for a chance to get inside. Jane remains humorous and straightforward despite all the accolades. The attention to detail is phenomenal and I know I haven't described a quarter of what there is to enjoy here. *Children over 12 welcome. Jane strongly recommends 3-night stays!*

Rooms: 1 cottage: 1 queen with en-suite bath and shower, 1 twin, 1 separate shower room.
Price: $495 for two, $25 for each extra person. Minimum stay 2 nights. Singles full cottage rate.
Meals: Full breakfast provisions provided. Self-catering.
Directions: Directions and key location emailed when you book.

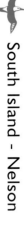

Te Puna Wai

Richard Hewetson and James Taylor
24 Richardson Street, Britannia Heights, Nelson
Tel: 03-548-7621 Fax: 03-548-7645
Email: stay@tepunawai.co.nz Web: www.tepunawai.co.nz
Cell: 021-679-795

The wide, open windows and verandahs at Te Puna Wai boast one of the best views in this bo
straight out over Haulashore Island and the Nelson harbour entrance, with the Tasman and Art
ranges to left and right respectively. The house is Richard and James's pride and joy, a n
Victorian (1857) villa with a fine, intricate façade, the whole building restored and painstakir
completed under Richard's generalship. Guests have a choice of three rooms. Downstairs
Haulashore apartment has its own balcony, bedroom and state-of-the-art kitchen (chrome
granite grey) and a gorgeously green, marble-tiled bathroom with underfloor heating; the Wak
room at the back also has a marble bathroom and the two rooms make a wonderful apartm
for families. Or there's the attic Fifeshire suite, my personal favourite for its open wall of a wind
looking down at the bay and up at the stars. Arabian Nights notions leap to the imagination. T
luxurious marble-tiled bathroom is full of whimsical design touches and has a wonderful full-len;
claw-foot bath. There is a first-floor sitting-room with blue sofas, mango walls and wooden floc
many books and a stunning verandah with a low parapet. Richard is a truly talented ling
(German, French, Spanish and Portuguese) and much travelled. He and partner James provic
stylish, visually energising city retreat. Te Puna Wai must be one of the happiest places I h
visited. *Friendly cat in residence and many canine visitors. High-speed Internet, guest PC, WIFI L*

Rooms: 3: 1 self-contained apartment with queen
kitchen & en/s shower; 1 queen room en/s showe
(can be part of apartment); 1 suite: queen, additior
ante-room with double & full en/s bathroom.
Price: $195 for side room B&B, $295 for attic roc
B&B, $325 for apartment, $480 for downstairs
double rooms let as one-party booking. Single, lon;
term & off-season rates available.
Meals: Complimentary drinks & full breakfast
included. Guests in apartment can choose B&B or
self-prepare breakfasts (provisions provided so not
self-catering).
Directions: Map on Te Puna Wai web site.

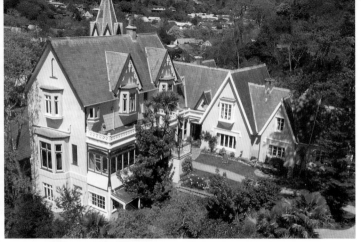

Warwick House

Nick and Jenny Ferrier
64 Brougham Street, Nelson
Tel: 03-548-3164 (freephone within NZ 0800 0222 33)
Fax: 03-548-3215 Email: enquiries@warwickhouse.co.nz
Web: www.warwickhouse.co.nz Cell: 027-688-243

Originally built in 1854 and known as 'The Castle' to Nelson locals, Warwick House's fame springs from its surprising turreted exterior and colourful past. 'Made in England' with Welsh-slate tiles, the property proudly guards the entrance to the valley, its impressive structure hogging the pick of the views from every window. When I arrived Nick was up a ladder, head in a trap door, ear taped to a phone and torch picking out yet another original arch waiting to be excavated. I therefore took the opportunity to digest the full magnitude of Warwick House's splendour, starting with the ballroom. Gigantic bay windows allow streams of light to run over the rich original matai flooring. A masterpiece of restoration, it seems to hang suspended in the leafy branches of an 80- to 90-year-old double tulip tree that reaches up from a garden far below. Nick and Jenny are a fascinating couple. They have lived and worked in Thailand, Indonesia, Burma, Hong Kong, Vietnam, Europe - the list goes on, yet Warwick House continues to surprise them with hidden staircases and rooms. You'll find tokens of their travels throughout – what better place to put a pair of 400-year-old, iron-clad Chinese doors than the entrance to the dungeon and tower? The suites are exquisitely fashioned in traditional Victorian grandeur and are truly superb. I only wish I had more room to describe them! *Vickie is the enthusiastic black lab in residence - and she loves walks! Central Nelson 5 minutes' walk away. Wireless broadband.*

Rooms: 3 suites: all kings with en-suite clawfoot bath and separate shower; 2 with private lounges.
Price: $250 - $395.
Meals: Full breakfast included. It is possible to organise meals for larger groups, enquire on booking.
Directions: Emailed on request.

Retiro Park Lodge

Robbert de Jongh and Victor Flores
152 Teal Valley, Nelson
Tel: 03-545-0118
Email: info@retiroparklodge.co.nz Web: www.retiroparklodge.co.nz

Retiro Park Lodge certainly does justice to the picturesque central park in Madrid after whic[h] was named. Many a walking track wind their way around the petite vineyard, olive and almo[nd] groves of the 50-acre farm. Donkeys, llamas and alpacas (all named according to the year in wh[ich] they were born) will befriend you if you feed them and I'm sure that Flavia, a sleek, boun[cy] greyhound with the enthusiasm of a puppy, will accompany you on walks if you let her. Robb[ert] has lived for over 20 years in Spain and has the collector gene. You'll find objects from all over t[he] world that capture the attention and imagination. A vast opulent bathroom in the main hou[se] echoes the Mediterranean in vivid terracotta and deep blues, while the impressive ba[rn] conversion is fresh and light and allows for a little more independence. Robbert and Vic[tor] encourage guests to dine with them on their first night, and I certainly had a fantastic time shoot[ing] the breeze with them over a leisurely meal. The couple share a sharp sense of humour and enthusiasm for the world that will keep you chatting for hours. Since Victor is a trained chef I c[an] assure you that both food and company will be wonderful, and I will be sorely jealous. The loc[ation] is only 15 minutes from Nelson with its numerous galleries, restaurants and activities. But Retir[o's] Spanish translation is 'retreat' and I would take the hint. *Your hosts speak English, Spanish and Dut[ch.] Tours of Abel-Tasman can be arranged through here. Wireless broadband.*

Rooms: 2: 1 queen with en-suite bathroom in the lodge and 1 queen with en-suite bathroom and kitchenette in converted barn. Additional single roo[m] in lodge and day bed in barn available on request.
Price: $250 - $275. Singles $150.
Meals: Full breakfast included. Picnic lunches & 3-course dinner by arrangement, both at additional cost. Dinner $150 (wine inc). Can be self-catering.
Directions: From Nelson travel 14km on SH 6 towards Blenheim. Turn R into Teal Valley Rd and travel a further 1.4km to private road. Retiro Park Lodge is signed on the right 200m on.

Cove Cottage

Sue and Nigel Hutchinson

Jetty 45, Double Cove, Picton
Tel: 03-573-4153
Email: doublecove@xtra.co.nz Web: www.doublecove.co.nz
Cell: 021-433-921

It's not everywhere you can go for a daybreak stroll in your pyjamas without fear of embarrassment, but at Cove Cottage that is exactly what I did. Lazily reclining on the second peninsula of Double Cove this unpretentious bach trails its gaze through blue topaz waters on both sides. Wedged between a rising backdrop of private woodland and the sea, this 'boat-access-only' spot is an entirely secluded resort in itself. Between much laughter and stories of Land Rover adventures through Africa, Kiwi-Sue and Brit-Nigel told me of quirky Cove Cottage's development from its humble origins as a ramshackle shed. Wonderfully friendly and fascinating people, they have injected the cottage with a full dose of character. The marine motif is subtle and interesting: driftwood framed mirror, old shell-shaded lights on pulley systems, flags and lighthouses. Also the 'sleep out,' a romantic hideaway with its own en-suite bathroom just up the path, is great for couples (although the beds can be twins if required). You won't be watching the TV with kayaks, rowing-boats, walks and art materials to play with, but you could always pop on 'Goodbye Porkpie' which was produced by your host! The deck next to the dock takes full advantage of a BBQ-friendly sunspot. Here I imagine many a sunset sinking into the night carried on a wave of fun, food... and probably booze. *Private walking tracks link directly to Queen Charlotte track walk (perhaps accompanied by friendly lab Fraser) and dolphin-watching trips are arranged as well as tours to bird and animal sanctuaries.*

Rooms: 1 self-catering cottage: 1 double room and 1 twin room with shared shower. Additional king/twin with e/s shower in the 'cabin.'
Price: From $250 - $350 per night. $60 for each additional person.
Meals: Fully self-catering. BBQ facilities and gas supplied. Can pre-arrange cupboards to be stocked beforehand.
Directions: 4km from Picton. Boat access only. Details of water taxis operating from Picton will be emailed on confirmation.

Map Number 3 & 4

Straw Lodge

Nettie Barrow and Jane Craighead

17 Fareham Lane, Blenheim
Tel: 03-572-9767 Fax: 03-572-9769
Email: strawlodge@xtra.co.nz Web: www.strawlodge.co.nz

What a cheery place! I defy any of you to leave Straw Lodge without a spring in your st
Interesting, super-friendly hosts, lots of wine, good food and charming accommodation made
you've guessed it, straw. Techniques have advanced since the days of the Three Little Pigs
here straw bales are plastered to create an atmospheric, well-insulated, rustic walling. Eight ye
ago this area was just paddocks, but now 19 acres of vines reach virtually to the doors of the gu
rooms in this picture-postcard setting in the Wairau Valley. Dinner was a very happy affair, help
no doubt by the 'in-house' sauvignon blanc and pinot noir, made by a local wine-maker fro
Straw Lodge grapes... and the trend continued at breakfast, minus the wine. In warm weath
(virtually the whole year in sunny Blenheim) meals are served outside on a long table un
trellises, a setting that reminded me of those country feast scenes from olive oil adverts. Gue
stay in apartments either side of the main house, but you're welcome, nay expected,
roaunfettered. There's a woody lounge with big beams and large fire, DVDs, CDs and TVs in
the rooms, a spa under the stars and private courtyards and BBQ areas. Definitely a wrench
leave. *Nettie and Jane also run a guiding company and can either guide or advise you about all so
of wine-tasting, walking, 4x4, fishing and cycling excursions. Complimentary golf clubs, mountain b
and wine-tasting available for guests.*

Rooms: 3: 2 Vineyard Suites, with king/twin +
double sofa-bed, & 1 double suite. All have en-s sh
Price: $255 - $348. Singles $235 - $295. Extra
person $75. Child (under 12) $50. Single night
booking surcharge $40.
Meals: Full gourmet cooked breakfast included.
Dinners $90 p.p. including wine. Vineyard platters f
two $60. Self-catering facilities plus BBQ courtyards
available for guests use.
Directions: From Blenheim, head towards Nelson
on SH6, then turn left onto SH63 towards the wes
coast. Travel for just over 7km to Fareham Lane on
your right. The house is 200m down here.

Old St Mary's Convent Retreat

Layonie Seque and Keith Denham
776 Rapaura Road, Blenheim
Tel: 03-570-5700 Fax: 03-570-5703
Email: retreat@convent.co.nz Web: www.convent.co.nz

Oh to have been a Marlborough nun! This really would have been quite some place to live: a large, handsome 1901 house with a beautiful kauri staircase and a first-floor chapel. Built almost entirely of native timbers for the Sisters of Mercy, it was transferred from the outskirts of Blenheim to its present vineyard-encircled spot in 1994, before conversion into luxury accomodation. Many of the original features, such as the stained-glass windows, are still intact; but fear not, the sleeping facilities have been significantly improved! You can expect antique beds, wooden floors, leather chairs and huge bathrooms. All the bathrooms have claw-foot baths (and separate showers), although the Chapel Suite, more apartment than room, has a double clawfoot which dominates the space. All the bedrooms look out onto the surrounding mountains, vineyards and olive groves and are blessed with ultra-modern heating/air-conditioning systems disguised behind wood panelling and rimu floors. Downstairs are the dining room and library, with a piano dating from 1901, huge comfy sofas and enough books to make you yearn for a downpour. My own favourite is the billiard room, a real gentleman's room with huge billiard table, red walls, leather sofas and well-stocked bar. Layonie and Keith are full of plans to expand and perfect the Convent, with a new lounge being built as we go to print. The convent is surrounded by 60 acres of working vineyards and parkland that boasts a creek with eels, a butterfly habitat and a pétanque court.

Rooms: 5: 1 "Hollywood" superking, 2 king, 1 queen, 1 super king/twin singles; all with en/s claw foot bath and separate shower.
Price: $550 - $750.
Meals: Full gourmet breakfast included.
Directions: Head out of Blenheim towards Picton. At the Spring Creek intersection turn left onto Rapaura Road.

Bec Spa Resort

Aloka and Leon Baumgarten
81 Cob Cottage Road, Blenheim
Tel: 03-579-4446 Fax: 03-579-4446
Email: info@becspa.com Web: www.becspa.com

My mother would have surely barked "close your mouth!" as I drove up to Bec Spa. The vie
here are outstanding, panoramic in the true sense of the word: 360 degrees of ocean, viney.
and mountain. Inside the house is, of course, no less impressive. Leon and Aloka are an extrem
well-travelled couple (American- and Sri Lankan-born respectively) and the house abounds w
curios, photographs and artworks gathered together from around the world. Everywhere yo
eye rests on something pleasing, whether it be a creation of nature or man-made. With sucl
sophisticated collector's eye at play, each room is enchanting: my attention was caught by t
many exotic objects to list here (but I definitely wanted to spend the night in that four-poster b
guarded by a laughing Buddha... two walls of windows slide back to let sunshine, oce
mountains and vineyards almost climb into bed with you). This is a place for a proper pamperi
Aside from the spa pool, steam room, pool and gym, there are massage therapies, body wra
facials and yoga all available. And the menu this year is Michelin-inspired. If you are not careful y
will be lulled into such a slow state of bliss - with all senses satisfied - that leaving Bec Spa m
become tricky... if not impossible! *Committed to sustainable environmental practices. Packa*
available.

Rooms: 5: I king with en/s shower over bath; I
queen with en/s shower and spa bath; 3 queens wi
en/s shower.
Price: $375 - $525. Prices for on-site spa (massage
facials, body wraps) vary.
Meals: Full breakfast included. Welcome wine
reception. Meals $125 per person including wine.
Directions: South from Blenheim on SH1 toward:
Christchurch 4km, turn R on to Cob Cottage Road
Bec Spa is at the top of the hill.

The Peppertree Luxury Accomodation

Werner and Heidi Pluss
3284 SH 1, Blenheim
Tel: 03-520-9200 Fax: 03-520-9222
Email: info@thepeppertree.co.nz Web: www.thepeppertree.co.nz

This 1901 homestead still drips with colonial charm, complete with verandah, wisterias, vines, rimu flooring, William Morris fabrics and croquet lawn. Heidi and Werner fell in love with New Zealand on a holiday trip from their native Switzerland, and never looked back - and more than a touch of the "old country" came smuggled with them: sherry decanters, chandeliers, garden dovecote, and, of course, Swiss Bircher muesli. The ten acres of grounds now play host to a boutique vineyard passionately nurtured by Werner (guests can become "godparents" to a vine), fifteen sheep, an olive grove and an abundant orchard – ducking my head under a kiwi fruit archway, I was able to pluck a feijoa straight from the tree, which is surely the epitome of an Arcadian New Zealand experience. Tucked away by the swimming pool is a little summerhouse-cum-gym, should one feel up to more than feasting on raspberries and a little gentle pétanque. The house is as pleasant as the grounds, with central heating throughout (something this pathetic Pom relishes), stained-glass windows making jewels of light on the hardwood floors, and each room sympathetically decorated. My favourite was the Dormer Room, white muslin balanced over lemon trees, and with its own spa bath. Heidi and Werner are interested by art and design (Sir Michael Fowler designed their gateway) which is evidenced even down to the design of their wine label. *Wireless broadband.*

Rooms: 5: 2 superking/twin with en/s shower; 1 king with en/s bath and shower; 1 king with en/s spa bath and shower; 1 queen with en/s shower.
Price: $400 - $540.
Meals: Full breakfast included. Meals by prior arrangement for a minimum of four people: $158 per person for 4-course dinner inclusive of wine.
Directions: South from Blenheim towards Christchurch on SH1. 4km from Blenheim, signposted.

Hapuku Lodge & Tree Houses

Rod and Belinda Ramsay

State Highway 1 at Station Rd, 12kms north of Kaikoura
Tel: 03-319-6559 Fax: 03-319-6557
Email: info@hapukulodge.com Web: www.hapukulodge.com

If ever there was a property that strove to and met unearthly levels of perfection this is it. Th
was originally a modest deer farm overlooking mountains to the west and sea to the east (and th
favourite surf-spot of nephew Paul). Some eager visits to this awesome spot with family a
friends inspired Tony to take the first steps towards the creation of Hapuku Lodge. W
architecture in the blood and a Wilson tendency for "the process to expand the idea" the origi
plan for a low-key B&B has expanded to become a fantastic landscape-complimenting structu
tailored outside and in to meet every possible need. Each room in the lodge is uniquely furnish
with hand-worked, rare and beautiful woods crafted from the collection of a family friend. I lov
the genius touches of swivel-back chairs in the lounge that allow you to rotate depending on wh
you want to talk to and the custom-made beds that guarantee you the best night's sleep in th
land. Tony's son Justin buzzed with enthusiasm as he showed me around the recently complet
tree-houses. Raindrop showers with a view, spa-baths and suspended sun-decks had m
desperate to come back for a return visit. The whole experience is one of innovative luxury. Th
120 acres are still roamed by deer and olive groves and support a wealth of fresh produce use
in the culinary delights of Hapuku's breakfasts, picnic lunches and communal family-style dinne
I've only mentioned a fraction of Hapuku's merits and cannot recommend it highly enough.

Rooms: 6 rooms in main lodge (3 king/twins and 3
queens all en-suite); 5 tree-houses (3 x 1-bedroom
and 2 x 2-bedroom); 1 self-catering olive house
apartment that sleeps up to a family of 5.
Price: Queens $310 - $390, king/twins $370 -
$460; tree-houses $380 - $850 (top rates include u
to 4 people in 2-bedroom treehouse); Olive House
apartment $520 - $670.
Meals: Full continental breakfast included in all room
rates. Dinner and lunch by arrangement.
Directions: Travel 12km north of Kaikoura on SH1
and turn right onto Station Road, signposted to
Hapuku lodge.

Austin Heights Boutique Bed and Breakfast

John and Lynne McGinn

19 Austin Street, On the Peninsula, Kaikoura
Tel: 03-319-5836 Fax: 03-319-6836
Email: austinheights@xtra.co.nz Web: www.austinheights.co.nz

ustin Heights sits above Kaikoura and commands sumptuous views down to the sea and across
the (often) snow-capped mountains. When I visited the beautiful garden was brightly ablaze in
e chilly autumn sunshine, so I was content to retreat into warmer quarters. The guest units with
eir two big bedrooms are situated above the McGinns' home. They have small kitchens with
yriad teas and coffees, bowls of fresh fruit, plus chocolates and biscuits for the middle of the
ght. And, for those brief hours when you're not charging around Kaikoura whale-watching,
olphin-watching, wine-tasting and sightseeing, a stereo, DVD player (plus movies) and flat-screen
y TV are your friends should you have need of them. The rooms are connected to the main
ouse by a long balcony where you can sit and applaud quietly as the sun sets gently over the
lls. John and Lynne can proudly claim all credit for the transformation of Austin Heights (including
e outdoor hydrotherapy spa) some few years ago. Now dab-hands in B&B they serve breakfast
nd advice in the main house at a long wooden table. This is a comfortable seaside base for
xploring the area's considerable charms and just a five-minute walk to the sea. It would make an
xcellent stopping point for two couples travelling together as you can make it into your own
rivate apartment. Gentle giant of a cat, answering to 'Oscar', in situ. *Free pick-up service from bus*
train. Handy to all major amenities. 10 mins' walk to the sea. WIFI.

ooms: 2 apartments: 1 superking with en/s
ower; 1 queen and 1 double sofa-bed with en/s
ower. Family apartment with shower and bath
ailable downstairs.
rice: $150 - $250.
eals: Full breakfast included. Several good
estaurants in the area.
irections: Heading north from the centre of
aikoura (signposted Christchurch) turn left into
carborough Street and keep going until you get to
ustin Street which is the 2nd turning on your left.

Charwell Lodge

Bill and Judy Clarkson

82 Medway Road, Hanmer Springs
Tel: 03-315-5070 Fax: 03-315-5071
Email: william.clarkson@xtra.co.nz Web: www.charwell.co.nz
Cell: 021-347-905

With uncanny timing, I arrived at what could have been an awkward moment as the lodge w full of Bill and Judy's friends who had all popped in after a big get-together in the mountains previous day. But we all got nattering so easily that I would have wanted to include Charwell ev if the rooms had resembled medieval penitentiary cells. Unsurprisingly, the bedrooms were wonderful with top-class linens, throws and curtains made by Judy and serene private verand with views over the southern mountains. And these views are mesmerising, across the spread the plains below with the broad Waiau River curling through, and (on my visit) the snow-topp mountains across the valley wreathed in mist. Relax in the jacuzzi and relish the perfection. T house was built in country style with old doors salvaged from demolition yards. The rimu fro door (complete with iron horse's head bell), for example, came from a girls' school Christchurch. There are a lot of African and South American artefacts from the couple's tin abroad and a David Shepherd painting in the guest living room that Bill carried rolled up in rucksack for months on end during their travels. I met Charlotte the goat and completely lost tra of time. Don't make the same mistake as I did and have to leave too soon. *Hanmer Hot Spri five minutes down the road. Closed Christmas Day.*

Rooms: 3: 1 king with en/s bath and shower; 1 queen with en/s shower; 1 superking/twin with en/ shower.
Price: $180 - $250. Singles $180. Enquire about winter specials. 'Pamper packages' available.
Meals: Full breakfast included. Packed lunches possible for day trips out. Dinners by arrangement. Complimentary glass of wine at 6pm.
Directions: From SH7 turn right into SH7A (signposted Hanmer Springs). Cross the ferry bridge and take the next right into Medway Road where th lodge is signposted.

Clearview Lodge

Robin and Sue Clements

8 Clearwater Avenue, Harewood, Christchurch
Tel: 03-359-5797 Fax: 03-358-9131
Email: relax@clearviewlodge.com Web: www.clearviewlodge.com
Cell: 021-727-883

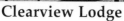

I was so overwhelmed by the presence of Clearview Lodge as I approached that I initially failed to notice the fully-fledged orchard and olive groves that were passing by. It may only be about ten minutes from the airport, but you could be halfway up Everest such is the spirit of peace and quiet here. Set in ten acres of vineyards and pure greenery, the lodge was built by Sue and Robin five years ago with future guests in mind. Bedrooms are therefore large and luxurious – mine had deep red walls, antique chairs, a TV (with Sky, if it matters), wifi and copious amounts of fruit and chocs. The bathrooms are, if anything, even bigger. From my balcony I could gaze freely across Sue's wild garden (with essential herb and veggie area) and out to the vines. It's a siren for local bird life, including a family of quails who surveyed me from the front lawn as I made my way towards the first meal of the day. Breakfast is an almost horizontally laid-back affair, taken at a table in front of long windows with yet more views over the grounds. Their cellar is well stocked with wines produced from their own vines (2006 from "best ever seen" grapes is about to be bottled) so I suggest you grab a glass or three and lie back in the spa pool – a perfect way to recover from any long and arduous flight. *Championship golf course and The Groynes just down the road. Also fully kitted-out and great for kids. Heated outdoor pool.*

Rooms: 3: all superking/twins, 2 with en/s bath and shower; 1 with en/s shower.
Price: $225 - $325.
Meals: Full breakfast included.
Directions: From airport turn left at the 2nd roundabout onto Russley Road (SH1). After 4km (becomes Johns Road) turn left into Clearwater Avenue and the lodge is the first driveway on the right.

Historic Hambledon

Brent and Claire Smith
103 Bealey Avenue, Christchurch
Tel: 03-379-0723 Fax: 03-379-0758
Email: hambledon@clear.net.nz Web: www.hambledon.co.nz

My first-ever night in New Zealand was spent at Hambledon, raising the bar very high for the that followed. Brent and Claire are proud of their magnificent, many-roofed 1856 home, wh thrills with its colourful walls and beautiful wood panelling. Hearts and wallets have gone into t restoration and conversion of this mansion back from a series of apartments to the unified build it once was and creating extensive cottage gardens. One big change from the house of yo though: imposing Victorian mansions were not meant to be this comfortable. I genuinely coulc wait for bed (sad, I know). I was sleeping in an antique half-tester awash with luxurious duv white cotton and soft gold curtains. Beside me a red carpet sidled up to pale green walls and windows, and a door led to a separate kitchen area and perky yellow shower room. Oth rooms were equally fine, some with four-posters, and all mixed antiques with many mode extras like hairdryers, bathrobes, TVs, videos, phones and fridges. The house is quite near a bu road, but it is double-glazed and perfectly quiet outside of rush hour. Breakfast was a you-wor need-lunch extravaganza — six cereals, five dried fruits or nuts, two stewed fruits, yoghurt, rai bread, fresh croissants and French toast with maple syrup, banana and bacon. I'm still digest happily.

Rooms: 4 suites: 3 with king/twin, 1 queen/twin. A with en/s shower and dressing room.
Price: $250 - $380. Single rates on request. Longe term self-catering accomodation available.
Meals: Full breakfast included.
Directions: Map on the website.

The Weston House

Leonard and Stephanie May
62 Park Terrace, Christchurch
Tel: 03-366-0234 Fax: 03-366-5254
Email: enquiries@westonhouse.co.nz Web: www.westonhouse.co.nz

This imposing neo-Georgian house (built in 1922) sits slap-bang in the middle of Christchurch. Technically guests stay in the servants' quarters, but have no fear, this is no 'Upstairs, Downstairs' arrangement. Bedrooms are English in feel but immaculately turned out in a way that I can never manage at home. The whole house has been given a lavish makeover and I don't think I have ever seen rooms with so many extras. Hidden in cupboards are telephones, bathrobes, corkscrews, more toiletries than you can shake a stick at, fridges, your own heating system and mohair rugs… to name but a few. No one seems to have told Stephanie and Leonard that they are under no obligation to provide everything for their guests. When I arrived Stephanie was in mid-conversation with two guests and the sound of laughter filled the air (always a good sign). Drinks are taken on the front terrace to catch the last of the sun and vicious games of croquet are often played out on the vast front lawn. Breakfast is a moveable and memorable feast and Stephanie admits that she is particularly famous for her salmon and brie omelettes. Fresh flowers and home-baking complete the picture. This grand residence may stand in the most prestigious street in town, but it's a totally un-stuffy place to stay and lots of fun. Incredibly central and a five-minute walk to the centre of town. *WIFI throughout house (and garden!). Also a computer dedicated to guest use - Photoshop & Picasa loaded - and Stephanie says she will even copy your photos to a disc... for free!*

Rooms: 2: 1 superking/twin with en/s shower; 1 queen with private bathroom with shower (but you are on your own landing, next to the bathroom).
Price: $400. No single rates.
Meals: Full breakfast included. Complimentary drinks served at 6pm. Restaurants surround you! Picnic hampers can be provided.
Directions: Eastern boundary of Hagley Park, corner of Peterborough St and Park Terrace. Stephanie or Leonard are happy to pick you up or drop you off at the airport too by the way.

Onuku Bed and Breakfast

Jenny and Bob Wilkinson

27 Harry Ell Drive, Cashmere, Christchurch
Tel: 03-332-7296
Email: bob.wilkinson@paradise.net.nz Web: onukubedandbreakfast.co.nz
Cell: 027-2451-360

At Onuku I was made to feel instantly at home by a rotund, very happy black labrador. By the time I was upstairs sitting comfortably with a glass of wine in my hand on a vast sofa overlooking the night lights of Christchurch I'd realised the cause of his good humour – life at Onuku himself, for the Wilkinsons, and for their guests is really pretty good. If I'd had a tail it would have been wagging too. Designed by a celebrated local architect the long and stylish contemporary open-plan sitting room boasts Persian rugs, native wood floors and floor-to-ceiling windows which offer a view out over the city to the Southern Alps and Pegasus Bay. Plans for a roof garden are also under way. Jenny is a keen bridge player and will play with guests, but be warned: she has played for the NZ national team for 12 years. Bob, when he's not working as a tour guide in NZ and Australia, can take guests golfing, fishing and walking. He is an expert on local flora and fauna. Both love to cook and Jenny has a particular passion for Thai food. I can certainly vouch for her excellent Kiwi cuisine. Onuku is only 15 mins drive from central Christchurch, but is right on the edge of Victoria Park so there's peace, quiet and walks aplenty from the house.

Rooms: 3: 2 queens en/s with shower; 1 twin en/s with shower and adjoining sitting room.
Price: $100 - $175. Extra person $50. Singles on request. Shuttle from airport by arrangement.
Meals: Full breakfast included. Dinner by arrangement: $30.
Directions: Drive south towards hills & continue on either Dyers Pass or Hackthorne Rds for about 3km until reach crossroads & Takahe (large stone building). Continue up L on Victoria Pk Rd & turn L at Longhurst Terr. Travel along this terrace until Harry Drive (3rd on R).

Ballymoney Farmstay and Garden

Merrilies Rebbeck
Wardstay Road, Christchurch
Tel: 03-329-6706 Fax: 03-329-6709
Email: info@ballymoney.co.nz Web: www.ballymoney.co.nz

Just a 20-minute drive from Christchurch airport I found myself out in the country on a true New Zealand farm. The Rebbeck family have been modifying their 100-year-old farmhouse for a while now, stripping back wood panelling, adding bits on, tending the two-acre garden. On my visit Merrilies was busy overseeing the extension job to her (temporarily!) al fresco kitchen. She has the arty genes - mother a painter, daughters' artwork on the walls - and her own wonderful eye for interiors. The farmhouse feels earthy and homely, but also very elegant, with wooden floors and kilims and seagrass matting. Merrilies wears many hats, farmer's and chef's among them. When I stayed we sat down together to lamb with potatoes, sweet potatoes, leeks and chestnuts, all from the farm, rounded off with home-made apple sorbet with galliano. That night, from beneath the snuggest of duvets, I scoffed at talk of imminent snow and after breakfast I was whisked around the property on a 4-wheel motorbike to admire Dexter cattle, Dorset horned sheep, saddle-back and kune kune pigs, white peacocks, black and white ducks and hens. I also advise a wander through the garden to the pond full of (mostly rare breed) bird-life, which the swans rule with wings of iron. Outside is a hot tub, set on a platform with views over the garden. Ballymoney is lots of fun.

Rooms: 2: Manuka Suite has king/twin with en-suite shower plus extra queen room with private bath and shower; Kowhai Studio with 1 queen and 1 single with en/s shower.
Price: $200 - $250. Singles $170.
Meals: Full breakfast included. Dinners $50 p.p. for 3 courses including wine. Kids eat free between 5 and 6pm.
Directions: From Christchurch take SH75 to Tai Tapu. Turn right towards Lincoln. After 2km turn left into Wardstay Rd. Travel 800 metres to Ballymoney on right.

Kawatea Farmstay

Judy and Kerry Thacker
Okains Bay, Banks Peninsula
Tel: 03-304-8621 Fax: 03-304-8621
Email: kawatea@xtra.co.nz

The drive into the Banks Peninsula was a great way to start my New Zealand tour, chugging al
the edges of volcanic highlands that plummet into the sea inlets far below and then curling do
the steep hillside roads to isolated farming communities such as Okains Bay. Kawate
surrounded by a high collar of green hills dotted with grazing cattle, and Thacker territory stretc
through 1400 acres of dramatic scenery which perhaps is wasted on the cattle, but not on y
Guests can take picnics out on foot to the Heads and safe, sandy, swimming beaches, and wall
in the hills is peerless. Back at the 100-year-old homestead all is superbly comfortable, with car
fireplaces, deep sofas, high ceilings, wooden floors and rugs, each room huge with its own de
views of the hills, the nearby flower garden, the sea. There's an aviary and a field of tame she
right by the house. This is a proper farm and you eat *en famille*, (beef, lamb, fish, fruit and
mostly home-grown), with breakfast taken in the sunny conservatory. When you stay, cons
how well you are looked after by Judy and Kerry, what a lovely house it is and how little you
paying for it all. *Kayaks available. Trips to seals, dolphins, penguins can be arranged. The penin*
rewards stays of longer than one night!

Rooms: 3: 1 queen and king-single with en/s
shower; 1 queen and 1 queen-single which share
guest bathroom with bath, shower and separate
toilet.
Price: $125 - $155. Singles $80 – $155.
Meals: Full breakfast included. Dinner by
arrangement: $35 pp.
Directions: From Christchurch follow highway
75km signed to Akaroa. 2km past Duvauchelle turn
left, signed Okains Bay Road. 11km to the house.

Maison de la Mer

Carol and Bruce Hyland
1 Rue Benoit, Akaroa
Tel: 03-304-8907 Fax: 03-304-8917
Email: maisondelamer@xtra.co.nz Web: www.maisondelamer.co.nz
Cell: 021-986-221

s we sat chatting on the sunny verandah, I listened with a landlubber's awe to Carol and Bruce's swashbuckling tales of adventures on the high seas. Well… three years spent living on yachts, sailing their family from Bruce's native Canada, down to the Caribbean and back. The house is as inspiring as its owners – my editor claimed their last incarnation, a B&B in Auckland, should have been "set on a pedestal and paraded around the world". Well, they've only done it again! Maison de la Mer is a truly wonderful house, full of antique furniture, Persian carpets and contemporary art. The bedrooms have individual styles, but all share under-floor heating, stunning views across the harbour, honesty bars, masses of fresh flowers, home-made shortbread and complimentary port (I particularly liked the nautically-themed Boathouse). Akaroa was originally a French whaling port and they must have left behind a few good recipes as the town now boasts three of the country's finest restaurants, all within easy walking distance of the Maison de la Mer. However, in the morning Carol, Bruce and their phenomenal breakfasts are very hard to beat. You should be keel-hauled or at least made to walk a plank if you don't find time to stay here. *Bush walks, penguins, fur seals and swimming with dolphins all available nearby.*

Rooms: 3: all queens, 2 with en/s shower, 1 with en/s shower and spa bath.
Price: $345 - $395.
Meals: Full breakfast included.
Directions: From Christchurch, highway 75 to the centre of Akaroa, past the Post Office, on the corner Rue Lavaud and Rue Benoit, on your left.

Onuku Heights

Eckhard Keppler
166 Haylocks Road, Akaroa
Tel: 03-304-7112 Fax: 03-304-7116
Email: onuku.heights@paradise.net.nz Web: www.onuku-heights.co.nz

I had been told to expect great views in New Zealand and was determined not to be too ea
impressed. Yet this carefully prepared insouciance counted for nothing when I reached On
Heights. My range of exclamations was found wanting. You approach the isolated 18
farmhouse up a winding gravel road that crosses several small streams. It's the highest prope
for miles, perched on the side of a hill. From the terrace at the front, home of a beautiful, hea
and beautifully-located swimming pool, the ground drops steeply away, sending the eye tumb
through vistas of pastures and trees to the turquoise blue of Akaroa Harbour and on to the
beyond. You're engulfed by nature, with a grove of enormous macrocarpa and 100-year-
totara, matai and beech in a 50-acre reserve. Then there are camellias, proteas, lillies, roses a
a small orchard (supplying much of the breakfast fruit). When not sheep farming, Eckhard
found time to restore the house: the bedrooms are great, floored with rimu and furnished v
antiques and expensive beds and there's an open fire in the guest lounge. Two rooms in the ho
look over that view, but there is also a separate, larger cottage room, looking to the rose gard
All breathtaking stuff, and you're just 15 minutes from Akaroa. *More great views from walking tra
(1 hour to 1 day) stretching over the 800-acre property. Heated swimming pool and sauna. Ho
trekking available; privately-guided rides on well-mannered Quarter Horses.*

Rooms: 3: all kings with en-suite shower.
Price: $240 - $330.
Meals: Full breakfast included. Dinner by prior
arrangement $40 - $60 p.p.
Directions: Turn left at the southern end of Akaro
(at the bakery) onto Rue Jolie. Follow signs to Onu
Marae. After the Marae, continue into Haylocks Rd
and farm is at the end.

Akaroa Country House

David and Sue Thurston

19 Bells Road, Takamatua, Akaroa
Tel: 03-304-7499; from UK call 0871 7207461 (10p/min. incl. VAT at all times) Fax: 03-304-7499 Email: takamatua@xtra.co.nz
Web: www.akaroacountryhouse.co.nz/com Cell: 027-4370-664

Fresh back from a day spent sailing, David and Sue soon uncorked a home-grown chardonnay on the verandah, just in time for us to watch the final throes of an autumn sun setting on the harbour waters. After merrily polishing off the bottle, talking a little shop, a little house and a lot France - another pair of local francophiles... did the French not get their colony after all? - I slipped way to my quarters for the night. At the end of a pebble-patterned path, across the bridge and downstream, there it sat crouching under trees and ferns in the twilight, my happy little cottage. Small but perfectly formed with daffodil-yellow walls and bluebell-blue shutters, claw-foot bath and doors it feels Scandinavian in its tasteful simplicity. Most importantly, it has a reassuringly high wrought-iron bed, so absurdly comfy and plumped up with embroidered linen pillows that once conquered I found it quite difficult to leave, even to go for a moonlit bath outside. Overlooking the rose garden, the barn is just as delightful. Furniture-maker David's masterful handiwork is everywhere from the barn's sleigh bed to the kitchen's rimu table. Supremely homely and so dreamy it has appeared in adverts, it is here in the kitchen that you'll enjoy one of the most deliciously fresh, homespun breakfasts in NZ. Fun and charmingly laid-back, this is an excellent place to while away a few days with great hosts relaxing into their lives on the peninsula - I'd advise you to follow their cue.

Rooms: 2 cottages: 1 queen with en-s bath, shower and outside bath; 1 queen with en-s shower.
Price: $110 - $145. Singles $110.
Meals: Continental breakfast (with the freshest farm eggs) included.
Directions: From Christchurch take SH75 towards Akaroa. Drive through Robinsons Bay until you get to Takamatua. Here, turn left into Takamatua Valley Road and then the take the first road on left-hand side and follow signposts for the house.

Boutique B&B

Barbara and John Morgan
107 Jefferis Rd, Waikouaiti
Tel: 03-465-7239 Fax: 03-465-7239
Email: info@boutiquebedandbreakfast.co.nz
Web: www.boutiquebedandbreakfast.co.nz Cell: 027-224-8212

Pulling up to Boutique B&B felt like stepping into the tea-stained pages of a Katherine Mans
story. Its bulk, to quote the great lady herself, lies "stretched upon the green garden like a slee
beast," a one-storey, wooden-slatted building framed by a balcony-covered veranda with pi
trellised by iceberg-white roses. Built as a hotel in the mid-nineteenth century, it was relocate
its present position in 1906. Inside, the morning sun streams right up to your pillow thro
windows looking onto grazing deer – and, if you're lucky, the resident peacock on his daily st
Lemon-coloured roses perch on the antique writing table and, in the sitting room, red fluffy s
promise afternoons spent drinking Darjeeling, eating cup-cakes and playing board games:
fridge is stuffed with home-baked goodies for just this purpose. Barbara is a fantastic cook, she
on a breakfast spread of home-made yoghurt, banana muffins, farm eggs and piping hot panc
stacks. Guests are an eccentric bunch - one insisted on playing his bagpipes in the garden - s
seems fitting that John, a deer farmer for thirty years, takes visitors on a decidedly idiosyncr
tour of the herd. Highlights include learning about 'The Roar' season, when feverish stags s
neighbours into a state of insomnia, and meeting Terrible Trevor, a 300 kilogram Yugoslavian S
with an attitude problem. My proudest moment, though, was blowing the shepherd's wh
pitch-perfect on my first attempt. An acquired skill I'm told.

Rooms: 3: all queens with en/s shower.
Price: $180.
Meals: Breakfast included: home-grown peaches &
rhubarb, freshly-squeezed OJ, home-made jams,
jellies, muffins, pancakes, muesli, scrambled eggs, fa
bacon, grainy bread.
Directions: Six miles south of Palmerston on State
Highway 1, turn right at Jefferis Rd. Look out for th
B&B symbol.

Glenfield House

Lyndsey and Guy
Farland
1 Peel Street, Dunedin
Tel: 03-453-5923
Fax: 03-453-5984
Email:
glenfieldhouse@xtra.co.nz
Web:
www.glenfieldhouse.co.nz
Cell: 021-564-615

Glenfield, built in 1884, is a relic of prosperous nineteenth-century Dunedin and reflects the fact that merchants of the time had both money and style… in spades. A step through the door is a step back to Victorian New Zealand – wood panelling, wooden floors and a dining-room dominated by an impressive carved kauri fireplace salvaged from nearby Larnach Castle. As you would expect in such a venerable building the bedrooms are all completely different. My favourite was the suite upstairs with free-standing claw-foot bath, luxuriously huge bed, separate sunroom and views all the way down to the town's harbour. Downstairs is a newly-opened room with a solid wood king bed, ornate pressed ceilings, and morning light streaming through stained glass windows. Down the corridor, the sunny garden room has french doors that burst open onto the blooming courtyard. Hosts Lyndsey and Guy, a young, laid-back couple, and their young children Lexi and Jackson, the smiliest sprogs in town, live in their own wing of the house. Lyndsey used to live in London and while there taught at Prue Leith's cookery school, and it shows. If you get the chance, don't fail to take her up on the fillet steak with cherry and port sauce. This is a Victorian townhouse with bags of original character, a place to don the slippers and sup on some vintage claret. And if all this over-indulgence leaves you thirsting for fresh air, Bali, the resident Lab, will happily take you on a walk down to St Clair Beach. *Closed Christmas Day.*

Rooms: 4: 1 superking with en/s bath & shower (sun room); 1 queen with en/s bath and shower; 1 queen with private bathroom with shower; 1 king with en/s shower and bath.
Price: $225 - $350.
Meals: Full breakfast included. Dinner, by prior arrangement.
Directions: Head south from the Octagon down Princes St, turn right (Casino) up Rattray St 100m, then left up Broadway. At lights, right into High St. At very top turn left into Peel St.

Elgin House

Roger and Carolyn Rennie
31 Elgin Rd, Dunedin
Tel: 03-453-0004 Fax: 03-453-0004
Email: inquiry@elginhouse.co.nz Web: www.elginhouse.co.nz
Cell: 027-656-8700

Within five minutes of arriving at Elgin House I was parked in a comfy armchair beside the fir glass of Otago red in my hand, a grin on my face, and feeling pretty good about life. Dunedin n be chilly at times – this is the 'Edinburgh of the South' after all – but inside this 1899 building warmth and peace. Roger and Carolyn are entertaining, laid-back hosts who have worked t South Island magic on Elgin, Carolyn is also an excellent cook with a great passion for food. Ha fled the corporate sphere (well, 'almost' in Roger's case) they are enjoying Dunedin's easy p of life, and it doesn't take long for you to do the same. The house has retained much c Victorian elegance: kauri floors, open fires, stained-glass windows and some impressively intri carvings in the wood-panelled hallway all lend great character, whilst more recent additior heating systems, vast beds and powerful showers – have made the house very comfortable Room themes and tipples here are one and the same, and come to suit every palette: the Champagne and Rosé on offer, for example, but I slept in my favourite room (and bevera Burgundy. Here my eyelids fell, gazing at the embers of my very own bed-side fire. Much be than the telly. Elgin House is a five-minute drive from the centre of Dunedin, a town famous its Victorian architecture and wildlife, particularly albatrosses and penguins.

Rooms: 3: all kings: 2 with en/s shower, 1 with shared bath/shower. 2 rooms can become a suite with shared shower.
Price: $250 - $350. $550 per night for suite.
Meals: Full breakfast included.
Directions: Approaching Dunedin from the north follow the Mornington signs, turn into High Street, continue into Mailer Street and L onto Elgin Road. Approaching Dunedin from the south, take 1st L a motorway at the Fire Station onto Mornington Roa which becomes Elgin Rd.

Mt Rosa Lodge

Brian and Maureen Dennis
Lot 19 Mt Rosa Estate, Gibbston Back Road, Queenstown
Tel: 03-441-1484
Email: info@mtrosalodge.co.nz Web: www.mtrosalodge.co.nz
Cell: 021-575-100

As dusk turned to darkness, I wound my way up through row upon row of ghostly autumn-veiled vines, onwards past rabbits and the odd live (!) possum. Spirited by this little discovery, I stepped into the warm glow of the lodge. But before you could say leather chair, crackling fire and chilled pinot gris all previous excitement was forgot as I sank deeply into my own comfort, wholly absorbed and delighted by my new find. Brian and Maureen, experts in the fields of wine and food respectively, moved down from Auckland to live within the vineyards of the Gibbston Valley and to purpose-build a lodge amongst them. Mt Rosa occupies a quite sensational vantage, the vines running from the edge of the verandah all the way down the valley ahead, stopping only when the ground rises to form the snow-peaked mountains of Coronet Peak and Cardrona. Beautifully built in keeping with its surrounds, the lodge is 21st-century rustic with underfloor heating, Egyptian cotton linen, Italian tiled bathrooms and windows large and plentiful. Its neutral-coloured walls are the perfect backdrop to the natural schist fireplaces, rocky features and heavy wooden furnishings. Except for touches of the exotic in the vibrant flowers in vases, oriental trunks and silk cushions this is Central Otago living through and through... relaxed, warmly sophisticated and best savoured with an accompanying glass of local pinot.

Rooms: 2: 1 superking/twin with en-suite shower and spa bath, 1 king/twin with en-suite shower.
Price: $280 - $400. Singles on request. If you stay for 3 nights, a free meal is offered.
Meals: Full or continental breakfast included. Dinners by prior arrangement $65 pp for 3-courses and pre-dinner drink.
Directions: Take SH6 north from Queenstown towards the Gibbston, past the bungy bridge and Peregrine vineyard. Turn right into Gibbston Back Road and go straight through the stone gates at Mt Rosa Station, Mt Rosa Lodge is directly ahead.

Twin Peaks

Margaret and Derek Bulman
661 Frankton Rd, Queenstown
Tel: 03-441-8442 Fax: 03-441-8575
Email: bulman@twinpeaks.co.nz Web: www.twinpeaks.co.nz
Cell: 021-685-520

Do the bedrooms have walls? Is the lake in the sitting-room? Twin Peaks is a stunning mod design with a glassed-in cloister that runs along the back of the house. If the big sliding walls of bedrooms are open you can see straight through the house and out to Lake Wakatipu. "Wo is a word that sprung childishly to mind as I slumped down in a broad expanse of armchair in sitting area. The lake seems to stretch out from beneath the house itself, seen through huge s of glass that jut triangularly like a ship's prow. No one could say that Twin Peaks does not m the most of its view. On the other side of the lake rise the Remarkables, a range of sk mountains with those two peaks after which the house is named. Outside is a barbecue area bedrooms have an oriental openness to the design, clean marble in the bathrooms and all-g showers. And while the house itself might be cool and minimalist, leaving you unsure if you inside or outside, Margaret and Derek are contrastingly warm, direct and friendly people w have clearly loved meeting all their guests. You are offered early evening drinks with them, a go time to sort out all that there is to do in Queenstown. *Biking and walking track to Queenstown, boating, white-water rafting, parapenting, skiing, flights to Milford Sound.*

Rooms: 2: both queens with en/s showers.
Price: $340.
Meals: Full breakfast included. About 130 restaura in Queenstown.
Directions: From Frankton village go 2.4km in the Queenstown direction on State Highway 6A. Twin Peaks is on your left. There is no large B&B sign. Look for number 661 on the letterbox and go to t end of the driveway.

Spaview Luxury Accommodation

Andrew Mitchem
Hensman Rd, Queenstown 9300
Tel: 07-827-4537 Fax: 07-827-4537
Email: info@spaview.co.nz Web: www.spaview.co.nz
Cell: 021-121-6268

It wouldn't take a detective to work out why this GG inspector will turn a limey shade of green if she meets any reader who spent a week at Spaview. The eponymous spa is a bubbling outdoor pool, deep and warm and perfect for immersing tired limbs in after a day of strenuous ski-ing, tramping, bungy-jumping, or canyon-swinging – this is Queenstown after all. Unfortunately, I didn't make it into the waters. But the view, ah the view! I was there when the jagged, snow-dipped peaks of The Remarkables were drenched in late-afternoon sun. Forget outdoor activities; if I had the choice I'd spend an entire week in the spa (at the risk of developing decidedly wrinkly fingers). If, though, you are a skier, the house is well set-up. There's plenty of storage space for poles, boots and so on. Plus there are two hot-water tanks, useful for a house that sleeps up to nine. Inside, you can put on your PJs, curl up in the leather sofas, turn the spot-lighting down and gaze out to Lake Wakatipu and the mountains beyond through the floor-to-ceiling windows. Bedrooms are simple, modern affairs with magnolia walls, black lacquered furniture and patterned covers. There's a large sitting room with a smaller adjoining area - an ideal space for children to watch DVDs and find general sanctuary from the oldies. Finally, the gleaming kitchen comes stocked with tea, cakes, flowers and wine – best enjoyed in a spa pool, of course!

Rooms: 5: 1 single, 4 doubles and 3 bathrooms, 1 with bath and shower, and 2 with showers.
Price: $600 - $800 per night. Peak months are from Jul - Sep and Dec - Apr. Off-peak months are May - Jun and Oct - Nov.
Meals: A chef can provide meals by prior arrangement, and the kitchen can be stocked.
Directions: Emailed on booking.

Mountain Range

Stuart Pinfold and Melanie Laaper

Heritage Park, Cardrona Valley Rd, Wanaka
Tel: 03-443-7400 Fax: 03-443-7450
Email: stay@mountainrange.co.nz Web: www.mountainrange.co.nz

Road weary as I was, I felt quickly invigorated by Stuart and Melanie who greeted me on arriv took my bags, placed a glass of local red in my palm and shepherded me towards the hom made cakes. Just over a year has passed since this delightful and fresh-faced couple launch themselves onto the B&B scene and they are still as enthusiastic as ever. It's a dream environment they have here - a large weatherboard and schist stone lodge built on a qu parkland plot, surrounded by grass, two minutes outside Wanaka. The lodge was designed make the most of the light and does so admirably. A homely sitting-room lures you in with its lar fire, comfy sofas, Sky TV, DVD collection and book exchange. I could not resist this warm he of the house for a minute, not even to slip outside and into the new Canadian-style hot tub in t garden - more fool me. And finally to sleep, in a spotless, understated bedroom with its suprem bed, its spa in the en-suite bathroom (all the bathrooms have heated floors) and its views ov frosty lawns to distant mountains. Those mountain views - of the Aspiring, Crown and Crin ranges - pop up on all sides of the lodge, which is terribly handy for those who like their so sharpening moments easily accessible. *Hiking, fishing, biking, golf and excellent skiing.*

Rooms: 7 superkings/twins; 1 with en-suite spa and shower, 6 with en-suite shower.
Price: $200 - $330.
Meals: Full breakfast included.
Directions: From Queenstown via Cardrona: lodg is on R after Café Fe, just before Wanaka. From Wanaka: follow signs to Cardrona, turning up Cardrona Valley Rd, and lodge is next L after Golf Course Rd. Press buzzer on gates to enter.

Lime Tree Lodge

Rebecca Butts and Sally Carwardine

672 Ballantyne Road, Wanaka
Tel: 03-443-7305 Fax: 03-443-7345
Email: revive@limetreelodge.co.nz Web: www.limetreelodge.co.nz
Cell: 021-529-118

No matter which way you look from Lime Tree Lodge's manicured garden, some distant, grandly-named mountain will stare right back at you. The lodge, humbled and alone among its rocky neighbours, is uniquely positioned on a huge, flat plain, so that with a single quick and dizzy spin you can view them all at once. Although just a quick drive away, I felt perfectly removed from the bustle of town as I pondered the panorama, not quite knowing where to rest my eyes – so I stepped inside and set my sights on some well-needed R&R instead. Dominated by a superb, craggy schist fireplace the living area is stylish-yet-put-your-feet-up-and-sink-into-the-sofa-right-now comfy all at the same time. Though new to the business, your hosts Sally and Rebecca seem instinctively to know just what you'll need. For me this meant cracking open a bottle of local pinot noir, preparing a delicious tray of nibbles, including Rebecca's whitebait 'fluffs' fresh from the pan, and stoking the fire till it crackled. Perfect. All the rooms are fresh and contemporary, but just as cosy. Plenty of light streams through French windows from Rebecca's lovely garden, which is just the spot for croquet and sunset barbeques of fresh salmon or local butterflied lamb … though don't tell the lodge's pets Rosie and Georgie, who are currently lambs, but destined for full sheep status one day. *Swimming-pool and 5-hole pitch and putt golf course on site. Children over 8 welcome.*

Rooms: 6: 4 rooms (2 superkings/twins, 1 king/twin, 1 queen) all en/s shower; 2 superior suites (1 superking/twin & 1 twin/bunk sharing en/s bath & shower; 1 superking/twin en/s shower), each with private lounge, satellite TV, CD/DVD & bar/fridge; 1 with log fire, kitchenette and dining area.
Price: $350 - $550. Singles $20 off room rate.
Meals: Full breakfast included. Complimentary apéritifs, all-day tea, coffee, home-baking, fresh fruit, mineral water and transfers to and from Wanaka & airport also included. Dinner by prior arrangement.
Directions: Leave Wanaka on SH6 towards Queenstown. Lodge is signed on right-hand side 6km from town. 7 mins from Wanaka.

Map Number 5   Entry Number 86

The Stone Cottage

Belinda Wilson
Dublin Bay Rd, Wanaka
Tel: 03-443-1878 Fax: 03-443-1276
Email: stonecottage@xtra.co.nz Web: www.stonecottage.co.nz

Belinda looks after her guests with a quiet, friendly competence. Dublin Bay is where her fam
had a holiday home and now she has returned. The Stone Cottage is her home and that
Brandy her dog, while the floor above houses an apartment and a smaller studio where gue
stay. You are fully self-contained up there with kitchen(-ette), breakfast matériel provided in t
fridge each morning (croissants, cereals, jams, fresh fruit, lots of teas), TV and video (and video
music, magazines. The smaller of the two has its own wooden deck and chairs while you can s
the lake from bed in the other. The house is secluded and surrounded by a spectacular spring a
autumn garden. It was hiding coyly under a frosty May rime when I was there, but the progno
was excellent! A four-minute stroll will take you down to Lake Wanaka, ideal for swimming w
its sandy beach and framed, as always in New Zealand, by a background of mountains. Whe
not chilling out in the garden or fishing on the lake, many of Belinda's guests are doing t
outdoorsy activities for which Wanaka is increasingly famed… including skiing. Belinda is there
you want her very relaxed company.

Rooms: 2 apartments; 1 sleeps 4 (queen and twin
beds, bath/shower); the other has a superking and
en-suite shower.
Price: $250 - $280. $40 per extra person.
Meals: Full breakfast provisions provided for you to
cook your own. Dinners by prior arrangement $55
$70.
Directions: From Wanaka take State Highway 6 fo
about 1.5km. Turn left where signed to Lake
Hawea/West Coast. Follow over the bridge up the
hill, turn left where signed to Dublin Bay Rd. Follow
signs to house for 3km.

Fiordland Lodge

Robynne and Ron Peacock

472 Te Anau - Milford Highway, Te Anau
Tel: 03-249-7832 Fax: 03-249-7449
Email: info@fiordlandlodge.co.nz Web: www.fiordlandlodge.co.nz

That's quite some window they've got there. You're out in the country 5km from Te Anau, near a lake, near the mountains. Any window stands a good chance of impressing. But this one? Wow. Entering Fiordland Lodge you're assaulted by a wall of glass rising some 30 feet, through which you look westwards across the grassland to Lake Te Anau and the forested lower slopes of Mt Luxmore. The large sitting area that confronts this view has deep armchairs and sofas, with a bar in the corner in case it all gets too much. In the middle of the room vast supporting trunks of silver beech compete for attention with a river stone fireplace that uses old bridge beams from the Milford Road. Everything in this building, built in 2002, is natural. Smart bedrooms use earth colours, chunky beams and relaxing spot lighting. Bathrooms are particularly handsome, with basins on wooden benches, more natural tones and big wicker baskets. And sumptuous dinners - included in the lodge prices - are served in the dining-room, which also looks west. Away from the lodge there are many natural activities - Ron was a National Park ranger and guides fishermen, bird-watchers and nature lovers in the Fiordland National Park. There are also two cheaper chalets, where dinner in the lodge is an optional extra.

Rooms: 10 rooms in lodge: 9 lodge rooms, all kings/twins, all en-suite showers; 1 Executive Suite, with king/twin, 1 en-s spa/shower; 2 log cabins, with queen bed and 3 singles, 2 en-s spa/shower.
Price: Room rates are for 2 people, incl' dinner, bed & breakfast. Lodge rooms $540 (winter) - $840 (summer); Executive Suite $640 (winter) - $1,040 (summer); log cabins $440 (winter) - $640 (summer). Extra adult $200, child $150.
Meals: Full breakfast and 4-course dinner, *table d'hote*, included for all.
Directions: Follow signs to Milford Sound out of Te Anau. After just under 5km, you'll see Fiordland Lodge sign-posted to the right.

Nokomai Station

Brian and Ann Hore

SH 6 (Queenstown - Te Anau Highway)
Tel: 03-248-8850 and 03-248-8837 Fax: 03-248-8841
Email: nokomai@xtra.co.nz Web: www.nokomai.co.nz
Cell: 027-242-9480

Far, far from the madding crowd, on an astonishing 100,000 acres of Southland farmland you f
Nokomai. One of the largest privately-owned stations in the country, it's home to 50,000 shee
2,000 cattle, horses and dogs as well as the station's staff and families. The location is a rurali
dream and the drive in no less so. Leaving the Queenstown road, you criss-cross the Matau
River three times before turning along the banks of Nokomai Creek and onwards to the far
which sits at the end of a light-filled valley. Accommodation is in three comfortable, purpose-b
cottages where you can either self-cater or have your meals provided. There is plenty to do he
it is not a place to arrive at 6 and leave at 8 the next morning. You can watch the seasonal fa
activities, walk forever, borrow mountain bikes, fish for trout on the famous Mataura River (20
of which runs through the property), or you can even try your hand at 'golfcross' - trust a bur
of Kiwis to invent a form of golf that's played with a rugby-shaped golf ball and posts! Your ho
can also arrange 4x4 trips, horse treks into the hills or, most glamorously, 'flightseeing' trips w
Nokomai helicopters. You can hire man and machine to go just about anywhere, from a tour
the station to Milford Sound, and do almost any activity: he'll even drop you on a mountain t
at sunset with a bottle of champagne.

Rooms: 3 self-catering cottages: 2 with 1 king/twin
with 2 kings/twins in different rooms.
Price: $250 for one bedroom cottage. $320 for 2
bedroom cottage.
Meals: Full breakfast included. $15 p.p. for packed
lunch. Dinner $65 p.p. (includes beer and wine).
Directions: From Queenstown, head towards Te
Anau on Hwy 6. Turn left 5km south of Athol onto
Nokomai Road. Go 12km to the station.

Mahitahi Lodge

John Birchfield and Jacqui Low

State Highway 6, Bruce Bay
Tel: 03-751-0095 Fax: 03-751-0195
Email: stay@mahitahilodge.co.nz Web: www.mahitahilodge.co.nz
Cell: Freephone in NZ 0800-751-009

Night was falling when I finally drove into Bruce Bay - and out the other side again. Quite a feat when you consider that there are only three permanent dwellings in this tiny West Coast settlement. Once the site of a thriving road-building town (in the thirties the village hall hosted black-tie balls complete with swing orchestra), Bruce Bay is now a close-knit rural community. Within five minutes of my locating Mahi Tahi, I was safely ensconced in front of the roaring fire, chatting away with a glass of pinot noir in hand. Jacqui is an accountant by trade, while John, a self-professed "hunter-gatherer" has a background in forestry and fishing. His fingers are the deepest shade of green, so naturally the jade-coloured broccoli and iron-rich new potatoes at supper were home-grown. Ask him to take you on a tour of the area and you'll find out about the growth cycle of the kahikatea tree, local Maori history and how to pan for gold - he has his very own concession. The couple built the house themselves from salvaged indigenous wood. Upstairs is a soaring loft space drenched in natural light, with wooden beams, rose-brown rimu furniture and walls painted the colour of bark. The forest theme continues into the bedrooms. I stayed in 'Rimu' a cosy affair with a russet-maroon bedspread and chocolates on the bed. The bathrooms have under-floor heating as well, perfect for drying off soggy boots after a long day's tramping.

Rooms: 3: Rimu Room and Totara Room both super-king or twin rooms with en/s shower; Matai Family Room with queen bed, shower, adjoining kitchenette and lounge with sofa bed.
Price: $295 inc. breakfast.
Meals: Cooked breakfast included: eggs, bacon, porridge, plus cereals, fresh yoghurt and jams. Evening meals, $65 inc. wine.
Directions: Thirty miles south of the Fox Glacier on State Highway 6. On your left-hand side as you drive through Bruce Bay.

Holly Homestead B&B

Gerard and Bernie Oudemans

State Highway 6, Franz Josef Glacier 7856
Tel: 03-752-0299 Fax: 03-752-0298
Email: stay@hollyhomestead.co.nz Web: www.hollyhomestead.co.nz

Gerard and Bernie had just completed breakfast when the Greenwood Guides first barged i
their lives having heard good things about them in town. It was an immediately comforting sce
wooden table, pieces of toast in racks, the smell of real coffee and freshly-baked bread. This 1S
former farmhouse has been stripped back to its wooden heart: weatherboarded walls, polish
floors, panelled ceilings, wooden windows. But the Oudemans continually improve it – m
recently a spacious new kitchen area allowing for plenty of elbow room at the breakfast table.
rooms have comfortable beds and percale sheets, while upstairs there's a tiny balcony v
wisteria and jasmine on one side and a roof terrace (facing the mountains and the sunset) on
other. Gerard and Bernie, both New Zealanders, have been in the B&B business since 2000
are rightly enthusiastic about their magnificent region. They are still unstuffy and refreshir
modest about what they offer, although "we're getting better at blowing our own trumpet." /
so they should, if only for the spectacular views from breakfast table, "clouds permitting!" Be
adds. So self-deprecating you know you're going to like it. *Good base for Okarito, Franz Josef*
Fox Glacier explorations. Scenic flights, guided glacier hikes, kayaking, horse-trekking, white he
sanctuary tour, kiwi tours at night. Children 12+ welcome. Wireless available.

Rooms: 5: 2 superkings/twins, 1 superking, 2 quee
3 with en-suite shower and 2 with en-suite bath ar
shower. Sitting-room for guests.
Price: $200 - $400. Check website for minimum
night requirements and winter specials.
Meals: Full cooked breakfast included. There are
plenty of restaurants in town for lunch and evening
meals.
Directions: On main road 1.5km north from the
Franz Josef village centre.

Awatuna Homestead

Pauline and Hêmi Te Rakau
9 Stafford Road, Awatuna, Hokitika
Tel: 03-755-6834 Fax: 03-755-6876
Email: rest@awatunahomestead.co.nz Web: www.awatunahomestead.co.nz

very laid-back, very happy home. If I were a bit older, I'd probably write about the vibe. Here the unspoilt coastal bush near Hokitika, Hêmi and Pauline's B&B manages to get everything ght. Take the opportunity to relax by the open fire in the guest lounge accompanied by Maori-peaking Hêmi's intricate knowledge of local history and cultural stories. Throw a fine wine list and auline's tempting cooking into the mix and you won't find many that venture out at night in search f restaurants. The three handsome guest rooms are beautifully decorated in various colour chemes, with furniture picked up by Pauline from, oh, all over the place. The Goldsborough is e grandest with its elegant decor and double spa bath. And there is also a self-catering partment. Outside are six acres of gardens and farmland with a spa pool (under cover for rainy ays) where you can sit and gaze at the Milky Way. Accompanied by the bird life you can fish on e nearby beach or go walking on a short walk to a look-out point in the bush. This is as much promise to return as a write-up. Two dogs, two cats, two horses and sheep in residence. Hêmi estores Morris Eights and if you're well behaved you might even get a spin in one.

Rooms: 4: I self-contained apartment with I queen oom and I twin room sharing bathroom bath/shower); I superking/twin with en/s spa bath & hower; I queen en/s shower; I twin en/s shower. Guest lounge. Wireless email/fax facility.
Price: $240 - $350. Singles $30 less than the oubles.
Meals: Dinners $65 p.p. by prior arrangement, vine (list available) not included. Full breakfast served n the homestead included. In apartment $20 p.p.
Directions: From Greymouth follow signs to Hokitika. At Awatuna turn L into Stafford Rd, signed, nd over the train tracks. Homestead is on L.

Bird's Ferry Lodge and Ferryman's Cottage

Alison and André Gygax
Bird's Ferry Road, Charleston
Tel: 0800-212-207
Email: info@birdsferrylodge.co.nz   Web: www.birdsferrylodge.co.nz
Cell: 021-337-217

Only three years old, a mere fledgling, yet Bird's Ferry Lodge seems nonetheless to h
seamlessly nested upon its hilltop where it sits content, quietly musing on the far-reaching,
lined views. As I chatted with Alison and André from a snug sofa I tried to keep my attentior
Greenwood Guides and away from the cinema-screen-sized window that frames the w
dramatic scene. Merlot and Mick, two whiskered, smiling, people-loving terriers, won me c
at once, while the warming presence of an Aga in the kitchen (as rare as a traffic jam in N
Zealand) reminded me of home. For Alison, a Celtic catering manager who just loves to coc
was a must-have. Here foody treats are conjured from home-grown produce and resic
chooks lay your eggs for breakfast. Originally from Cape Town, André has lived in New Zea
for the last 23 years and, with a past career as a guide, his knowledge of the country far exce
that of any local. He recently qualified as a masseur, and the massage room is newly set up, if
should feel the need for even more relaxation. At the end of the road, in 12 secluded acre
the new cottage, with quirky driftwood furniture made by André, and disturbed only by kiwi
at night. An old-fashioned bath sits out at the front, perched over views stretching from se
snow-covered mountain, just awaiting the glories of sunset. Here there is no TV, no landline
no clock… just a wealth of peace, seclusion and beauty. WIFI.

Rooms: 3: 2 queens with en/s bath/shower; 1 tw
with en/s shower. All rooms have private deck &
access. Self-catering cottage: 2 queens, 1 twin.
Sharing bath/shower.
Price: $200 - $300. Lodge stays of more that 2
nights include half a day's guiding with André. Cott
tariff includes breakfast hamper.
Meals: Full breakfast included for lodge. 3-course
dinners by arrangement: $65. Made with local
produce. Half a bottle of wine included.
Directions: 17km south of Westport & 8km nor
of Charleston on SH6. Signed on L coming from
Charleston (R from Westport). Turn off at sign & g
1.7km along private gravel rd. Lodge at end of roa

hand-picked
things to do
and
places to eat

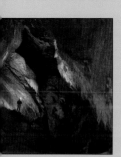

NORTH
ISLAND

THE NORTH ISLAND IS A JIGSAW of different landscapes from the winelands of the south and east to the central volcanic belt, western caves and tropical north. You could hug a giant tree in Northland, surf in Raglan, explore the caves of Waitomo, ski on a volcano, tramp around bubbling geysers in Rotorua, white-water-raft in Taihape and sip wine in Hawke's Bay in a week if you really wanted to, but you'd be utterly exhausted. The best – but least heeded - piece of advice that I can give is to take your time. A week is virtually no time to see either island. You are far better off reading this book in depth, choosing a few great things to do and see and giving yourself the time to enjoy them in a relaxed way... rather than trying to tick off the whole of New Zealand in a fortnight. Even if you are visiting from Europe and think you will make the trip only once.

There are a number of ways to tackle the North Island. Whether you work your way south from Auckland after catching the sun in the 'winterless north,' or you head north from windy Wellington after breezing around New Zealand's culture capital, you will pass through the volcanic centre. The Taupo Volcanic Zone arcs from Mt. Taranaki on the west coast through to Mt. Ruapehu and Tongariro in the Central Plateau. It then continues up through the enormous crater lake of Taupo and the active heart of Rotorua before finally reaching the coast at Mt. Maunganui in the Bay of Plenty and spilling offshore to White Island. The unique geology is down to the wrestling activity of two tectonic plates. In the North Island the Pacific Plate is subducting beneath the Indian Australian Plate. As one plate is forced below the other it generates immense friction and heat, which is vented through surface volcanic activity. (In the South Island the subduction is taking place in the other direction but this time the plates buckle along the Alpine Fault forming the mountainous ridge of the Southern Alps.)

If you have flown a long distance to get to Auckland, you will undoubtedly need to deal with the jetlag. Give yourself a couple of days to gather your wits in the 'City of Sails,' before venturing onto the Hauraki Gulf or over to the deserted west coast beaches. Then head to Northland where you can dive, island hop, sandsurf and enjoy a civilised tasting or two in the Matakana wineries. Alternatively take the quick drive over to the lush Coromandel Peninsula for some of the country's finest beaches and most relaxed inhabitants.

If you've crossed over from the South Island it's worth lingering in Wellington for a few days and sponging up the culture. There are a variety of routes that you can take north from Wellington. Bear off to the east and you pass through Wairarapa and on to Hawke's Bay, both regions of underestimated and spacious beauty, where farmland rolls out to meet the rugged windswept coasts and wineries bask in the region's extra sunshine. Napier's lively art deco scene is a beacon in the area. Watch out for stray wild goats as you wind on from Hawke's Bay and out to the East Coast, an area that remains, for the greater part, undiscovered. I don't think I have ever seen anything as green as the grass that rolls through the valleys of this region.

If you have time, drive around the cape of the East Coast on your way to the Bay of Plenty. These areas are home to much of the country's Maori history and current Maori population. The Bay of Plenty is easily accessible to everything: the beaches in the north, the geothermal spas in the centre, the ski fields further south and the CBD of Auckland. The volcanic activity is a big draw for both the Bay of Plenty and Central Plateau regions. Spend your time wisely here. There is an awful lot to see and do, but much of it is pretty commercial. The beaten track is obvious and some must-see things are popular for a reason, such as the thermal parks and Maori shows. But do take the road less travelled and visit the marine volcano of White Island or head off into the woodland wilderness of the national parks. With skiing in winter and absurdly good tramping all year round, the Central Plateau, lying just below Rotorua, rates highly in any season.

If you head south from Auckland or west from the Bay of Plenty you enter Waikato and King Country. This area is distinguished by rolling farmland, country gardens, the surfer-friendly coastline and the underground landscape of Waitomo Caves. Push a bit further southwest and the prominent and extraordinary form of the great volcano Mt. Taranaki will loom into view. The fertile landscape continues through Wanganui and Manawatu where rivers (great for rafting and fishing) prevail. Finally head back to Wellington via the Kapiti Coast and Kapiti Island bird sanctuary before crossing over to the dramatically different South Island.

Northland

North Island

Northland

South Island

Highlights

• Explore the secluded bays, long white beaches, velvet-green rolling hills and sleepy fishing settlements of the Whangarei Heads. This is one of the most beautiful, and gladly, least visited parts of Northland.

• Dive or snorkel the fantastic Poor Knights Islands, go inside the biggest sea cave you'll ever see and round off the day with a pizza in Tutukaka's quiet harbour.

• Join in the Maori boat-racing, flag-raising, canon-firing celebrations of Kiwi life on Waitangi Day, 6 February at the Waitangi Treaty Grounds, or come here each day of the year to watch re-enactments of Maori and European histories on stage.

• Learn to sail in the stunning coastal waters of the Bay of Islands. Swim, snorkel or take a rod and fish for your dinner.

• Head north to the pohutukawa-lined, golden shores of Coopers Beach and Doubtless Bay, stopping off for lunch in picturesque Mangonui.

• Try your hand, and body, and nerves at sand-boarding down dunes after hot-footing the length of 90-mile Beach, racing the tide, from Cape Reinga. Even better, fly its length if you can.

• Feel very small indeed as you contemplate Tane Mahuta, New Zealand's most gigantic kauri tree in the Waipoua Forest Sanctuary.

WARKWORTH
WINERIES
Ransom Wines

'Fabulous - keep it quiet or tell everyone!' reads a jubilant whisper in the guest book. Firmly placing myself in the latter category, there'll be no hushing here... Ransom Wines is one of my favourite vineyards. In a truly captivating setting, this is a winery at peace with itself. It is New Zealand through and through, quite set apart from the usual. There is simple quality in everything from the contemporarily rustic architecture to the wine taster's platters of spreads, cured meats, marinated vegetables and crusty bread. And the wines, a range from classic French grape varieties, are fantastic. But I shall let them speak for themselves.

Prices: *$18 per head for the lunch platters. Wines $17 - $38 per bottle. Tasting flights are a $5 donation to charity or $10 if you sit at the bar.* **Contact:** *Marion Ransom, 46 Valerie Close, Warkworth;* **Tel:** *09-425-8862;* **Fax:** *09-425-8864; info@ransomwines.co.nz; www.ransomwines. co.nz*

WARKWORTH
NATURE AND ACTIVITIES
Sheepworld

I'd always thought New Zealand was Sheepworld until I happened upon this place. Just off the highway outside Warkworth you can look, listen and learn as sheep dogs display their mental prowess shepherding sheep to and fro. Admittedly, the dogs win paws down in the 'brainy' stakes (I didn't get the chance to see ducks giving them a waddle for their money in the Dog and Duck show so can't comment on that), but one can't help but feel some sympathy for the shivery-looking sheep herded into a corner post-shave. The shearing operation is a fast and fascinating one however, and you'll soon feel less sympathetic once you slip into the your new woollen socks and jumper.

Prices: *Full admission $17.50 adult, $8 child includes Sheep and Dog show (at 11am and 2pm) and entry to the park and its 30-acre eco-discovery trail. Black Sheep Café and woollen products shop open daily. Dog and Duck show at 2pm on the weekend.* **Contact:** *Marianne Vacher, State Highway 1, 4km north of Warkworth;* **Tel:** *09-425-7444;* **Fax:** *09-425-7666; info@sheepworld. co.nz; www.sheepworld.co.nz*

MATAKANA
EATING AND DRINKING
Matakana Village Farmers' Market

Traditional (but with a cosmopolitan twist), medieval-type wooden stalls allow up to 31 local growers and food producers to sell fresh fruit, gourmet spray-free veggies and a myriad of other products every Saturday. There's Swiss organic chocolate, eggs, jellies and preserves, cheeses, mussel fritters, chutneys and pickles, olive oils, breads, specialty meats, honey, flowers and more. I tucked into a hearty breakfast accompanied by a freshly-brewed espresso coffee before wandering by the river to watch musicians perform. This is a proper, organic posh-nosh heaven, with a heady market atmosphere that's quick to soak up. Hours: 8am - 1pm all year round.

Contact: *Michael Kessell, 2 Matakana Valley Road, Matakana;* **Tel:** *09-422-6889;* **Fax**: *09-422-6889; mihou@paradise.net.nz; www.matakanavillage.co.nz*

MATAKANA
WINERIES
Ascension Vineyard

Family-run warmth and wine-country graciousness make the perfect blend here at this fantastic Matakana vineyard. Fifth generation wine-makers, Darryl, Bridget and family produce highly sought-after, hand-crafted wines and happily take their food as seriously as its accompaniment in their award-winning restaurant. This is a very special and exceptionally friendly place where lots of events are put on to entertain throughout the year from jazz concerts and comedy theatre to their big, not-to-be-missed, autumnal harvest dinner (includes grape stomping!).

Prices: *Cellar door wine prices $22 - $50. Restaurant main dishes: lunch $18 - $26, dinner $22 - $32.* **Contact:** *Darryl and Bridget Soljan, 480 Matakana Road, Matakana;* **Tel:** *09-422-9601; info@ascensionvineyard.co.nz; www.ascensionvineyard.co.nz*

PAKIRI BEACH
NATURE AND ACTIVITIES
Pakiri Beach Horse Rides

The Haddons (that's Laly, Sharley, daughter Olivia and son Ben) are descended from the Maori chief who discovered and settled next to the beautiful, unpopulated 15km stretch of white sand surf beach at Pakiri. Ride out on one of their 125 horses and experience the freedom, splendid isolation and beauty of this special place. Few rides are as exhilarating as this one; after tracing the line of the Pacific you'll canter off into the dunes and through groves of pohutukawa trees ablaze with red flowers in summer. Rides from one hour to several days.

Prices: *$50 for on hour, $220 full day (including lunch). Self-catered accommodation on the beach can be provided. Licensed café on site.* **Contact:** *Sharley and Laly Haddon, Taurere Park, Rahuikiri Road, Pakiri Beach;* **Tel:** *09-422-6275;* **Fax:** *09-422-6277; pakirihorse@xtra.co.nz; www.horseride-nz.co.nz*

KAIWAKA
EATING AND DRINKING
Café Eutopia

Far beyond unusual, this place is a complete one-off product from the mind of owner, fantasy author and artist Peter Harris. One part café to one part "ongoing sculptural project", Peter has transplanted his fantastical visions into reality. Step onto the bridge and enter the dream-like courtyard of Eutopia with its lotus fountain surrounded by five domes. Right on the side of the highway, heading north, this is the place to stop and refuel on organic, GM-free food and coffee.

Prices: *Breakfasts: muesli $10.50, toasties $9.50.* **Contact:** *Karen Harris, State Highway 1, Kaiwaka;* **Tel:** *09-4312-999; Fax: 09-4312-999; karen@eutopia.co.nz; www. eutopia.co.nz*

Pakiri Beach Horse Rides

northland

 ## WHANGAREI
EATING AND DRINKING

Vinyl Café

Vinyl is definitely groovy. Menus are presented on old LPs, the atmosphere is chilled and the service friendly. They take their food, however, very seriously (as do I!). Juicy meats, so-fresh-it's-flapping fish and an adventurous brunch menu had me salivating at the thought. Tuesday - Friday from 5.30pm. Thursday 5.30pm - 8.30pm live entertainment. Saturday and Sunday 9am till late. Closed Monday.
Prices: *Mains from $28 - $34. Weekend brunch from $10 - $18.* **Contact:** *Helen Smith, Cnr Riverside Drive & Vale Road, Town Basin, Whangarei;* **Tel:** *09-438-8105; info@vinylcafe.co.nz; www.vinylcafe.co.nz*

A Deco

"Fantastic! Fantastic! Fantastic!" proclaims one happy customer, undoubtedly not the first to rave so highly about this stylish and intimate restaurant. As the name suggests, there's a classic art deco theme throughout from the wonderful building to the elegant presentation of the dishes. Nothing here disappoints. The very friendly staff is entirely on the ball and the food, well, I think a long and meaningful 'mmmmm' should suffice. Try Brenton's famous pumpkin tortellini on spinach with sage butter and the pina colada crème brûlée with pineapple sorbet. This is the kind of place you wish you could transport to your hometown, which makes the savouring of it all the more sweet... while you can. Dinner from 6pm.
Contact: *Brenton Low, 70 Kamo Road, Kensington, Whangarei;* **Tel:** *09-459-4957; bridget.candy@pernod-ricard-nz.com*

 ## WHANGAREI
NATURE AND ACTIVITIES

Zion Wildlife Gardens

Craig Busch is so legendary in the lion world (among the humans, not the lions) that I saw a documentary about the 'Lion Man' himself on the plane over to New Zealand. The guy certainly has a way with big cats, and none come bigger than Samson, father to a pride of twelve Barbary lions. Extinct in the wild, there are just 250 of these mighty felines in captivity making Zion Wildlife incredibly important in the conservation and understanding of the species. Also at home here are ten white lions who originate from South Africa, two cheetahs and nine royal white Bengal tigers. Take a tour to meet the lions at close range and learn about these incredibly rare creatures whose fragile existence belies their powerful presence.
Prices: *Guided tour through the gardens: 60 mins, $60 adult, $30 child. Cub Encounter tour is an 80-minute private tour: $200 adult, $50 child. Ask about tours with Craig himself.*
Contact: *Renee Woodleigh, Gray Road, Kamo, Whangarei;* **Tel:** *09-435-0110; zion@zionwildlifegardens.co.nz; www.zionwildlifegardens.co.nz*

Ransom Winery

TUTUKAKA
EATING AND **DRINKING**

Marina Pizzeria

Tim, a recent import from the UK, is the cheery chap who runs this great little pizzeria bang on the boat-filled Tutukaka harbour. Sit out on the deck and get stuck into a Landlubber Pizza (spicy hot, certainly packs a punch) or the terrific 3-Metre Swell (top-filled, local seafood combo). You can take away but with a fantastic position like this, you'd really be missing out.

Prices: *Pizzas: $13 - $19 small, $17 - $23 large. Open 10am - 8pm, Thursday to Sunday.*
Contact: *Tim Green, The Marina, Tutukaka, Whangarei;* **Tel:** *09-434-3166.*

TUTUKAKA
NATURE AND **ACTIVITIES**

Dive! Tutukaka

Jacques Cousteau ranked the Poor Knights Islands as one of the top ten dive sites in the world and to dive these sub-tropical waters is on most divers 'must do' lists. These guys run a fantastic, friendly and very professional operation from Tutukaka harbour. There are over 100 dives to choose from and all equipment is provided. There are kayaks on board so that you can paddle around the island's arches and caves between dives. Basic, advanced and specialty (wreck diving, underwater photography etc) courses are available. A 'Perfect Day' cruise is also available for non-divers where you can view the fishes from an underwater camera.

Prices: *$225 for a 1-dive day includes tea and coffee on board and the use of kayaks from the boat. Ask about their yummy $10 lunches. A try dive is $275 and a refresher course is $275 for 2 dives. The Perfect Day cruise is $129 for a day cruise.* **Contact:** *Kate Malcolm, Marina Road, Tutukaka, Whangarei;* **Tel:** *09-434-3867 or freephone 0800-288-882;* **Fax:** *09-434-3884; info@diving.co.nz; www.diving.co.nz*

Cave Rider

You'll certainly not miss out by seeing the Poor Knights Islands from this non-diving perspective. They are the only nesting ground for the Buller shearwater and home to several endemic species of flora and fauna, nine types of prion bird, gannet colonies, native cuckoos, melodious bell-birds, seals and the odd whale. Not only this but, most excitingly, amongst the extraordinary scenery of cliffs, arches and tunnels is Riko Riko, the world's biggest sea cave. Scuba gear? Trust me, you'll be just fine without it.

Prices: *Two and a half hour round trip: adults $90, Children 5 - 12 yrs $45. No children under 5.* **Contact:** *Kate Malcolm; Marina Road; Tutukaka; Whangarei;* **Tel:** *0800-288-882 (freephone within NZ) or 09-434-3884; info@caverider.co.nz; www.caverider.co.nz*

Bush'n'Bike Adventuring

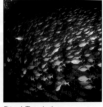
Dive! Tutukaka

Culture North

BAY OF ISLANDS – KAWAKAWA
NATURE AND ACTIVITIES
Bush'n'Bike Adventure Company

This combination of quads, horses and go-karts is a sure-fire hit. Splash through rivers and 4WD along rugged bush tracks and challenging terrain. Alternatively, amble quietly through the spectacular river valley setting on horseback. First-timers and old-timers can all come along for some great, family fun.

Prices: *Quad bikes $75 for 1.5 hr tour, 2.5 hr tour by arrangement. Passengers: $55 adults, $25 children for 1.5 hr tour. Off-road go-karts: $75 for 1 hr, $40 for half and hour. Horseback Adventures are $55 pp for a 1.5 hr trek. Kid quads and pony rides $15. Prices are subject to alteration.* **Contact:** *Jorvar and Cheryl Jensen; Tirohanga Road (off SH10), Kawakawa, Nr Paihia;* **Tel:** *09-404-1142;* **Fax:** *09-404-1143; info@adventurecompany.co.nz; www.adventurecompany.co.nz*

BAY OF ISLANDS - PAIHIA
EATING AND DRINKING
Swiss Café and Grill

Originally from Switzerland and Austria, the Amslers own GG favourite Chalet Romantica just up the hill. Inge's warmth and charm shine just as brilliantly down here in this, her very popular little restaurant. Very friendly and attentive staff serve traditional alpine fare from Wiener schnitzels, cheese fondus, apple strudels and Mövenpick ice creams. Fresh seafood (snapper, scallops, prawn and calamari) and fillet steaks are amongst the more Kiwi offerings from the grill. This place is totally unique, very relaxed and comes brimming with character.

Prices: *Prices vary from $18.50 - $29 for main meals.* **Contact:** *Inge and Ed Amsler, 48 Marsden Road, Paihia; Tel: 09-402-6701.*

Pure Tastes

Inspired by many global cuisines, much of the food here is bold in flavour with a contemporary edge, challenging diners to open their minds, not just their mouths, and broaden their palates to try something new and exciting. Signature dishes on the menu include a starter of tempura Ludbrook (as in Christine from GG''s fantastic Ludbrook Guesthouse) figs with blue cheese & orange, main course of tomato mussels & pearl couscous, eggplant caviare & sticky mustard dressing and an infamous dessert of dark chocolate tart with espresso gelato & apple chips. With such comely dishes as these need I say more…?

Contact: *Paul Jobin, 116 Marsden Road, Paihia;* **Tel:** *09-402-0003;* **Fax:** *09-402-6026; info@puretastes.co.nz; www.puretastes.co.nz*

Pure Tastes

Bush'n'Bike Adventuring

All smiles aboard the Earl Grey

northland

BAY OF ISLANDS - PAIHIA
NATURE AND ACTIVITIES

Gungha II, Bay of Islands Sailing

During my research Mike and Debbie's sailing trips got unanimous double-thumbs-up recommendations from sources far and wide. After leaving Canada 15 years ago, the Careres sailed *en famille* over 100,000 ocean miles throughout the Pacific before landing on Northland shores. Fortunately they never quite shuck off their sea legs and now offer day-sailing adventures on their beautiful yacht Gungha II. Tasty morning snacks, an island stopover, snorkel gear, kayaks and a yummy fresh lunch are included. These trips are superb value for an experience that I guarantee will be unique, personal and funny.

Prices: *Adults $85, departs Paihia and Russell daily.* **Contact:** *Mike Carere, Paihia Harbour, Paihia;* **Tel:** *09-407-7930 or freephone within NZ 0800-478-900;* **Fax:** *09-407-7930; bayofislandssailing@xtra.co.nz; www.bayofislandssailing.co.nz*

Earl Grey Fishing Charters

Join professional saltwater fishing guide Captain Steve Butler aboard his boat, Earl Grey II, fishing around the Bay's 144 islands, an area so abundant with sea life that it is often referred to as being an 'angler's El Dorado'. Yellowtail kingfish, snapper, mao mao and John Dory are among the tasty fish that you might bring in from sea to plate during the course of your day. Judging by the big fish Steve holds on his flyer photo and the wide grins on the faces of those that go with him, you can expect a day as fishy as it is fun.

Prices: *$220 per person for a 6-hour share charter, $880/6-hour sole charter, $1,200/day sole charter. Salt-water fly-fishing & marlin/tuna fishing also available.* **Contact:** *Wendy and Steve Butler, Bay of Islands;* **Tel:** *09-407-7165;* **Fax:** *09-407-5465; wendy@earlgreyfishing.co.nz; www.earlgreyfishing.co.nz*

The Treaty and grounds of Waitangi

New Zealand's founding document, an agreement between the British government and 50 Maori chiefs, was signed on the grounds of Waitangi in 1840. In return for giving Queen Victoria rights to buy their land, Maoris were granted all the rights and privileges of British subjects, quite extraordinary considering the times and the very different form of race relations (or non-) just over the pond between the British and the Aborigines.

However a few differing meanings, lost in translation between the two versions of the treaty (English and Maori), have caused considerable controversy over the text that continues to this day.

Differences aside, each year on 'Waitangi Day' on 6th February, New Zealanders of all origins come here to commemorate the founding of their nation. Ceremonial celebrations including flag-raising, canon-firing and fireworks mark the event. The highlight of the day is the launch of the 120-warrior long-canoe Ngatokimatawhaorua. This impressive 35-metre Maori war canoe is made from the trunks of three kauri trees and is named after the vessel in which Kupe discovered these shores.

northland

Going Kayaking

Pick up a paddle and go kayaking with Logan and Camilla for a jumping fish's eye view of the Bay of Islands. Venture through mangrove forests and historical sites and discover islands and their sandy beaches as you cruise through the straits with their marine inhabitants. Dry bags for your cameras are complimentary. Morning tea and lunchtime food are provided.

Prices: *Full day from $90 pp, half day from $60 pp.* **Contact:** *Logan and Camilla Going, Paihia;* **Tel:** *Freephone 0800-024-646 (within New Zealand only); goingkayaking@xtra.co.nz; www.goingkayaking.co.nz*

Salt Air

They say the only way to see the Bay of Islands is by boat, but this must have been before Salt Air started flying over the islands on their half-day Cape Reinga tours. Everyone gets a window seat and you can chat with the pilot as you fly up the wild west coast for a bird's eye view of Ninety Mile Beach. Not that you'll have much to say – the views are so awe-inspiring you'll probably be stuck for words. Touch-down for some nibbles and then a drive down Te Paki quicksand stream (easy on those nibbles) before tobogganing down giant sand dunes and then flying home, this time down the east coast that's all dotted with lovely islands. Salt Air also offer day tours to Cape Reinga and the Bay of Islands from Auckland for those with time-restricted itineraries who can squeeze in a spare day in Auckland.

Prices: *$375.00 per person. Children under 4 years can travel on parent's lap FOC otherwise full fare will apply.* **Contact:** *Grant Harnish and Wendy Hopkinson, The Hangar, Marsden Road, Paihia;* **Tel:** *09-402-8338 or freephone (within NZ) 0800-472-582;* **Fax:** *09-402-8302; info@saltair.co.nz; www.saltair.co.nz*

Salt Air

Waitangi Golf Course

This club is a favourite among locals and it's not hard to see why. The 18-hole championship standard course overlooks the whole bay and all of its islands and is a joy to play.

Prices: *Green fees for non-affiliated members: $45.* **Tel:** *09-402-7713;* **Fax:** *09-402-7713; waitangigolf@xtra.co.nz; www.waitangigolf.co.nz*

BAY OF ISLANDS – PAIHIA
CULTURE AND HISTORY

Culture North - Treaty of Waitangi Sound and Light Show

You're in 'birth of the nation' territory up here and you can watch history unfold before your very eyes and on the ground where it took place. Kupe's first landing, the meeting of the Maori and European cultures and the signing of New Zealand's founding document are all brought to life in these stunning evening productions. Maori culture, story-telling and live drama are combined with impressive lighting and sound effects in their unforgettable, atmospheric visions of the past.

Prices: *$55 pp for 2 hrs. Includes pick-up transport.* **Contact:** *Kena Rameka Alexander, Waitingi Treaty Grounds, Paihia;* **Tel:** *09-402-5990;* **Fax:** *09-402-9301; culturenth@xtra.co.nz; www.culturenorth.co.nz*

BAY OF ISLANDS - PAIHIA
CULTURE AND HISTORY
Paihia Matariki Festival
The Matariki Festival shows off art, food and Maori skills in a bonanza of events that take place throughout June. I happened upon it too late to be able to attend any of the festivities, but I longed to be at the traditional Maori kite-making workshop, the celestial navigation tour complete with tales of the ancestors, and of course the celebration of local food! Dates, times and places change yearly.
Tel: *09-402-7932; godsiff@xnet.co.nz*

 BAY OF ISLANDS - OPUA
CULTURE AND HISTORY
Studio Opua
Just opening when I passed through Opua, Matthew (a celebrated New Zealand ceramicist himself) is making a collection of local art and designware. He objects to the description "eclectic" (as I recollect, he preferred "random"), but I think it suits this gallery and workshop perfectly. New Zealand's burgeoning young talent is represented here, and Matthew's involvement means that the selection on display is varied and challenging. Most pieces are for sale should your heartstrings be irretrievably caught.
Contact: *Matthew Nisbet, 1 Beechy Street, Opua;* **Tel:** *09-402-7375; m@online.gen.nz; www.online.gen.nz*

 BAY OF ISLANDS - RUSSELL
EATING AND DRINKING
Kamakura
This local haunt boasts a stunning location right on the waterfront in Russell. After exploring this little historic harbour town treat yourselves to a great dinner or lunch. Clean-tasting seared Thai beef from the hills or chargrilled NZ game fish fresh from the bay were on offer when I dropped by, sadly with no time to dine… I'd strongly advise you not to follow my lead.
Prices: *Starters: $15 - $23, mains: $29.50 - $33, desserts: $12 - $20.* **Contact:** *Mark Ruston and Lesley Cook, The Strand, Russell;* **Tel:** *09-403-7771;* **Fax:** *09-403-7733; markandlesley@paradise.net.nz*

 BAY OF ISLANDS - RUSSELL
NATURE AND ACTIVITIES
Fernz Eco Tours
Friendly and knowledgeable, Fern offers 'a little bit different' days out around historic, seaside Russell. Shunning big crowds, small-choice or little-time type tours, flexibility is the order of the day as she weaves Maori culture, local stories and stunning scenery into the itinerary you so desire. From eco-tours, ancient kauri rainforests, beach walks, oyster farm tours and tastings, underground glow-worm and limestone caves, ancient hot mineral pools and local food and wine visits the list of things to choose from goes on… authentic, Kiwi, fun.
Prices: *Half-day tours $125. Full-day tours $220.* **Contact:** *Fern Jobbitt, 24 Kingfisher Road, Jacks Bay, Russell;* **Tel:** *09-403-7887;* **Fax:** *09-403-7887; info@fernzecotours.co.nz; www.fernzecotours.co.nz*

BAY OF ISLANDS - KERIKERI
EATING AND DRINKING

Café Jerusalem

This is the kind of place that no matter how short your stay is in town, one visit just never seems enough. Tucked back from Kerikeri's main street, you can sit on a quiet cobblestone courtyard under vines and tuck into some phenomenally tasty Middle Eastern food. The lamb schwarmas are the stars of the show, followed closely by the various vegetarian platters and lunchtime kebabs, all served quick as a flash by super friendly staff. Finish up your meal with some baklava, mint tea or a shisha. Only rarely do you find so much taste for so little money.

Prices: *Satisfying meals from $15.50 to $23.* **Contact:** *Cobblestone Mall, Kerikeri;* **Tel:** *09-407-1001; cafejlem@ihug.co.nz*

Café Cinema

Rolf is Dutch from Indonesia and Anita, Canadian: You can see and taste their homeland foodie influences in the great menu at this Kerikeri favourite. There's plenty of fresh locally-caught fish, typically cooked in four or five different ways each night and lots of the dishes have a distinctive and delicious Indonesian tang. Just next-door is the town's small, old-fashioned movie theatre. Spend an evening here and do one of their 'movie and meal' deals.

Contact: *Rolf and Anita, Hobson Avenue, Kerikeri;* **Tel:** *09-407-442.*

BAY OF ISLANDS - KERIKERI
CULTURE AND HISTORY

Historic Stone Store

From a kauri gum store to a mission supply house, then a general store and now after extensive conservation a museum, New Zealand's oldest standing European stone building has had many different guises in its time. Completed in 1836 by an ex-convict from New South Wales, the Regency-style building now contains relics and displays from its history. The country's very oldest building is Kemp House, just next door and built in 1821 - quite remarkable seeing that it's made of wood. Open daily from 9.30am to 5.30pm.

Prices: *$5 pp. Contact: 246 Kerikeri Road, Kerikeri;* **Tel:** *09-407-9236;* **Fax:** *09-407-9246; kkmission@historic.org.nz; www.historic.org.nz*

Fernz Eco Tours

Going Kayaking

Kerikeri's Historic Stone Store

Kerikeri Art and Craft Trail

Known as the 'cradle of the nation' Kerikeri is another of NZ's little enclaves famed for its artsy, slightly alternative way of life. I guess the backdrop of lush, verdant pastures, orchards and forests and its proximity to the Bay of Islands (though nicely set back from the tourist bustle) that draw the artistic crowd. Whatever it is, there are plenty of local painters, potters, wood-carvers and designers on this art and crafts trail to visit and watch at work. These trails are great ways to get your bearings on a place and to meet some local faces.
Contact: *09-407-3034;* **Fax:** *09-407-3036; lynda@kericopycentre.co.nz*

MATAURI BAY
NATURE AND ACTIVITIES

Kauri Cliffs Golf Course

Often rated one of the world's best, this par 72, championship golf course measures 6,510m and offers four sets of tees to challenge every skill level. Fifteen holes look out to the Pacific Ocean, six of which are played dramatically alongside cliffs that plunge to the sea. The remaining inland holes are beautiful and wind their way through marsh, forest and farmland.
Contact: *Matauri Bay Road, Matauri Bay;* **Tel:** *09-407-0100;* **Fax:** *09-407-0061; reservations@kauricliffs.com; www.kauricliffs.com*

KAEO
NATURE AND ACTIVITIES

Snow Cloud

Chris (appropriately surnamed Sale) has amassed huge experience over the years of the Southern Seas, collecting data on the distribution and breeding of various southern seabirds. He's also a thoroughly nice chap with heaps of knowledge about his local area's history and wildlife. You can help sail the Snow Cloud or just relax and take in the stunning, and I mean this in the fullness of the word, scenery of the Cavalli Islands and magnificent Whangaroa Harbour. Home-cooked food, sub-tropical beaches, walks and snorkeling are all part of this fantastic value day out.
Prices: *$80 pp for day trip, longer charters by arrangement.* **Contact:** *Chris, Marianne and June Sale, Te Ngaere Bay, Kaeo;* **Tel:** *09-405-0523; snowcloud@xtra.co.nz; www.kerikeri. net/snowcloud*

Cape Reinga or Te Rerenga Wairua: 'leaping-off place of the spirits'

Right up at the top of the North Island, Cape Reinga separates the Tasman Sea from the Pacific Ocean. Its lighthouse is spectacularly situated and presides over the two massive bodies of water as they clash and create the wild waters below. The site is of great significance to the Maori. According to their mythology, the spirits of the dead travel here on their journey to the afterlife in the spiritual homeland of Hawaiki. At Cape Reinga the spirits depart from the mainland by leaping off the ancient pohutukawa tree that stands nearby. They then turn briefly at the Three Kings Islands offshore to look back towards the land one final time before continuing on their journey.

MANGONUI
GUIDES

4x4 Paradise

Why go on the school bus when you can experience Cape Reinga and 90-Mile Beach from Gordon and Bev's ridiculously comfy, air-conditioned 4x4? This is the only serious way to do it: on tours tailor-made to suit your exact requirements and in a vehicle that can go where most others can't, or won't. Sit back and enjoy the stunning scenery of the dramatic northern shores and participate in a range of activities: swimming, sand tobogganing, fishing, digging for shellfish, quad-biking, golfing and wine tasting… the choice, as they say, is yours. Delicious picnic lunches with fine Northland wine as well as morning refreshments are provided.

Prices: *Vary depending on trip chosen.* **Contact:** *Jeanette Narbey, Mangonui;* **Tel:** *0800-494-392 or 09-406-0460; whathwhiwhi@xtra.co.nz; www.paradisenz.co.nz*

MANGONUI
EATING AND DRINKING

Waterfront Café and Bar

From snowboarder to chef, Paul's professions have taken him to high peaks and top restaurants all over the world. Teaming up with his sister Gerry, they have now taken over this great little restaurant/café and bar in Mangonui. Right by the village's sleepy harbour, days and boats alike idle past here at the Waterfront. I am sure you'll not find a spot more serene and incredibly beautiful than this to dine in the whole of NZ. The terrace makes a superb setting from which to sample local goodies like Whangaroa oysters, market fish and fresh lamb. Open for breakfast, lunch and dinner.

Prices: *Starters $4 - $17, mains from $24 - $28.50.* **Contact:** *Paul and Gerry Gordon, Waterfront Road, Mangonui;* **Tel:** *09-406-2245;* **Fax:** *09-406-2248; ggorgon@xtra.co.nz*

Mangonui Fish Shop

To this Mancunian, this was an eye-opener and a half. A chippy that fries your fish for you while you wait? A chippy with seafood salad, sashimi, fried oysters and crayfish on the menu? Unbelievable. And don't worry – the chips are excellent as well. Take your meal and drinks outside and watch the fish swim beneath the gallery floor as you eat. The only grit in the oyster? BYO vinegar – apparently it's a Pom thing.

Prices: *Breakfast, lunch and dinner range from $5 - $50. Licensed.* **Contact:** *Alan Wright Beach Road, Mangonui;* **Tel:** *09-406-0478; mangonui.fish@paradise.net.nz*

Kerikeri Art and Craft Trail

Jerusalem Café

Windswept beaches in the Far North

MANGONUI
CULTURE AND HISTORY
Butler Point Whaling Museum

With a whaling museum, a macadamia orchard, exotic and native flora gardens and a historic house, Lindo and Laetitia are exceptionally good jugglers of many interesting things. Butler Point is a historically important part of the Far North and, sitting on an old Maori fort, Butler House and its land preserves much of it. The Fergusons personally conduct tours through the house and museum and there are barbeque areas and picnics spots from where you can enjoy the ancient pohutukawa trees and expansive grounds over lunch. Recommendations from all quarters led me to this fascinating and unique place. Visits by appointment only.

Prices: *Adults $12, children $2, pre-school no charge. Reductions for groups.* **Contact:** *Lindo and Laeticia Ferguson, Butler Point, Mangonui;* **Tel:** *09-406-0006; butler.point@xtra.co.nz; www.butlerpoint.co.nz*

KARIKARI PENINSULA
NATURE AND ACTIVITIES
Carrington Resort Golf Course

Situated on the spectacular Karikari Peninsula, the unique feature of this course is that, despite its ocean-side location, it looks and plays like an inland golf course complete with rolling hills, vales and natural water hazards. The course is of tournament quality with 18 holes.

Prices: *$135 pp green fee. Club hire $40, carts $40. NZ affiliates $85.* **Contact:** *Maitai Bay Road, Karikari Peninsula;* **Tel:** *09-408-7222;* **Fax:** *09-408-7414; info@carrington.co.nz; www.carrington.co.nz*

The Mighty Kauri

With trunks as wide as a two-lane road, most trees don't come in proportions as gigantic as New Zealand's kauri. Growing to more than 50m tall and with trunk girths of up to 16m, they used to cover much of the top half of the North Island before the first people arrived 1000 years ago.

The Maori, who used their timber for boat building, carving and housing, and their gum for starting fires and chewing, first began felling them. Then, the arrival of European settlers saw the real decimation of the forests. Sailors were quick to realize that young kauri trunks made ideal ships' masts and the settlers who followed discovered that the more mature trees yielded timber of unsurpassed quality for building. The gum, too, became essential in the manufacture of varnishes.

The exploitation of forests increased with the demand for more and more cleared farmland. Whereas kauri forest once covered 1.2 million hectares of land; now they have been reduced to just 80,000 hectares.

Revered by the Maori people, who believe the trees possess their own spirit, they have named several individual trees including Tane Mahuta or 'Lord of the Forest', still standing (at a neck-achingly huge 51.5m tall!) after 2,100 years in the Waipoua Forest in Northland. Saved from destruction by their remoteness, the Waipoua forests are also home to the second and third largest kauri trees, Te Matua Ngahere and the McGregor kauri. If you are driving down to or from Auckland via the west coast then you must take the time and trouble to walk into the forest and see these giants. They are simply magnificent.

northland

KARIKARI PENINSULA
WINERIES
Karikari Estate Winery

This is New Zealand's northernmost winery and it is positioned on the achingly beautiful Doubtless Bay on the Karikari Peninsula. Several French grape varieties and Italian montepuliciano appear to enjoy the region and climate as much as I did, and duly prosper.

Contact: *Michael and Luciana Nijdam, Maitai Bay Road, Kaitaia, Karikari Peninsula;* **Tel:** *09-408-7222; info@karikariestate.co.nz; www.karikariestate.co.nz*

AHIPARA
NATURE AND ACTIVITIES
Tua Tua Tours

Skip the air-con of tour bus trips to feel the wind rush past as you experience the dunes of the far north beaches on these ATV quad bike tours. Climb up dunes and over remnants of ancient kauri forest as you check out archaeological sites, Tanutanu Beach and ride into the awesome Shipwreck Bay. This is brilliant fun and all trips are guided so you visit places most locals don't even know about. Your guide will assess your ability and give basic riding skills so that even if you've never been on a bike before, you'll know what you're doing. Take a good jacket, covered shoes and sunglasses and expect to take home plenty of dust, mud and good memories. Kids are very welcome.

Prices: *Reef Rider (reef and dunes, approx 20km): 1.5 hrs, single $90, double $100. Dune Rider (gumfields+dune/reef riding, approx 28km): 2 hrs, single $120, double $135. Gumfields Safari (approx 35km): 3 hrs, single $155, double $175. Booking essential.* **Contact:** *Ahipara, 15km west of Kaitaia;* **Tel:** *0800-494-288 (freephone from NZ) or 0274-858-453;* **Fax:** *09-409-4875; tuatuatours@ahipara.co.nz*

WAIHARARA
CULTURE AND HISTORY
Gumdiggers' Park & Ancient Buried Kauri Forest

A four-minute detour on the way to Cape Reinga brings you here, and unless you are an awful lot more informed than me, I can guarantee it will be an instructive experience. Dalmatian gumdiggers? Kauri gold? Gum spears? Tattoos and linoleum? Nope, I had no idea either, but this is a fascinating insight into an almost forgotten part of New Zealand''s heritage. There is also a gecko trail, and an onsite shop selling locally crafted kauri artefacts.

Prices: *Adult $10; child $5; family pass $25 (2 adults + 2 or more kids); under 8s are free.* **Contact:** *Heath Road, Awanui, Waiharara.* **Tel:** *09-406-7166; info@gumdiggerspark.co.nz; www.gumdiggerspark.co.nz*

Gumdiggers' Park

Poor Knights Islands Dive! Tutukaka

Carrington Golf Resort

Highlights

• Get sailing on the Waitemata Harbour in this the 'City of Sails'; even better if you can bag a space on one of the America's Cup yachts.

• Learn about the history, geology and wildlife of New Zealand at the Auckland Museum. Do this on a Sunday morning and spend the afternoon (during summer months) picnicking at the Domain and watching a free jazz concert.

• Have a long and lazy lunch in front of the super-yachts at the Viaduct Harbour, before taking a walk through Downtown to the Sky Tower, the Southern Hemisphere's highest platform.

• Hop on the ferry to historic Devonport, climb Mt Victoria for 360 degree views of the city or walk up to the old garrison atop the other volcanic cone of North Head. Afterwards, bathe at lovely Cheltenham Beach.

• Explore the islands of the Hauraki Gulf: the city-suburb of Waiheke, volcanic Rangitoto and the wild frontier of Great Barrier.

• Spend a day tramping in the lush forest of Waitakere National Park. Stop in at the Arataki Centre for information about the area's flora, fauna and cultural history. Carry on west till you hit the coast and some of Northland's rugged, great-for-walking beaches like Piha and Karekare.

North Island

Auckland

South Island

AUCKLAND CENTRE
EATING AND DRINKING

One Tree Grill

This is a posh-nosh venue without the attendant snobbery. Staff are ultra-friendly, and ultra-knowledgeable about the food, the wine and the combination of both. Guy Malyon (yes, he is a distant cousin and no I didn't let that cloud my judgement, honest governor) has nurtured a casual, neighbourhood-eatery atmosphere whilst at the same time creating a top-notch menu. The New Zealand fish blew my mind: spiced snapper fillet served on sweet-corn fritters, sashimi timbale, and tea-crusted rare tuna loin, all as fresh as a springtime daisy. (Incidentally, One Tree Grill is a pun on the restaurant's location in residential One Tree Hill.)

Dinner is served Monday to Saturday from 5pm; lunch is Monday to Friday from 11.30am.
Prices: *Fixed menu from $55.* **Contact:** *Guy Malyon 9-11 Pah Road, Greenwoods Corner, Auckland;* **Tel:** *03-625-6407;* **Fax:** *03-625-6406; info@onetreegrill.co.nz; www.onetreegrill.co.nz*

Auckland: a city of sails and sailors

No explanation is really needed to describe why Auckland has acquired the moniker 'city of sails' – just take a look at all those lovely sailboats jammed into its Waitemata Harbour, all bobbing neatly in line. With a population of just over one million, Auckland is said to have more boats per capita than any other city in the world. With its temperate, sea-faring-friendly climate and the stunning island-speckled Hauraki Gulf off the end of the deck, it is abundantly clear why yachting is such a hugely popular pastime here. One of the highlights of the city's year is the Auckland Anniversary Regatta at the end of January, with over 600 yachts taking part.

Number 5

With its strict 'life is too short to drink bad wine' philosophy, Number 5 is already a winner for me. Set in an old redbrick house with burgundy walls, dancing fires and cosy, candlelit dining areas, the setting here is intimate and warm. Food, such as double-roasted duck on creamy potato mash and caramelised citrus jus or white veal rack, is beautifully presented and completely delicious. And, of course, a fabulous (and mostly New Zealand sourced) wine list is accompanied by a jolly sommelier to help you make your choice.

Prices: *Open Mon - Sat 6pm until late. Starters $13 - $18.50, mains $25.50 - $37.50 and desserts $13.50;* **Contact:** *Martina Lutz, 5 City Road, Auckland;* **Tel:** *09-309-9273;* **Fax:** *09-309-9174; info@number5.co.nz; www.number5.co.nz.*

Cin Cin On Quay

Far and away the most popular restaurants in the harbour, this is a sophisticated yet relaxed place that you can return to again and again and never be disappointed. Whether it's pork belly, salmon or lamb, all dishes present great-quality NZ produce in delicious and innovative ways. Right on the waterfront, Cin Cin is at the heart of all the action and is a great place to eat, talk, drink and watch.

Prices: *Open 7 days, from 10am till late. Starters $17 - $19.50, mains $28 - $38 and desserts $14.* **Contact:** *Cristina Magni, 99 Quay Street, Auckland;* **Tel:** *09-307-6966;* **Fax:** *09-307-6523; email@cincin.co.nz; www.cincin.co.nz.*

Revive!

Intoxicatingly fresh and healthy aromas will seemingly lift you up from the busy downtown street and into this invigorating, oasis-like vegetarian café and juice bar. Jeremy is passionate about whole, organic foods and produces delicious hot meals, salads and juices and smoothies made from happy, wholesome ingredients. I stopped by before catching the nearby ferry to Waiheke and my salad and fruit shake combo kept me fuelled up all day.

Prices: *Salads and hot meals (change daily) $7.90 - $13.90, juices and smoothies $5.90 - $6.90. Heaps of vegan, wheat-free options, semi-organic with an extensive salad bar with 12 different options. Open Mon - Thurs 11am - 9pm, Fri 11am - 2.30pm.* **Contact:** *Jeremy Dixon, 16 Fort Street (at the bottom of Queen Street), Auckland Central;* **Tel:** *09-307-1586; info@revive.co.nz; www.revive.co.nz.*

AUCKLAND CENTRE
NATURE AND ACTIVITIES

The Pride of Auckland

Brent's gang of four shipshape and 50ft yachts have trademark blue-and-white sails for cruising and dining around Auckland's nautical playground, the Hauraki Gulf. With no bonus points for effort and the emphasis on enjoyment for all, participatory roles can vary from the calm 'eating/relaxing/tanning oneself' combo (my preference) to taking the helm for some full-on match racing action. Includes entry to the NZ National Maritime Museum.

Prices: *Choose your cruise to coincide with your favourite meal of the day, from $58 pp for coffee and cake to $95 pp for dinner. A half-day adventure cruise is $153 pp.* **Contact:** *Brent Pasley, Cnr of Quay & Hobson Streets, Downtown, Auckland, 1143;* **Tel:** *09-373-4557;* **Fax:** *09-377-0459; sail@prideofauckland.com; www.prideofauckland.com.*

America's Cup Experience

Not only can you experience the thrill of sailing an America's Cup yacht, but you can also participate in racing on one. Meet up with the professional crew who take you through safety and race briefings before departing through the America's Cup village and past the super yachts to take positions for practice. Alternatively take the more laid-back option of a two-hour sailing trip. Sails are hoisted and passengers become the crew and are encouraged to take the helm. Exert energy on the grinders or simply sit back and enjoy the action as you sail down Auckland Harbour. No experience is necessary and all instruction is provided by friendly crew on board the yachts.

Prices: *2-hour sailing experience: $91 adult, $75 child. 3-hour racing experience $131 adult, $118 child.* **Contact:** *Viaduct Harbour, Auckland Central;* **Tel:** *09-359-5987; info@ explorenz.co.nz; www.explorenz.co.nz.*

Healthy Pickings at Revive!

Some Woolly Natives at Nikau Cave

Outside the National Maritime Museum

auckland

Kelly Tarlton's Antarctic Encounter and Underwater World

Come as close as you dare to a broad-nosed seven-gill shark, proudly displaying (behind 7cm of glass) some of the most powerful jaws on the planet. Plunge under Auckland's waterfront and travel through the clear viewing tunnel and meet other fascinating creatures of the deep, like giant stingray, dainty sea-horses, huge crayfish and feisty piranha. In the Antarctic Encounter, you can travel in a snowcat through snow and ice and get a fish-eye view of the penguins as they swim under water.

Prices: *Adult $28, children (over 15) and seniors $21, children (4 - 14 yrs) $14. Discounts if you book online. Family passes available as well.* **Contact:** *23 Tamaki Drive, Orakei, Auckland;* **Tel:** *09-528-0603;* **Fax:** *09-528-5175; info@kellytarltons.co.nz; www.kellytarltons.co.nz.*

Sky Tower Vertigo Climb

For the best views of Auckland, go no further (not that you can) than the very top of the highest man-made platform in the southern hemisphere. After fifteen minutes of easy yet totally exhilarating climbing inside the mast of the tower, you'll find yourself 300m above ground. Most of the two-hour experience is spent at the top enjoying the amazing view all the way over the Hauraki Gulf to the Coromandel Peninsula as Vertigo guides point out the city highlights. With drink and rest breaks along the way, guides will amaze you with facts on behind-the-scene tower construction and local volcanic activity.

Prices: *Two-hour guided tour: adult $145, children (under 14) $75.* **Contact:** *Jamie Whitburn, Sky Tower, Auckland Central;* **Tel:** *09-368-1917; info@4vertigo.com; www.4vertigo.com.*

Auckland Zoo

Come and see the two 'icons' of New Zealand, the kiwi and the tuatara, relaxing at home in their special public viewing nocturnal shelters, the only ones of their kind in town. Watch the kiwis forage for small bugs and worms in the moonlight dimness and peer through glass into a replica den to spot the closest living relative to the dinosaurs hiding in the leafy undergrowth. You'll see the usual zoological suspects here from tarantulas, hippos, NZ songbirds and Oz, their dashing new Sumatran tiger.

Prices: *Adults $18, children (4 - 15 yrs) $9, students $14. Family concessions are available.* **Contact:** *Motions Road, Western Springs, Auckland;* **Tel:** *09-360-3800;* **Fax:** *09-360-3818; aucklandzoo@aucklandcity.govt.nz; www.aucklandzoo.co.nz.*

AUCKLAND CENTRE
CULTURE AND HISTORY

NZ National Maritime Museum

New Zealand's maritime heritage is rich with tales of exploration, discovery, design and success. To discover the history of the nation you must understand its vital relationship with the seas that surround it. Located in the heart of the Viaduct Harbour in the 'City of Sails', this is one of the finest maritime museums in the world. You can view the widescreen presentation of the first Polynesian migration to New Zealand, step inside some of the life-size exhibits and learn about the sailing feats of the late Sir Peter Blake, NZ yachting legend.

Prices: *Museum entry: adults $16, children $6. Heritage harbour cruise: adults $15, children $7. Under 5's go free and concessions apply for students, seniors and families. Combined rates available for museum and harbour cruise.* **Contact:** *Pam Smith, Cnr Quay and Hobson Streets, Viaduct Harbour, Auckland;* **Tel:** *09-373-0800;* **Fax:** *09-377-6000; museum@nzmaritime.org; www.nzmaritime.org.*

AUCKLAND CENTRE
CULTURE AND HISTORY
Auckland Art Gallery Toi o Tamaki

With the most extensive collection of national and international art in the country, Auckland Art Gallery or 'Toi o Tamaki' remains the largest art institution in New Zealand, with a collection numbering over 14,000 works. These include major holdings of New Zealand historic, modern and contemporary art, and some outstanding works by Maori and Pacific Island artists. There are also many European paintings, sculptures and print collections from 1376 to the present day and busy programmes of international touring exhibitions.

Prices: *Open daily 10am - 5pm except Christmas Day and Good Friday. Entry to the gallery is free. Admission charges apply for special exhibitions: adult $7, concession $5. Family Passes and Multi Passes available.* **Contact:** *Corner Wellesley and Lorne Streets, Auckland;* **Tel:** *09-307-7700;* **Fax:** *09-302-1096; gallery@aucklandartgallery.govt.nz; www.aucklandartgallery.govt.nz.*

NEWMARKET
EATING AND DRINKING
Sahaa

This superb little restaurant is a real off-the-beaten-track, local haunt. You don't often come across quality Algerian, Morrocan and Tunisian flavours in NZ. In fact this is the only one of its kind on the whole North Island, something that makes Sahaa's menu shine even brighter. Naturally, tagines are the specialty here and the setting is positively North African exotic with a private, traditional low-seating area, a family dining room complete with Moroccan fountain, colourful pottery on the walls and dainty glass cups from which to sip your mint tea.

Prices: *Entrées $10 - $24, mains $20 - $26.* **Contact:** *Makh and Dianna Benyettou, 475 Khyber Pass Road, Newmarket, Auckland;* **Tel:** *09-523-4578;* **Fax:** *09-523-4578; sahaarestaurant@hotmail.com.*

PARNELL
EATING AND DRINKING
St Tropez Bistro and Wine Bar

St Tropez is refreshingly laid-back for the fine restaurant that it is. Jean-Christophe serves some of the best French food in the country, decadent and oh so good. Order a gloriously rich pâté with fresh crusty bread, then confit de canard or poisson Grenobloise and - voilà! - let yourself be transported to the South of France and feel its glow until your last spoonful of tarte tatin with chantilly cream goes down. Put simply by an NZ Herald reviewer, "they know about the food and the wine, and why it is what it is".

Prices: *Open for dinner, plus lunch on Fridays only. Mains $25.50 - $29.50. Desserts $11.50. Open Monday to Saturday, Sundays only. Function bookings avaialble on request.* **Contact:** *Jean-Christophe, 149 Parnell Road, Parnell, Auckland;* **Tel:** *09-309-0996; info@sttropez.co.nz; www.sttropez.co.nz.*

Non Solo Pizza

Walk into Non Solo Pizza and prepare yourself not just for an edible but a visual feast as well. With a marble fireplace stacked with logs at one end, a delicious food selection at the other and one of the loveliest outdoor courtyards in town at the back, this is definitely a place to feel good in. From contorni, antipasti, pizza, pasta, insalate, secondi and dolci, all the food is as properly Italian as it sounds... and, of course, as authentically delicious.

Prices;: *Pizza $21.50 - $24.50. Pasta: main $24.50. Salads and other dishes $7.50 - $30.50. Desserts and cheeses $10.50 - $15.00.* **Contact:** *Vivienne and Antonio Crisci, 259 Parnell Road, Parnell, Auckland;* **Tel:** *09-379-5358;* **Fax:** *09-379-5359; nsp@nonsolopizza.co.nz; www.nonsolopizza.co.nz.*

PARNELL
NATURE AND ACTIVITIES
Parnell Rose Gardens

Just around the corner from Parnell are the beautiful Rose Gardens, with over 4,500 different bushes of the flower, all laid out in beds within the Dove-Myer Robinson Park. The gardens are sited just above Judges Bay, sloping downwards with pleasant shaded pathways and numerous fine, mature trees. This is a great place to while away a sunny afternoon looking out over the harbour and its busy container wharves from the cliff-top edge. From late spring to early autumn the brilliant displays of rose bushes are at their best.

Prices: *No entrance fee. Open daily during daylight hours.* **Contact:** *Auckland City Council, 85 Gladstone Road, Parnell, Auckland;* **Tel:** *09-302-1252;* **Fax:** *09-525-5308; parnellrosegarden@xtra.co.nz.*

PARNELL
CULTURE AND HISTORY
Auckland Museum

Housed in one of the nation's finest heritage buildings and with spectacular views of Auckland City and the harbour, Auckland Museum tells the story of New Zealand. Three expansive levels follow the emergence of a nation through the loss and suffering of war, explain its uniquely ancient natural history, and showcase a collection of priceless Maori and Pacific treasures. Definitely worth seeing is a performance of the story of Aotearoa through traditional song and dance by the Maori cultural group, Manaia. They perform three times every day (four times a day from January to March). For kids there's a fantastic hands-on discovery centre - touch real fossils, discover drawers full of creepy-crawlies, go face to face with enormous cockroaches and watch frogs catch their breakfast!

Prices: *Open daily 10am - 5pm. Admission free but $5 donation per adult greatly appreciated.* **Contact:** *Domain Drive, Parnell, Auckland;* **Tel:** *09-309-0443;* **Fax:** *09-379-9956; info@ aucklandmuseum.com; www.aucklandmuseum.com.*

Sahaa

Parnell Rose Gardens

Auckland Museum

auckland

Exploring the Hauraki Gulf

The gulf around Auckland is dotted with lots of lovely islands. There are 65 of them in all, some within minutes of the city, others a little further offshore. Many are easily accessible on ferries from central Auckland. For more information on times of crossings visit www.fullers.co.nz.

Here's a bit of info on some that you might like to visit:

Waiheke gained a reputation in the 1960s for the 'alternative' lifestyles of its residents and its artisan culture, though now it has become more like a dormitory suburb of the city. With white sand beaches, vineyards and olive groves, this is still a great place to visit and is easily accessible at less than half-an-hour's ferry journey from downtown Auckland.

Rangitoto is the youngest island in the gulf. It emerged from the sea just 700 years ago in a series of volcanic explosions. Its volcanic landscape supports over 200 species of moss, plants and trees including tree daisies, manuka, orchids and the largest pohutukawa (also known as the 'NZ Christmas tree' due to its flaming red flowers over Dec/Jan) forest in the world! There are some 10 or so short and long walks around the island and from the summit there are magnificent views over the Hauraki Gulf, the Waitemata Harbour and Auckland City.

Tiritiri Matangi in Maori means 'wind tossing about'. As its name suggests this is an island of dramatic, steeply rising cliffs and, despite extensive planting programmes attempting to return the forest to its original glory, it remains largely bare. 25km north of Auckland, it is an open sanctuary and the public is free to visit and venture down the five main walking tracks to enjoy some of New Zealand's rarer fauna and bird life.

Great Barrier Island is decidedly remote. It is the largest island in the gulf, about half the size of the city's metropolitan area, and lies 90km north-east of Auckland. Very rugged with narrow ravines, steep cliffs, jagged pinnacles and a deeply indented coastline, the 1100 residents live the type of alternative and artsy lifestyle of the former residents of Waiheke. The island is a real haven of peace and tranquility, wilderness, and rare birdlife. Scenic drives, wonderful walking tracks among native forest and bush, long white surf beaches, fishing and good diving all make this a great destination. Catch a ferry from the city or alternately take a 30-minute flight.

Kawau Island can only be reached from Sandspit in Warkworth, a little further up the coast, although if you stay at Kawau Lodge, [G] Dave will happily come and meet you on the mainland with his boat to take you over. It is best known for Mansion House, built in 1846 and home of former New Zealand governor Sir George Grey. He turned the island into a zoological park importing a variety of animals including kookaburras, peacocks and parma wallabies which, thought to be extinct in Australia, can sometimes still be seen.

PARNELL
CULTURE AND HISTORY

Summer Jazz Concerts at the Domain

What could be more pleasant than listening to top-quality jazz and other classical sounds whilst sitting on the beautiful grounds of the Auckland Domain and looking out over the shimmering Hauraki Gulf? I can't really find an answer, except perhaps to do it with a picnic and some wine. Pop into the Pandoro Bakery (open 7 days) on nearby Parnell Road, turn up just before the 2pm kick-off and make a thoroughly pleasant Sunday afternoon of it.

Prices: *Free for all. From 2pm every Sunday for three months over summer (Dec - Feb). Look for the Music in Parks section on the aucklandcity.govt.nz web site for dates.* **Contact:** *Auckland Domain Band Rotunda, Parnell, Auckland;* **Tel:** *09-379-2020; www.aucklandcity.govt.nz.*

PONSONBY
EATING AND DRINKING

Bambina

Ponsonby Road spills over with boutique designers, fine dining and wine bars, and on Sunday morning it felt like the place to see and be seen - and nowhere more so than Bambina. Get there early enough and grab a seat on the big square table so you can rustle away behind all the weekend newspapers. Extensive menu and reliably excellent food.

Contact: *Peter Wren, 268 Ponsonby Road, Ponsonby, Auckland;* **Tel:** *09-360-4000;* **Fax:** *09-360-2985; bambina@xtra.co.nz.*

The Ponsonby Belgian Beer Café

This Belgian beer café was recommended to me by real-life Belgian-Aucklanders, Bart and Thérèse from Ascot Parnell. With its distinctly European-brasserie atmosphere, the Ponsonby is now famous for its moules-frites-bière combo. Housed in what used to be the old Ponsonby Post Office, a full range of Belgian beers on tap and tasty Belgian cuisine have replaced its postage stamps and mail boxes. There's a great selection of Lambic (fruit), Trappist (monk) and (Belgian favourite) Kwak beers to go with their delicious pots of mussels and fries.

Prices: *Mussels, served by the steaming pot: $17. Mussel platters: $16.50. Beers $7.15 - $14.50 a bottle.* **Contact:** *Steve Oakley, 1 - 3 St Mary's Road, Ponsonby, Auckland;* **Tel:** *09-376-6092;* **Fax:** *09-376-6095; hardi.and.alexa@xtra.co.nz; www.theponsonby.co.nz.*

Shimmering waters around Waiheke Island

WAIHEKE ISLAND
GUIDES
Ananda Tours

Jenny is utterly charming and seemingly has the knack of being in many places at once, all fantastic and all of them somewhere on gorgeous Waiheke Island. Genuinely friendly (and genuinely local!) guides reveal as much or as little of the island, its people and its natural splendours as you wish them to. Homespun galleries, award-winning vineyards, lush gardens, world-class restaurants, white sand beaches and wild bush walks will be your stepping stones through a very colourful and informative day.

Prices: *Prices start at $95 pp for a full day tour. Lunch and ferry tickets additional.*
Contact: *Jenny McDonald, 20 Seaview Road, Ostend, Waiheke Island.* **Tel:** *09-372-7530*
Fax: *09-372-7531; anandatours@ihug.co.nz; www.ananda.co.nz.*

WAIHEKE ISLAND
WINERIES
Mudbrick Vineyard and Restaurant

Tired of the rat race across the waters, Robyn and Nick bought this plot of land and began the toil of planting, planting and more planting. Now the roots have spread to encompass an award-winning vineyard, an acclaimed restaurant constructed from bricks of, yes you guessed it, mud, potager gardens and a quirky cellar shop. 'Pure relaxation' is how most guests and the Joneses themselves describe the feeling of sitting on the terrace, sipping wine by the fireplace and looking out over the vines and back to the city.

Prices: *Entrées range from $15 - $22, mains $33 - $38, desserts $15.* **Contact:** *Nick and Robyn Jones, Church Bay Road, Oneroa, Waiheke Island;* **Tel:** *09-372-9050;* **Fax:** *09-372-9051; info@mudbrick.co.nz; www.mudbrick.co.nz.*

WAIHEKE ISLAND
CULTURE AND HISTORY
Connells Bay Sculpture Park

A large Easter Island styled wooden head carved by a Samoan artist watches over one of the country's finest collections of contemporary sculpture which brings together art and nature in its most beautiful forms. John and Jo provide a two-hour guided walk as you wander along an elaborate system of paths through nikau palms and pungas and view some mind-boggling kinetic sculptures as well as stunning views that sweep over the Hauraki Gulf. Open by prior appointment only, mid-October to mid-April. Bookings are essential and children must be supervised.

Prices: *Adults $30 and children $15. (Fees and donations are paid to Creative Arts Trust to promote its charitable activities and support NZ sculptors.)* **Contact:** *John and Jo Gow, Cowes Bay Road, Waiheke Island, Auckland;* **Tel:** *09-372-8957; info@connellsbay.co.nz; www.connellsbay.co.nz.*

Lopdell House

WEST AUCKLAND
GUIDES

Bush and Beach Eco-Tours

Bush and Beach offers interactive, enjoyable, guided full- or half-day eco-tours in the greater Auckland region. Walk in the unique Waitakere rainforest with giant tree ferns and ancient kauri trees and on the wild west coast's black-sand beaches - incredibly just a thirty-minute drive from downtown Auckland. Or enjoy a half-hour scenic flight to untamed Great Barrier Island. Here you walk on pristine white-sand beaches, cross lush wetlands to natural thermal springs and visit the island's only farm where you find endangered brown teals (friendly little ducks). At a nearby stream, monster eels can be fed... if you dare. Or spend the day on the Coromandel Peninsula and enjoy the amazing landscape of mountains, forest-covered backbone, stunning coastline and sheltered bays and coves that make this a favourite holiday spot. This unique area is steeped in history associated with kauri logging and gold mining.

Prices: *Wilderness Experience: 12.30pm - 5.30pm, $125 pp; Coast and Rainforest Walk: 10am - 5pm, $185 pp; Auckland's Untamed Island Tour: 7.15am - 5.30pm, $545 pp; Coromandel Day Tour: 7am - 7pm, $285 pp. Refreshments and city pick-ups provided. Min 2 people.* **Tel:** *09-837-4130;* **Fax:** *09-837-4193; bbl@bushandbeach.co.nz; www.bushandbeach.co.nz.*

WEST AUCKLAND, TITIRANGI
CULTURE AND HISTORY

Lopdell House Gallery

En route to Auckland's stunning west coast beaches and the Waitakere Ranges is the peaceful little village of Titirangi. A building that wouldn''t look out of place in the South of France, is home to Lopdell House Gallery, Waitakere City's Regional Art Gallery. Natural light and airy spaces, concrete pillars and polished timber floors, are the perfect framework for touring exhibitions that reflect the excellence of contemporary New Zealand art and the cultural diversity of the city. Afterwards drop by to the Hardware Café, Java Central, with experienced baristas serving great coffees and lunchtime snacks.

Prices: *Admission is free. Open daily from 10am - 4.30pm.* **Contact:** *Lesley Smith, Corner Titirangi and South Titirangi Roads, Titirangi, Waitakere City.* **Tel:** *09-817-8087;* **Fax:** *09-817-3340; info@lopdell.org.nz; www.lopdell.org.nz.*

WAIKARETU
NATURE AND ACTIVITIES

Nikau Cave

Nikau Cave's formations are dazzling. The only crowds you find in this tiny family-run operation are the tightly-packed and twinkling glowworms that map the contours of the rock in luminescent dots. A wonderful and mildly challenging trip that will convert even the most adamant of surface dwellers. Extensive gardens, farm and bush walks also on site. New café planned for summer 2007.

Prices: *Adult $25 - $30, child $15 - $20.* **Contact:** *Anne and Philip Woodward, 1779 Waikaretu Valley Road, Waikaretu, Auckland.* **Tel:** *09-233-3199;* **Fax:** *09-233-3131; info@nikaucave.co.nz; www. nikaucave.co.nz.*

Spotting the glowworms in Nikau Cave

Coromandel

Highlights

North Island

Coromandel

South Island

• Get out the binos at the Firth of Thames near Miranda. Thousands of birds, especially the ones from Siberia and the Arctic, have flown as far as you have (and much more cheaply) to reach these shores for some winter sun to breed.
• Follow the 'crimson trail' of summer-blooming pohutukawas (aka the NZ Christmas tree) as you drive north up the coast from Thames. Cross over the peninsula's forest-clad mountain spine and come down the east coast's rugged coastal route.
• Venture into the impressive Coromandel Forest Park, an area steeped in kauri logging history. Choose one of the many trails and walk past milling remnants and through nikaus, ferns and the remaining kauris of this luxuriant, dense forest.
• Potter around low-key Coromandel Town and take the time to visit local artists' workshops and quirky establishments – don't miss the brilliantly fun Waiau Waterworks on Highway 309!
• Follow the unsealed west coast road to the real land's end at Fletcher Bay. This place is magical: deserted beaches, walks in forests and along the coast and splendid views (all across the Hauraki Gulf) abound.
• Last but definitely not least, kayak in the idyllic marine reserve around Cathedral Cove and discover some of New Zealand's most gorgeous beaches at Hahei, Matarangi and Whangamata.

COROMANDEL PENINSULA
CULTURE AND HISTORY

Homegrown Festival

All around the Coromandel, all through May, is the Homegrown Festival. It celebrates 'Coro' food, Kiwi music and local art, so whatever your niche there will be something to delight you. Events are as disparate as a 'Catch a Cray' day at The Alderman Islands, one-act plays performed in Coromandel Town, and skateboarding in Thames. The website lists the year's events and schedules so you can tailor-make your festival experience to suit your own particular quirks of interest.

Contact: *carl@thecoromandel.com; www.homegrownfestival.co.nz*

 ## MIRANDA
NATURE AND ACTIVITIES

Miranda Shorebird Centre

As well as having three of its own endemic species, Miranda is a very popular wintering spot for birds; great news for birders. Thousands of nesting shorebirds from Siberia and Alaska flock here each year, arriving exhausted and hungry at the end of the last leg of their epic journey. It is a remarkable tale of migration, and it is told here at the Miranda Shorebird Centre. Even without the birds, this is also a lovely, undeveloped shore of shell-banks and tidal flats that make for great walking ground with views over to the Coromandel stretching out into the blue horizon. September to March is the main breeding season for a variety of Arctic birds.

Contact: *Firth of Thames, 283 East Coast Road, Pokeno, Miranda;* **Tel:** *09-232-2781; shorebird@xtra.co.nz; www.miranda-shorebird.org.nz*

Kauri 2000

The Coromandel was once home to magnificent forests of kauri. However, after years of logging during the 19th and early 20th centuries, very little of it now remains. Kauri 2000 is a very special organisation that seeks to organise and encourage re-planting. For just $10 you can have a kauri seedling planted on your behalf by volunteers and you'll receive a certificate giving you your tree's exact location. A great excuse for returning to the Coromandel to see your little tree grow big. For further information contact Kauri 2000 Trust, T/F 07-866-2656, www.kauri2000.co.nz.

THAMES
NATURE AND ACTIVITIES
Rapaura Watergardens

Rapaura is a 64-acre tranquil haven of soothing native greenery. Marvel at the summer water lilies in the 14 lily ponds, and take the bush walk through the tree ferns and native trees up to the cascading waterfalls. The gardens are a veritable paradise of peace. I loved the sculptures and art pieces scattered around, echoing the beauty of the surroundings. Sally and Sacha have just opened the Koru at Rapaura cafe/restaurant, where they serve 'dam' good coffees and delectable (trust me on this one) home-baked food.

Prices: *Adults $10, children (aged 5 - 15) $4.* **Contact:** *Sally and Sacha Sank, 586 Tapu-Coroglen Rd, Tapu, Thames Coast;* **Tel:** *07-868-4821;* **Fax:** *07-868-4821; info@rapaura.com; www.rapaura.com*

COROMANDEL TOWN
EATING AND DRINKING
The Peppertree Restaurant

Superb fishes of the day - try orange roughy with prawns and scallops - juicy local beef, lamb and interesting vegetable concoctions explain why this is the most popular restaurant in town. Situated in an old country-style cottage with a laid-back, wrap-around balcony, its roaring fires, adjoining bar and great service help enormously. "Our lunch here [of local crayfish] will retain a fond place in our memories for the rest of our lives," said one lifelong-happy customer. Well, this place definitely gets my vote too.

Prices: *Mains from $22.50 - $32.50. Various seafood platters and indulgences at differing prices depending on season;* **Contact:** *Richard and Jennifer Savage, 31 Kapanga Road, Coromandel Town;* **Tel:** *07-866-8211; peppertreerandb@xtra.co.nz*

Umu Cafe and Restaurant

Head no further than Umu for hearty café breakfasts where happy, friendly staff serve great coffee and superb corn fritters, among other things. It's open daily from brunch to dinner and the menu's awash with local seafood as well as pizzas, NZ lamb and cake. Big colourful paintings by local artists dress the walls and the atmosphere is delightfully relaxed and calming a lot like Coromandel Town itself....

Prices: *Lunches from $7.50 (for delicious wraps) to $22.50, dinners $21.50 - $30, pizza $13 - $22 depending on size and toppings.* **Contact:** *Josie Fraser, 22 Wharf Road, Coromandel Town;* **Tel:** *07-866-8618; umucafe@xtra.co.nz*

Water-based tomfoolery at Waiau Waterworks

Pohutukawa in bloom

Resident Chief Spider at Waiau Waterworks

coromandel

COROMANDEL TOWN
NATURE AND ACTIVITIES

Waiau Waterworks

"Arrive wondering, leave smiling." There are over 40 water-powered gadgets, sculptures, toys and playgrounds (for adults!) in this whimsical wonder of a place. From fathoming the giddy sticks and flying foxes, to water-jousting on wooden steeds and spinning in the human hamster wheel, each contraption here is as eccentric, humorous and fun as the last. You'll laugh, play and delight at this interactive and totally unique park where the novelty never wears off. Barbeques and picnic spots are dotted amongst the trees, lawns and streams or there's a café for insanely good coffee and delicious home-cooked foods.

Prices: *Adults $10, children $5. Under 5's go free. Discounts for larger groups.* **Contact:** *Chris and Kay Ogilvie, 471, 309 Road, Coromandel;* **Tel:** *07-866-7191;* **Fax:** *07-866-7191; info@waiauwaterworks.co.nz; www.waiauwaterworks.co.nz*

Driving Creek Railway

The trains climb up through native forest, through short tunnels, high trestle bridges (one of which is double-decked) and five reversing points up to the terminus, the Eyefull Tower. From here, grand sweeping views of the Hauraki Gulf and islands, and forest-covered mountains are to be enjoyed. Owner Barry Brickell originally built the narrow-gauge railway to bring clay and firewood down to his potteries below.

Prices: *Hour-long round trip is $20 adult, $11 children. Pottery is sold in the 'station' shop.*
Contact: *Barry Brickell, 380 Driving Creek Road, Coromandel Town;* **Tel:** *07-866-8703; railway@drivingcreek.co.nz; www.drivingcreekrailway.co.nz*

WHITIANGA
EATING AND DRINKING

Purangi Estate Winery

This vineyard is so wonderfully rustic and antiquated you can almost hear the dusty shelves groan under the weight of organically-grown bottles of wines and ciders - almost as loudly my own groans the morning after I polished off (with friends!) a bottle of their splendid feijoa liqueur. All fruit and herbs are gathered here on the estate to make traditional, fortified and fruity alcoholic beverages. Sit by the pine log fire in 'The Buttery' brasserie or in the heat of the summer in the shade on kiwi-fruit vines and taste their delicious feijoa and kiwi liqueurs. You can also retrace the exploration of the Purangi River by Capt. Cook on a cruise that starts at Cook's Bay and ends here at the original 'Top Landing' right on the Purangi Estate. This place is effortlessly charming, delightfully quirky and off-the-tourist-beaten-track; a must-see that's definitely worth the effort. Open 7 days, 9.30am - 5pm. Summer until 11pm. Call for details about the Winery River Cruise (capacity 10).

Contact: *450 Purangi Road, Whitianga;* **Tel:** *07-866-3724;* **Fax:** *07-866-2948; info@purangi.co.nz; www.purangi.co.nz*

Natural Waterworks at Waiau Waterworks

The Pepper Tree Restaurant

The Coromandel Peninsula

WHITIANGA

WHENUAKITE

PAEROA

🍽️ WHITIANGA
EATING AND DRINKING

The Fire Place

Right on the marina, this place does exactly what it says on the packet. Several open fires add to its attractive cosiness, indoor palms and warm wooden interiors lending it a slight colonial-in-the-tropics feel. And the food is fantastic. There are crisp-based pizzas with a variety of exciting toppings, juicy lamb and chicken from the rôtisserie, and daily specials of fresh fish, fresh pasta and curry amongst other taste-bud temptations.
Prices: *Pizzas $20, light meals from $15.00 - $21.00, mains from $30.00 - $36.00.*
Contact: *Harry and Ben Williams, 9 The Esplanade, Whitianga;* **Tel:** *07-866-4828;*
Fax: *07-866-0102; thefireplace@xtra.co.nz*

The Scallop Festival

Innovate and creative scallop recipes, wine stalls, Indian seafood, and belly dancers, all by the harbour in Whitianga. I half-fancied my chances at the scallop opening competition, but perhaps I would be better off settling for sipping a coffee and tucking into some succulent Coromandel scallops (opened by another, of course!) at the Jazz Brunch. A 'shucking good time' is promised for all. Tickets for this year's third festival sold out in six days, so be prepared to scramble. Four-day event.
Prices: *Entry for the Saturday is $30.* **Contact:** *Jo-Anne Inansci, Whitianga;*
Tel: *09-402-7932; carl@thecoromandel.com; www.scallopfestival.co.nz*

🌲 WHITIANGA
NATURE AND ACTIVITIES

Arts & Crafts @ Baycarving

If I, with my two left thumbs, can create my own bone-carving, I defy anyone not to do the same. Pick out the design you want, or, if you are streets ahead of me in confidence and artistic ability, draw up your own design and start working! Two hours, plenty of help, and a cup or two of coffee later, I walked away with my very own bone pendant. The pleasure of crafting for oneself is immense: it felt like claiming a little piece of New Zealand. No better way to spend a wet - or even a dry - afternoon.
Prices: *Between $35 and $80, depending on design.* **Contact:** *12 The Esplanade, Whitianga;* **Tel:** *07-866-4021; info@baycarving.co.nz; www.baycarving.com*

Waiau Waterworks

Outside The Fireplace in Whitianga

Ohinemuri Estate Winery

WHITIANGA
CULTURE AND HISTORY

Moko

Just across the road from the hotspot (literally) of Hot Water Beach is this equally hot little art space. Pacific- and New Zealand-style sculptures and wall-art lurk in the garden and in open-plan rooms, and the jewellery and design-ware in the shop is some of the best I've seen. This is definitely the setting in which to while away time waiting for the tide to turn.

Contact: *Simon Buchanan and Sonya Corlett, 24 Pye Place, Hot Water Beach, RD1 Whitianga;* **Tel:** *07-866-3367;* **Fax:** *07-866-3367; moko.hotwater@xtra.co.nz; www.moko.co.nz*

Pamper yourself at a Hot Water Beach

Dig yourself a hole in the sand on Hahei's Hot Water Beach and sit in your very own natural spa pool, heated by thermal waters that brew just below its surface. If you want to cool off in the sea, do be especially careful - the waters here have currents and are dangerous for swimming.

WHENUAKITE
EATING AND DRINKING

Colenso Café and Shop

This absolute gem of a café is situated just before the turn-off (coming from the south) to Hahei and Hot Water Beach. Everything about it is just so, well... very very pleasant. All the food is hearty, fresh and utterly mouth-watering, even just to look at, from muffins, quiches and cakes to great coffee and juice freshly squeezed from their orchard fruits. There is also a great shop full of local, great-quality crafts and arts. Set in the country amid beautiful herb gardens, I'd not be surprised if the café is actually a clever ruse so that owners Ruth and Andy never have to spend any time away! Open 10 - 5 daily. Closed for August.

Contact: *Ruth and Andy Pettit, Main Road, State Highway 25, Whenuakite;* **Tel:** *07-866-3758;* **Fax:** *07-866-3759*

PAEROA
WINERIES

Ohinemuri Estate Winery and Restaurant

"A day without wine is like a day without sunshine." Quite. It was with thoughts like these that Horst and Wendy uprooted from Germany to the beautiful Karangahake Gorge to start making wine from their garage. Nearly 20 years on, this fun, family-run boutique vineyard is going strong with a restaurant now serving excellent food in the old stables and its lovely, rustic courtyard. Close to Auckland, this is a destination in itself with walking tracks, history and entertainment (à la Horst) aplenty.

Prices: *Wines prices from $19 - $25 per bottle. Restaurant prices from $11 - $25 for lunches and all day breakfasts.* **Open** *10am to 5pm.* **Contact:** *Wendy and Horst Hillerich, Moresby Street, Karangahake Gorge, Paeroa;* **Tel:** *07-862-8874;* **Fax:** *07-862-8847; ohinemuri.wines@paradise.net.nz; www.ohinemuri.co.nz*

Waikato and King Country

North Island

King Country

Waikato

South Island

Highlights

- The English-style countryside around Cambridge. This rural village is famous for breeding and training thoroughbred horses. You may even catch a spot of cricket on the green.
- The rolling landscapes, country gardens and rich farmland of the Waikato. This is hobbit country and the most beautiful of shires.
- Wriggle into a wetsuit, grab a board and catch some impressive waves at Raglan.
- Dramatic Pirongia Mountain on the Waikato horizon. This distinctive landmark's many peaks were created by a series of volcanic eruptions.
- Waitomo Caves. There are a whole heap of cave-experiencing options from the dry glowworm trips, to the slightly wet (well, pretty drenched) serious adventure caving and black-water rafting.
- Grab a brochure and explore the private gardens of Te Kuiti, the sheep shearing capital of the world.

HAMILTON
EATING AND DRINKING
Hamilton Farmers' Market

Every first and third Sunday come rain or shine Hamilton Farmers' Market lays out a feast of local produce for you to sample and buy - fruit, vegetables, sausages, eggs, herbs, flowers, coffee and more....

HAMILTON
NATURE AND ACTIVITIES
Hamilton Gardens

There are 58ha of gardens in the heart of Hamilton. This massive town-set oasis includes five different-themed garden collections that arouse each sense with colour, smell and birdsong.
Tel: *07-838-6782.*

Surfing at Raglan

The Raglan coast is one of the world's surfing hot spots and, although I'm not a surfing dudette (my board rides only on snow I'm afraid), I'll attempt to direct you in the right direction from what I've been informed.

Supposedly (word on the street says) Manu Bay has the longest, most consistent left-hand break in the world which means, if you catch a colossus of a wave, you can cruise for a massive distance with "guaranteed nice lines and perfect peelers", according to one surfer in the know. This surf spot is also known as 'The Point' and was featured in the 1966 cult surfing film 'Endless Summer.' Whale Bay, renowned for an awesome left point break, offers great surfing on all tides. It's particularly good if you're after a hollow wave — sounds a little scary to me! Be warned. Raglan may excel in its surf conditions but rocky ledges and reefs command respect and require a certain level of skill to overcome. "This is not grommet territory", i.e. you need to know what you're doing in the water.

Raglan has attracted the likes of musical surf lover Jack Johnson to its wave-washed shores and has a truely laid-back vibe. If you're not up for floating on a board, boogie-, surf- or otherwise. You'll love the tiny seaside town and can happily frolic in the action-packed waters.

RAGLAN
EATING AND DRINKING
Aqua Velvet

If I were to open my own café, it would be modelled on Aqua Velvet. A friendly, bohemian atmosphere with welcoming staff, properly cooked porridge (I don't like it when the oats are still hard!), a soaring roof with space for birds to fly in and out, and an impressive music roster. International musicians are a common sight (and sound) in Raglan.
Prices: *$10 for a coffee and porridge.* **Contact:** *17 Bow St, Raglan;* **Tel:** *07-825-8588.*

Absolute Adventures   *Spellbound*   *Absolute Adventures*

RAGLAN
CULTURE AND HISTORY

Soundsplash Reggae Festival

Soundsplash is an eco-focused open-air reggae festival held 500m from the beach in Wainui Reserve (a handy natural amphitheatre). The festival usually takes place in early February.

Prices: *Tickets are around $100 and are available from Ticketmaster and all NZ post shops, Raglan Info Centre, or via http://www.motherland.co.nz.*

Whaingaroa Creative Market

Raglan is one of New Zealand's creative hot spots, so no need to explain what this market will be like really. It's a celebration of life's special and unique things: home-original art and designware, funky fashion clothing and jewellery, delicious food and preserves, lively entertainment and a friendly, vibrant atmosphere. To quote GG owner Jenny Thomson "a whole lot of things are going down." Second Sunday of the month.

Prices: *Free!* **Contact:** *Old School Arts Centre, Stewart St, Raglan;* **Tel:** *07-823-0023; market@raglanartscentre.co.nz; www.raglanmarket.com*

The kiwi, a flightless bird

Kiwis are endemic to New Zealand and belong to the family of flightless ratite birds, which includes emus, cassowaries, ostriches, rheas and the now extinct moa. This is a peculiar little bird with shaggy hair-like feathers, cone-shaped body and primitive claws.

Vital Statistics:

• *Kiwis are nocturnal, hence the fact they are pretty damn hard to spot in the wild (especially when you consider their dwindling numbers).*
• *Their wings are only between 30 – 50mm in length and end in a primitive dinosaur-style claw.*
• *They are the only bird whose nostrils are arranged at the tip of their beak (and a hugely long beak at that).*
• *Their sense of smell is so acute they can sniff out a worm 3cm under ground.*
• *There are 4 species and 6 varieties/taxa of kiwi: the northern brown, okarito brown, southern tokoeka, Haast tokoeka, little spotted and the great spotted.*
• *The females lay eggs proportionally larger to their body than any other bird (roughly 1/4 of her size!).*
• *They have cat-like whiskers to aid movement in the dark.*

Due to the country's isolation New Zealand's lack of predatory mammals has previously allowed for the kiwi's chilled-out ground-dwelling lifestyle. Unfortunately, with the relatively recent introductions of rats, possums, dogs and cats the kiwi has had a bit of a hard time trying (and usually failing) to hide or outrun his new aggressors, and their eggs have made many a possum breakfast. Their noisy rummagings also make them easy prey. Many conservation schemes are now set in place and areas are pest-proofed to save New Zealand's heritage bird.

Jet Collective

The Jet Collective is a group of artists and designers who wanted to sell their own work on their own terms, so they set up and now run their own shop. They make funky hand-made clothing, bags and jewellery at excellent prices. I bought two beautiful belts and a wooden mushroom necklace; all were one-off pieces and cost the same amount in total that I would have paid back in the UK for each item.

Prices: *$40 for a hand-made bag.* **Contact:** *Bow St, Raglan;* **Tel:** *07-85-8566; people@jetcollective.co.nz; www.jetcollective.co.nz*

OTOROHANGA
EATING AND DRINKING

The Little Tart Café

Run by a bubbly mother and daughter duo this tiny (dare I use the word cute?) café is well worth a look-in. The counter brims with freshly-made, filling-packed sandwiches, yummy cakes and home baking.

Contact: *Zenna and Tami Boroevich, 13 Maniapoto Street, Otorohanga;* **Tel:** *07-873-6611.*

The Copper Tree

Warm and stylish, the Copper Tree restaurant was a faultless spirit-lifting remedy for a lonely Mothering Sunday evening (yes, even intrepid travel writers get a little home-sick at times). Streaks ahead of its small town setting, the food and service were superb. Groups of diners seemed particularly taken with their choice of top-notch pizzas while my delicately-presented stuffed chicken breast was not the only piece of art to please the eye (the restaurant spills into a gallery of interesting local pieces).

Prices: *Dinner: $7 - $14 entrees; $20 - $28 mains; $9 - $13 mains.* **Contact:** *Jenny Herford, 80 Maniaoto Street, Otorohanga;* **Tel:** *07-873-7777; hangaelect@xtra.co.nz*

OTOROHANGA
NATURE AND ACTIVITIES
Otorohanga Kiwi House

For those wishing to spot a real-life version of New Zealand's national symbol this is the place to do it. Night and day have been reversed at the Otorohanga kiwi house with the aid of an artificial moon and good old black-out techniques. These wacky nocturnal birds were a lot bigger than I expected. When you consider this charity-run conservation operation also houses one of New Zealand's largest walk-in aviaries and displays more bird knowledge than is safely recordable in a day you'll feel guilty not paying more than the ridiculously low entry fee.

Prices: *The cost of entry is $12.00 for adults and $4.00 for children (5-16 years old) accompanied by adults. Children under 5 years old are free.* **Contact:** *Maggie Hughes, Alex Telfer Drive, Otorohanga;* **Tel:** *07-873-7391;* **Fax:** *07-873-7356; admin@kiwihouse.org; www.kiwihouse.org.nz*

Waitomo Caves and Glowworms.

These cave-lurking, occasionally cannibalistic, creatures can only survive in dark, damp and still places where their light will shine uninterrupted and no wind will tangle their sticky lines. Waitomo Caves provides the perfect habitat. Glowworms are technically glowing maggots but it was felt that 'glow maggots' wouldn't have quite the same tourist-attracting ring. The worms spend most of their lives feeding; attracting flying insects with their light, catching them in their sticky threads and reeling them in. When they finally pupate and become an adult fly, the fungus gnat, they survive for only a few days, just long enough to mate and lay a batch of eggs. In short glowworms spend their lives fishing, eating and mating. I know quite a few people living in similar fashion.

Vital statistics:

- They glow to attract food and burn off waste. Chemicals in their tail react with oxygen to produce light – bioluminescence.
- Glowworms are sensitive to vibrations so the more noise you make the brighter they will glow.
- The larvae are about the size of a matchstick.
- If a fellow worm or glowworm fly gets caught in another's thread they will be eaten (hence they are cannibals).
- The adult fungus gnats have no mouth and starve to death after a couple of days.

En masse in the dark glowworms are one of New Zealand's most stunning sights but pick them out with a torch individually and they'll gross you out. Both ways they are utterly incredible and a must-see feature.

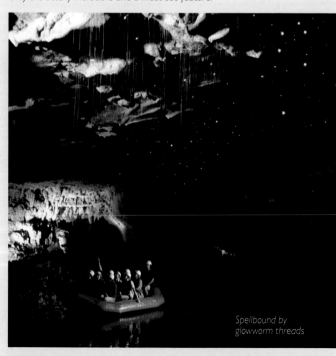

Spellbound by glowworm threads

Waitomo Golf Course

Waikato has 46 golf courses in total. One of the most recommended was Waitomo's easy-going country course. The 18-hole course measures up to championship standard yet is as friendly as they come.
Tel: 07-873-7978

 ## WAITOMO CAVES
NATURE AND ACTIVITIES

Spellbound

Brought to you by the man who invented (and coined the phrase) 'black-water-rafting', Spellbound offers an enthralling (and dry) cave-venturing alternative. The galaxy of glowworms and the intricate knowledge possessed by this small and personable operation have impressed the likes of (no less than) Sir David Attenborough. For the best glowworm appreciation Waitomo has to offer Spellbound remains absurdly modest and incredibly good value.
Prices: *Adults $55 pp, children (4-14 yrs) $20 pp, children (0-3 yrs) free.* **Contact:** *Peter and Libby Chandler, Waitomo Caves Museum, 21 Waitomo Caves Road, Waitomo Caves;* **Tel:** *07-878-7640 or freephone 0800-773-552 (within New Zealand) (0800 SPELLB);* **Fax:** *07-878-7622; info@glowworm.co.nz; www.glowworm.co.nz*

Absolute Adventure

Rigged up in overalls, harness, helmet and gumboots I was exposed to 'Lucky Strike' (the McKay's impressive formation-filled cave) and its many rocky challenges. This is serious caving action and my most amazing experience to date. Groups of no more than 4 abseil, squirm and clamber under the watchful eyes of an inconspicuous guide. Adrenaline rush guaranteed, a towel and change of underwear recommended... that's what they say!
Prices: *Mission trip: 2 hrs underground, 4 hrs in total $100. Expedition trip: 4 hrs underground, 6 hrs in total $175. Free CD of photos from trip.* **Contact:** *Justine and Kieran McKay, Waitomo Museum of Caves, Waitomo Caves;* **Tel:** *07-878-8274; justine@absoluteadventure.co.nz; www.absoluteadventure.co.nz*

Rolling Hills of Waikato

Bay of Plenty

North Island

Bay of Plenty

South Island

Highlights

- Walk on the moon-like surface of White Island.
- Rotorua is one of the primary Maori settlement hotspots and there are stacks of cultural shows and experiences to choose from. The young and enthusiastic members of 'Mitai' run the most authentic and energetic show.
- Rotorua's natural hot spas and thermal parks wil bring out the budding geologist in you. The area is one big colourful volcanic playground.
- Cruise over to Mokia, the Sacred Island at the heart of Lake Rotorua. The site is bursting with Maori history and is an ecological sanctuary.
- Zorb down a hill... see 'Zorb Rotorua.'
- Head to 'The Mount' for sun, sand, sea, surf, scuba-diving and seafood. The upbeat small town of Mt. Maunganui lies at the foot of its hiking-friendly mountain and makes a great day trip.
- Follow the Katikati mural trail where picture-painted buildings are all the rage.

TAURANGA
EATING AND DRINKING

Slowfish

Slowfish is influenced by the slow food movement, and why would you want to hurry, sitting opposite Mt Maunganui Main Beach, looking over the sea? To encourage you to linger (as if any such encouragement is needed), Josh and Brigitte offer a *smorgasbord* of delights. Unfortunately I chose the 'energy salad', stuffed full of good nutrition and off I went... but if you had time, what a delight it would be to kick the sand out of your shoes and indulgently wind down.

Contact: *Josh and Brigitte, Shop 5, Twin Towers, Mt Maunganui, Tauranga;*
Tel: *07-574-2949; slowfish@wave.co.nz; www.slowfish.co.nz*

TAURANGA
NATURE AND ACTIVITIES

Tajo Ostrich Farm

Ostriches are bizarre, beautiful birds... and huge (at 2m tall they certainly tower over me). Here you can feed the adults (if you can reach), take a farm-tour trailer ride and watch chicks hatching. An on-site farm shop is stocked with everything 'ostrich' from ostrich leather handbags to ostrich-oil hand cream.

Contact: *Susan Binks, 1130 Troutbeck Road, Galatea, Tauranga;* **Tel:** *09-412-2525;*
Fax: *09-412-2526; tajo@ostrichmeat.co.nz; www.tajo.com*

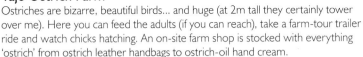

TAURANGA
CULTURE AND HISTORY

Montana National Jazz Festival in Tauranga

For five days over Easter, Tauranga throbs to the harmonious notes of the longest-running jazz festival in the southern hemisphere. Featuring the best of New Zealand and world jazz in a beautiful seaside setting, the experience is perfect for both jazz buffs and those of us that can't really tell a wrong note from a right one but can tap our feet to the beat, and love the fine wines and the sunshine.

Contact: *Jo Bond, Tauranga;* **Tel:** *07-577-7018; festival@jazz.org.nz; www.jazz.org.nz*

The inquisitive inhabitants of Tajo Ostrich Farm

135

🔺 OHAPE
🌲 NATURE AND ACTIVITIES
Ohope Golf Course

This local 18-hole par 71 course is surprisingly and impressively challenging. The coastal fairway is set against a backdrop of volcanic White Island and prominent Whale Island.

Contact: *Harbour Road, Ohope;* **Tel:** *07-312-4486; ohope@golf.co.nz*

White Island

The lunar landscape of White Island that breaks through the surface of the sea is something I've only ever touched upon in fantasy or science fiction novels. Here, vivid beds of yellow and white sulphur crystals grow alongside effervescent fumeroles and towering crater walls shelter a spectacular lake.

Aside from being a site of continual scientific intrigue the volcanic peak was previously farmed for sulphur. In 1914 part of the western crater rim collapsed creating a lahar that killed all 10 workers. Supposedly only Peter the Great, the camp cat, survived. The ruin of the old factory can still be seen on the island. White Island may be moody, but the level of volcanic activity is always closely monitored. The opportunity to don a hard-hat and gas mask and tentatively step into such a surreal landscape is a one-off. PeeJays run a superb guided tour from Whakatane to White Island's highly protected shores. They provide all safety gear, in-depth knowledge and lunch aboard the PeeJay herself. You'll need a full day and a good camera. They also have a great café back at base where you can exchange the lingering hint of sulphur for a far more pleasurable smell of coffee and freshly-made snacks. Dolphins and other marine life flourish in the surrounding fertile waters (which are incredible for fishing and diving) so keep your peepers open on the boat trip over.

PeeJays White Island Tours: 15 Strand East, Whakatane. www.whiteisland. co.nz. Tel: 07-308-9588 or freephone 0800-733-529, Fax: 07-308-0303.

Another excellent way to see White Island is by air. Enquire about scenic flights with Air Discovery (224 Aerodrome Road, Whakatane Airport 07-308-9558).

ROTORUA
EATING AND DRINKING

Bistro 1284

When I popped in to Bistro 1284, a local lady was excitedly discussing birthday feast plans with Damon who was taking every detail on board. She gushed about the lamb and the wine, and I tried my best to look like the sort of person you'd want to invite to a birthday party. As a lamb and beef ambassador, and consistently voted as Rotorua's best restaurant, all meat dishes are stamped with the 'hallmark of excellence'. Try the slow-roast lamb belly with whipped potato, green peas and jus for size or get down there and start your own party.

Prices: *Entrées $16.50 - $17.50, mains $31-$33, desserts $15;* **Contact:** *Damon McGinniss, 1284 Eruera Street, Rotorua;* **Tel:** *07-346-1284;* **Fax:** *07-346-1284; dine@bistro1284.co.nz; www.bistro1284.co.nz*

You and Me Restaurant

This not-to-be-missed dining experience is very easy to miss if you don't know where to look. Eyes peeled for the tiny glowing sign above the not-so-obvious doorway and staircase that leads up to the swanky first-floor restaurant. Once through the portal 'You and Me' has all the fine attributes that a good restaurant should have. All the locals know where it is, and now you do too, so make sure you join them.

Prices: *Mains $32 - $35.* **Contact:** *Hiroyuki Peraoka, 1119 Pukuatua St, Rotorua;* **Tel:** *07-347-6178; yoshiko23@xtra.co.nz*

Sirocco's Café Restaurant

A cosy café-restaurant with the kind of atmosphere I could have happily enjoyed all afternoon if work (it's a hard job but someone's got to do it) hadn't caused me to press on. Sirocco's offers a Mediterranean medley of modern food from pasta dishes to paella. I opted for a simple but scrumptious vegetarian dish, which arrived promptly, piled high with roasted vegetables and flavour. Choose to munch outside on the deck or dine inside amongst local art and warmed by a pot-bellied fire.

Prices: *Mains $25-$35.* **Contact:** *Lynda Stewart, 1280 Eruera Street, Rotorua;* **Tel:** *07-347-3388; l_stewart@xtra.co.nz*

Sirocco's Café Restaurant

Slowfish

Bistro 1284

Seismic Gastrobar

Seismic, meaning: earthquakes and earth-shakes in the geothermal history of the region; and a blend of Maori and Croatian heritage in the owners. This funky little gastrobar serves an adventurous lunch and dinner menu, an extensive brunch list, and, after the kitchens have been closed, you can take the wine list outside onto the terraces and pour over it to your heart's content.

Prices: *Starters from $6.50. Mains from $19.50 - $32. Opening Hours: Weekdays 11.30am - 10pm (kitchen closes). Bar licensed till 3am.* **Contact:** *Tapa and Marija, 1158 Whakaue Street, Rotorua;* **Tel:** *07-348-2082;* **Fax:** *07-348-2083; info@seismicgastrobar.co.nz; www.seismicgastrobar.co.nz*

Geothermal Rotorua and Mt. Tarawera's Big Bang.

Rotorua is renowned for its lively geothermal activity. You will be easily distracted from the eggy odour of the sulphur by the sight of billowing springs, sputtering geysers, bubbling mud and simmering puddles. It was the vibrant colours that took me by surprise... lime green lakes, ever-changing bright orange and yellow residue and turquoise waters. The thermal parks can be relatively commercial but are still definitely worth a look. Waiotapu Thermal Park is the most colourful geothermal area and houses the Lady Knox geyser who blows her stack daily at around 10am. Freebie parks include the mud-bubbling Kuirau Park (the boiling lake emits continual clouds of steam that roll out over the highway) and Craters of the Moon on the way into Taupo.

On June 10th 1886 Mt. Tarawera erupted in a violent shower of red-hot volcanic bombs and buried the Maori villages of Te Ariki and Te Wairoa under 20 metres of mud. The noise of the explosion was so loud it was heard in Christchurch. The Pink and White Silica Terraces, a fan-like geological marvel considered the eighth wonder of the world, were completely annihilated. You can visit the buried village of Te Wairoa, learn more about the 1886 eruption and wander the park and excavation sites.

ROTORUA
NATURE AND ACTIVITIES

Zorb Rotorua

You, the soon-to-be zorbanaut, have a number of zany zorbing options at this Kiwi-born escapade. The hectic hill-rolling bubbles were invented here and continue to diversify. Choose from the original harness ride Zorbit, the Zorb-tri-riffic ride or the 'wash cycle' Zydro (you and the zorb plus water - warm in winter, cool in summer). Absolutely barmy and hilarious fun.

Zorb Rotorua

Prices: *Zydro, $49 or $81 with wet pack; Zorbit, $59 or $91 with wet pack; Zorb-tri-riffic or any three rides $108 or $140 with wet pack. (The wet pack consists of t-shirt, shorts, towel and a bag to put it all in, or you can just bring your own).* **Contact:** *Haylee Bloor, Cnr of Western Rd and SH5, Ngongotaha, Rotorua;* **Tel:** *07-357-5100;* **Fax:** *07-357-5102; rotorua@zorb.com; www.zorb.com*

Arikikapakapa Golf Course

Possibly one of the strangest golfing experiences you're ever likely to have. Arikikapakapa sits upon a fuming stew of thermal activity that creates wild undulating fairways pock-marked with simmering vents. The layout is excellent, although you may need a supply of spare balls, as I doubt many strays will be recovered easily.

Prices: *Non-NZ affiliated visitor $60, NZ affiliated $30, NZ resident $40.* **Contact:** *Jill Kirby, Fenton Street, Rotorua;* **Tel:** *07-348-4051;* **Fax:** *07-348-1384; info@rotoruagolfclub.co.nz*

Agrodome

The list of attractions here took my breath away. Founded by an internationally renowned sheep shearer, the Agrodome hosts a 160-hectare working sheep farm. You can encounter hands-on farming experience of sheep, alpacas, cattle, deer, goats and ostriches, watch sheep being sheared or, buy more wool than you ever could knit (erm, that might just be me). Not only this but Agrodome is also a mecca for the more adventurous amongst us, with bungy, freefall 'extreme body flying', the Zorb, the Swoop (43 metre-high giant swing), the Swheeb (a human-powered mono-rail race track) and helipro trips all on offer.

Prices: *Between $22 (agrodome show) and $405 (island helipro trip). Opening hours: 8.30am - 5pm.* **Contact:** *Western Road, Ngongotaha, Rotorua;* **Tel:** *07-357-1050;* **Fax:** *07-357-5307; marketing@agroventures.co.nz; www.agrodome.co.nz*

PeeJays White Island Trip

Adventures at Agrodome

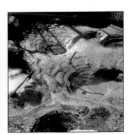

Bubbling Volcanic Mud in Kuirau Park

bay of plenty

ROTORUA

Raftabout

100% Kiwi-owned and -operated, Raftabout consider it their mission to take you hurtling down the highest commercially rafted waterfall in the world, through thrilling rapids, and past Maori sites of legend. I am assured that these guys are models of professionalism and experience - and that the scenery is amazing, if you can bear to take a look. More placid rafting and more extreme options available too.

Prices: From $85 - $155. **Contact:** *Kylee Stevens and Stephen McNab, 811 State Highway 33, Okere Falls, Rotorua;* **Tel:** *07-343-9500;* **Fax:** *07-343-9503; info@raftabout.co.nz; www.raftabout.co.nz*

Paradise Valley Springs - Trout Springs & Wildlife Park

The opportunity to stroke a lion cub had me sold before I'd even arrived at Paradise Valley. If there are cubs in situ you can enter their enclosure, watch them play and even give them a pat. After that you can watch the adults play at feeding time, a majestic display of power and teeth as you can imagine. Any enclosures are impressively spacious and indicative of the animals' natural habitat, but the majority of wildlife here roams virtually free. Stroll the 150m bushwalk and hand-feed the trout, eels, wallabies, deer and goats as you go.

Prices: From $24 for adults, $12 children 5-15, free for under-5s. **Contact:** *Kay Clarke, Paradise Valley Road, Rotorua;* **Tel:** *07-348-9667;* **Fax:** *07-349-3359; paradisev@xtra.co.nz; www.paradisevalleysprings.co.nz*

ROTORUA
CULTURE AND HISTORY
The Historic Elms Mission House

Alfred A. Brown (1803 - 1884) bought a slice of land from the Maori people where he built a mission station in 1844 and called his home 'The Elms'. He would probably still recognise the property today with its small chapel and freestanding library in the garden as it remains virtually unchanged from the early European settlement years. The library provides a home to most of the original books and the late-Georgian décor remains true to the period style.

Prices: Admission for adults $5, children 50 cents. Grounds open daily free of charge. **Contact:** *Bruce Heaton, Mission Street, Tauranga;* **Tel:** *07-577 9772;* **Fax:** *07-577 9782; theelms@enternet.co.nz; www.theelms.org.nz*

Rotorua Museum

Raftabout

Ohope Golf CLub

St. Faith's Anglican Church and Tamatekapua

The Tudor building of St. Faith's church is an extraordinary sight. Gently hissing and simmering puddles create an eerie yet strangely calming ambience around the church and the concrete graves that rest above ground. An etched image of Christ hovers frozen in a window and looks as if it is walking on Lake Rotorua. Christ is depicted in a *korowai* (a Maori chief's cloak) and the insides of the church are distinctly adorned with Maori carvings and woven wall panels, a symbolic expression of Maori faith embracing Christianity. Opposite St. Faith's church is the Tamatekapua meeting house, the main gathering place of the Arawa tribe, and an equally impressive building.

Prices: *Free of charge.* **Contact:** *Ohinemutu.*

Tamatekapua, Ohinematu

Kiwi Fruit

Kiwi fruit became an all-out marketing success in the 1930s when a chap called Jim McLoughlin planted the first orchard in Te Puke and sold the fruit at the local market. Previous to McLoughlin's success, kiwis were known as Chinese gooseberries, but their presence grew so rapidly in the New Zealand market (many farmers became instant millionaires from the plants flourishing success in the Bay of Plenty region) that they have now become a New Zealand icon. Make sure you sample both the traditional emerald green Hayward variety and the more recent gold-fleshed Zespri variety. Both are delicious.

Agrodome

The Mission House

Tajo Ostrich Farm

Central Plateau

North
Island

Central
Plateau

South
Island

Highlights

- Lake Taupo. You can fish in it, swim in it, dive in it, boat on it and skydive over it.
- Drive the volcanic loop highway (it's famous for a reason), take on the volcano-crested Tongariro National Park, breeze around Taupo's thermal parks or fly over the lot. Fire and ice (the mountains are snow-capped) come together in an astounding way at the North Island's raging core.
- Base yourself in Ohakune, a small time après-skiing village with stacks of character and an awful lot of carrots (it's the New Zealand carrot capital). Here you can see and drink long after the sun has set.
- Don skis, poles and that daft woolly hat you've always been too embarrassed to wear and clatter onto the Whakapapa and Turoa ski fields.

central plateau

WHIRINAKI
GUIDES

Whirinaki Rainforest Guided Walks

Prepare to be humbled by this dramatic, towering and mystical forest as you tread the ancient thoroughfares of the *tangata whenua* (the original people of the land). The spirit of Whirinaki rainforest is intoxicating and its history is fascinating. As you are guided by the descendents of the original Maori settlers they will tell you about their traditions and tribal practices, divulge the real stories of the Urewera region and expose the secrets of this ancient rainforest - an amazing experience.

Prices: *1-day eco-culture walk $155 pp, 1-day private guided walk $325 pp, 3-day rainforest stay tour $745 pp. Prices valid until end Sept 2008.* **Contact:** *Chris Birt, Whirinaki;* **Tel:** *07-377-2363 or freephone 0800-869-255 (within New Zealand); info@indigenousbynature.co.nz; www: indigenousbynature.co.nz*

TAUPO
EATING AND DRINKING

The Bach

With a cracking lake-side position and panoramic views of Tongariro National Park, The Bach might just be the most

> ### Interesting fact
>
> *Geothermally-charged Taupo is the country's biggest lake. At 43km long and 28km wide, it is actually the crater of a mighty volcano that erupted in 181AD.*

enticing eating location in Taupo. The restaurant, with its beachy rondavel-style thatched roof, was once a classic Kiwi bach. It is still rustic and cosy inside and flaunts a torch-lit garden out front for al-fresco dining. The service is impeccable and the food as impressive as the view.

Contact: *Daniel Kemp, 2 Pataka Rd, Taupo;* **Tel:** *07-378-7856;* **Fax:** *07-378-7856; daniel@thebach.co.nz; www.thebach.co.nz*

The Volcanic Kitchen

Sean Wakelin's pizzas with their crisp bases and explosive flavours won 'A touch of Italy's' recognition in a national pizza challenge. Prepare for some imaginative topping combinations. For an easy and fail-proof meal, this is the place to go.

Contact: *Sean Wakelin, 113 Tongariro Street, Lake Taupo, Taupo;* **Tel:** *07-377-1537; volcanickitchen@xtra.co.nz*

The Brantry

Prue and Felicity, a dynamic sisterly duo, have made quite a name for themselves and Taupo's food scene with their decadent dinners featuring such unique New Zealand tastes as 'confit of hare with roasted watermelon, drizzled with a vanilla and honey dressing'. Prue, previously an NZ beef and lamb ambassador chef, is the mastermind behind the food while Felicity takes care of the rest.

Prices: *Mains $29-$33.* **Contact:** *Prue and Felicity Cambell, 45 Rifle Range Road, Taupo;* **Tel:** *07-378-0484; brantry@xtra.co.nz; www.thebrantry.co.nz*

Whirinaki Rainforest Guided Walks

TAUPO
NATURE AND ACTIVITIES
Windsor Charters

Fancy some trout for supper? If so, you may need to enlist Bruce and Angela's help because you can't buy the fish in shops in NZ but there are many restaurants where you can BYO fish. Though famous for its brown and rainbow varieties (it's not unusual to land a 5lb one), there's a lot more to this lake than just fishes and rods. Good old Kiwi hospitality, magnificent scenery and Maori rock carvings are among the highlights of a day spent boating with the Christoffersens. Fishing tackle and tuition are provided.

Prices: *Charter rates from $360 for half day to $800 for a full-day hire with lunch provided.*
Contact: *Bruce and Angela Christoffersen, 46 Rokino Road, Taupo;* **Tel:** *07-378-8738;*
Fax: *07-378-8748; windsor-charters@xtra.co.nz; www.troutfishingtaupo.com*

Mt. Ruapehu and Tongariro National Park.

There is nothing quite as novel as skiing or snow-boarding on a stratovolcano, particularly when it's still active. Mt. Ruapehu and its three main peaks demand respect from skiers, hikers and onlookers alike. Tahurangi (2,797m), Te Heuheu (2,755m) and Paretetaitonga (2,751m) surround the brooding (lake-filled when it's not erupting) crater and are a formidable sight.

Ruapehu has the largest developed ski area in New Zealand, made up of two main ski fields. Whakapapa (pronounced 'fakapapa') spans the northern side and Turoa the southern. The season runs roughly from July to October unless volcanologist mountain monitors advise otherwise....

The 1995-96 eruptions (yup, that recent!) meant skis and snowboards remained safely packed away and powder-lovers were sorely disappointed. The 1995 season ended abruptly when the Department of Conservation issued hazard warnings advising people to stay off the mountain. Activity on the mountain had been closely monitored since 1994 and there have been a number of episodic eruptions and lahars (mud slides) since. The experts are always one step ahead of Ruapehu's internal churnings and they serve up warnings accordingly. Heed their advice and take the opportunity to ride on this remarkable mountain if the all-clear is given.

Tongariro National Park is a great park for trekkers. The Tongariro Crossing passes between Mt. Tongariro and Mt. Ngauruhoe, rumbling past cold mountain springs, lava flows, steam vents, an active crater, deep-green lakes and wonderful views. The terrain is steep and frequently difficult, so a decent level of fitness is essential. Ensure sturdy footwear, equipment and clothing and be aware of the weather.

Mt Ruapehu and Mt Tongariro

central plateau

OHAKUNE
EATING AND DRINKING

Altitude 585

I'm told Altitude is packed every night in season, and it was still buzzing when I visited in May. I had a delicious and rich Thai red curry and my friend had salmon with potatoes. Although there was not even a single snowflake to be found on Mt Ruapehu's summit, both choices would have been suitably filling after a hard day's skiing.

Prices: *$24.50 for a red Thai curry.* **Contact:** *John McGrath, 75 Clyde St, Ohakune;* **Tel:** *06-385-9292; info@altitude585.co.nz; www.altitude585.co.nz*

Utopia Café

There is no better place to start the day... or end it. In fact, you may as well have lunch there as well, or at the very least buy something to take away. Utopia Café's legendary breakfasts have fuelled many mountain-goers while others have been enticed off the peaks with early après-ski/après-trekking urges. One happy ski bum wrote, "Utopia has coffee that rocks, spectacular paninis, phat [meaning 'very good'] breakfasts, a bad-boy [extensive] wine selection, toasty open fire & style sounds (um, good music I presume?). Its après-skiing at its finest." Stylish and buzzing... I couldn't agree more.

Contact: *Dawn, 47 Clyde Street, Ohakune;* **Tel:** *06-385-9120; Fax: 06-385-9120*

The Projection Room

Killer cocktails (I hear the mojito is very good) and spot-on tapas-style nibbles. This is one of Ohakune's major music venues. Whether you're eating, drinking or listening (probably all three) you'll be swept up and along by the relaxed and upbeat atmosphere.

Contact: *Paul Stieglbauer, 4 Thames Street, Ohakune Junction;* **Tel:** *06-385-8664; wicked_edge@xtra.co.nz*

Another splendid waterfall in Whirinaki Rainforest

East Coast

North
Island

East Coast

South
Island

Highlights

• Circumnavigate the East Cape on SH35, a route virtually untouched by tourism. The rugged landscape is an astounding combination of coastal beauty, pohutukawa trees and dense inland forest. Potter from one isolated bay to the next, relax on remote beaches and observe the strong Maori influence in this region before bagging a photo of the East Cape Lighthouse and Tolga Bay Wharf (the longest pier in NZ). Don't forget your surfboard.

• Lose yourself in Te Urewera National Park tramping its Lake Waikaremoana Great Walk (ensuring that you find yourself again of course).

• Experience the truly wild east by foot, mountain-bike or kayak in the Raukumara Ranges. Keep an eye out for the rare blue duck and expect many a frog sighting.

• Drag yourself out of bed in time to catch the sunrise over Gisborne (it's the first city in the world to see the dawn of each new day).

• Unwind in Morere hot springs.

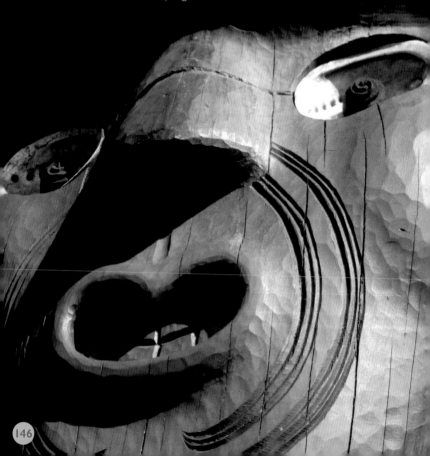

MORERE
NATURE AND ACTIVITIES
Morere Hot Springs

This is definitely worth a stop-off when driving from Napier to Gisborne. Steaming away, hidden in lush jungly forest, Morere's natural hot springs come in a variety of temperatures and contain a cocktail of rich therapeutic minerals. Set in 364 hectares of nature reserve you can take a 20-minute stroll or a 3-hour trek before soothing your body in the healing waters (which, if you're interested, are often referred to as 'fossilised sea water' and emerge from a fractured fault-line running across the Mangakawa Valley). Geoff, the man in charge, swears he's getting younger by the day from his regular soaks.

Prices: *Entry for adults $5 and children $2.50, non-swimmers $2.50. Private Pools $3 pp for half an hour. Towels $2. Light snacks and drinks available from on-site shop.* **Contact:** *Geoff Prickett, State Highway 2, Morere, Gisborne;* **Tel:** *06-837-8856;* **Fax:** *06-837-8873; morerehotsprings@xtra.co.nz; www.morerehotsprings.com*

Random Fact

Taumatawhakatangihangakoauauotamateaturipukakapikimau ngahurunokopokaiwhenuakitanatahu, near Mangaorapa, East Coast is the longest place-name in the world.

GISBOURNE
EATING AND DRINKING
The Works Café and Bar

This captivating dock-based building is the only survivor from a line of original 1906 warehouses. The old freezing works, with thick brick walls and a high concrete ceiling (perfect cellar conditions) was rescued at the last minute and still holds the demolition scars on its right-hand side. Now the character-charged Works Winery houses the cellar door for Thorpe Brothers Wines and Tiritiri vineyard and The Works Café offers first-rate meals or light bites, top coffee and knock-your-socks-off cocktails day and night.

Contact: *Tony Taylor, Cnr The Esplanade & Crawford Rd, Gisborne;* **Tel:** *06-863-1285;* **Fax:** *06-863-0596; info@gisbornewinecompany.co.nz*

Feeding a wild Stingray with Dive Tatapouri

East Coast landscape

Feeding Deer at Knapdale eco-lodge

GISBOURNE
NATURE AND ACTIVITIES

Dive Tatapouri

Although they run excellent diving courses, this is more than just a dive crew. With superb eco-tours available you can dip in on various conservation projects (feed wild stingray and lend a hand protecting the blue penguin) or choose to get up close and personal with a shark (don't worry, a safety cage is included). The fascinating gliding, waddling and biting aquatic species all trigger informed asides from Dean Savage who, after 20 years' commercial diving experience, certainly knows his stuff.

Prices: *Prices vary depending on course and trips.* **Contact:** *Dean Savage, SH35, Tatapouri, Gisborne;* **Tel:** *027-4571-876; divetatapouri@xtra.co.nz; www.divetatapouri.com*

The Gisborne Mural Trail.

Graffiti may never have caught your imagination before, but I assure you the Gisborne's Mural Trail will. Banish the image of a bunch of insecure adolescents breaking out a can of spray paint and casting their identity on exposed sections of wall. Gisborne graffiti is truly Art. The city has flexed its creative muscles and commissioned a whole series of street paintings that depict historical scenes, the Tairawhiti Regiona and Tangata Whenua (the original people of the land). Follow the impressive trail throughout Gisborne. My favourite was the children's wall of tiles. 6,500 pupils from 39 primary and intermediate schools throughout the region have painted their self-portrait on a tile and the many oddly proportioned beaming smiles have given a highly successful face-lift to a previously ugly wall. Grab a Mural Trail leaflet from the tourist information centre and follow the painted path.

Eastwoodhill Aboretum

Eastwood Hill Arboretum, New Zealand's national home for trees, boasts the largest collection of northern hemisphere trees in the south. With six walking tracks of assorted lengths and difficulty you can explore the 150 hectares of lofty collaged canopies and remarkable homestead gardens for as long as you wish. Guided walks and 4WD tours are also available.

Prices: *Entry fee for adults $10, senior citizens $8 and children go free (accompanied by paying adult).* **Contact:** *Helen Hayward, 2392 Wharekopae Road, Gisborne;* **Tel:** *06-863-9003;* **Fax:** *06-863-9093; office.eastwoodhill@xtra.co.nz; www.eastwoodhill.org.nz*

Captain Cook

Captain Cook took his first steps onto New Zealand soil in Gisborne on the 9th October 1769. Both a monument to Cook and a statue of 'Young Nick' (Cook's cabin boy, Nicholas Young, who first spotted New Zealand on the horizon) are found in Gisborne.

Hawke's Bay

North
Island

Hawke's
Bay

South
Island

Highlights

• Slosh your way around the many wineries throughout the region. Everything grows in the Hawke's Bay sunshine and fresh local produce equates to superb food and wine.

• Keep your ears to the ground for local winery events. There is always something going on from live music to open air cinemas and elaborate culinary affairs.

• Enter the Art Deco time warp of Napier. The prominent local architecture of this seaside town is built on a fascinating history.

• Potter around Port Ahuriri and listen to the clink of sails. A beach boardwalk takes you to the harbour entrance where you'll find many crafts and antiques.

• Watch the gannets duck and dive at Cape Kidnappers.

NORTH ISLAND

 **NAPIER**
GUIDES AND **EXPERTS**

Vince's Vineyard Tours

Vince is an absolute character who may cause giggles between each sip of wine. As a close relative of one of New Zealand's pioneer wine-making families and with years of grape touring experience, he can pop the cork on all of Hawke's Bay's wine-making and drinking secrets.

Prices: *$55 per person. Includes free pick-up within Napier.* **Contact:** *Vince Picone, 9 Thurley Place, Bay View, Napier;* **Tel:** *06-836-6705; vincestours@hotmail.com; www.vincestours.co.nz*

NAPIER
EATING AND **DRINKING**

Westshore Fish Café

"Your pleasure is our pleasure" is the mantra at Peter and Hieke's Westshore Fish Café. Hieke insisted I try a portion of their beautiful fish and good ol' mushy peas, which I wolfed down with gusto, accompanied by some cheerful banter from local regulars. I left with the parting phrase, "if you're happy tell your friends, if you're not... tell us" ringing in my ears. This may help to explain why they're so inundated with everyone's friends and why I'm telling you.

Prices: *Starters $6.90 - $8.90, mains $9.90 - 19.90, desserts $5.50, kids meals $6.90. Vegetarian and non-fish lovers options available.* **Contact:** *Hieke and Peter Wijnsma, 112a Charles Street, Westshore, Napier;* **Tel:** *06-834-0227; hiekepeter@xtra.co.nz*

C.J. Pask Winery and 'The Great Long Lunch'

Over 200 metres of table, delectable food, wine and sociable banter contribute to the fun at Napier's famous Great Long Lunch. The 3-course meal remains a closely guarded secret until the 700 guests (one of which will be you) are seated and happily supping local wine. Throughout the long leisurely afternoon you'll be amused by live entertainment, more wine, great company and a super setting. CJ Pask winery is the main sponsor of the Great Long Lunch and one of New Zealand's leading producers of Bordeaux-style red wine. The winery is worth adding to your wine tour taste list.

Prices: *From $75 per person.* **Contact:** *1133 Omahu Rd, Hastings, Napier;* **Tel:** *06-83-3916 (Great Long Lunch), 06-879-7906 (C.J. Pask Winery), 06-879-6428 (C.J. Pask Winery); events@inhb.co.nz (Great Long Lunch) info@cjpaskwinery.co.nz (C.J. Pask Winery)*

Pacifica

This is a Napier favourite. It's set near the seafront and, as the name suggests, seafood features highly on the menu. Try yellow-fin sashimi, or fleshy John Dory, rounded off by a blackberry parfait with fresh blueberries, raspberries and, of course, kiwi fruit. New owners Rebecca and Jeremy Rameka took over recently so expect an enthusiastic welcome. Dinner from 6pm until late Tuesday through to Sunday. Reservations highly recommended.

Prices: *5-course tasting menu is $75 per person without wine.* **Contact**: *Rebecca and Jeremy Rameka, 209 Marine Parade, Napier;* **Tel:** *06-833-6335; info@pacificarestaurant.com; www.pacificarestaurant.com*

Earthquake

On 3rd of February 1931 a massive earthquake hit Napier and flattened it. The quake was so violent it raised 40 km² of submerged land and caused the area to grow considerably. Sadly 258 people died in the destruction and fires that raged in the aftermath. Although devastated, the area picked itself up, dusted itself off and began rapidly to rebuild. Being the trend of the time, art deco inspired the new elegant structures. The city is now a national monument and a joy to explore.

To commemorate the incident and celebrate the art deco style, The Brebner Print Art Deco Weekend is staged every year on the third weekend in February by the Art Deco Trust. The 'not-too-serious' festival is a flurry of fancy dress, jazz, wining, dining, classic cars, twilight toe-tapping and picnics à la Great Gatsby. Ensure you have enough 1930s dress-up to last the whole 4 days as you'll feel wildly out of place in regular clothing.

If you can't make the Art Deco Weekend keep an eye out for Bertie. Fresh from the 1930s, this local character is always happy to stop and chat.

Regale Eatery

This small and friendly eatery in Napier's bohemian, art deco district of Ahuriri serves delicious breakfasts and lunches. It comes highly recommended by one GG owner who hosted her son's wedding reception there. Regale, incidentally, is Italian for 'to delight and entertain with a feast'. Opening times: 8am - 3pm.
Contact: *3 Waghorne Street, Ahuriri, Napier;* **Tel:** *06-834-0835; regaleeatery@xtra.co.nz*

Soak at the Ocean Spa

This glass-fronted café overlooks Napier's Ocean Spa, with its hot pools and fountains, and beyond that the Pacific Ocean. Highly recommended by all Napier's GG owners, Soak is all clean lines and chrome finishes with cakes, coffee, all-day breakfast and a tasty-looking menu that includes coconut seafood laksa and spanakopita.
Prices: *$10 for a long-black coffee and a muffin;* **Contact:** *42 Marine Parade; Napier;* **Tel:** *06-835-8553; soakcaferestaurantnapier@hotmail.com*

NAPIER
NATURE AND ACTIVITIES
National Aquarium of New Zealand

Perched on the Pacific Ocean, New Zealand's top aquarium is home to a multitude of East Coast marine creatures from sea-horses to sting rays. Try and drag some children along; that way you have an excuse to go round and round on the travelator that spirals beneath the Oceanarium. Best of all, if you're qualified, you can go diving in one of the tanks.
Prices: *Adults: $14; children under 14: $7.50;* **Contact:** *Marine Parade, Napier;* **Tel:** *06-834-1404; info@nationalaquarium.co.nz; www.nationalaquarium.co.nz*

NAPIER
CULTURE AND HISTORY

Art Deco Trust

Learn more about the vibrant style and relevance of art deco in Napier on this quirky and highly informative walking tour of the city. If your legs are already suitably stretched, you can take a one-hour Vintage Deco Car Tour in a 1934 Buick or a 75-minute Deco Bus Tour. These tours explore Napier Hill, historic Ahuriri and homes and gardens of Marewa, Napier's Art Deco suburb.

Prices: *Morning walk at 10am ($10) and evening walk (from Dec 26th to March 31st only) at 5.30pm ($12) both leave from Napier's i-Site visitor centre. Afternoon walk at 2pm ($15), Vintage Deco Car Tour ($99, max 3 pp) and the Deco Bus Tour (11.30am, $28) depart from the Art Deco Shop. Bookings essential.* **Contact:** *Anne Corney, Art Deco Centre, 163 Tennyson Street, Napier;* **Tel:** *06-835-0022;* **Fax:** *06-835-1912; walks@ artdeconapier.com; www.artdeconapier.com*

Hawke's Bay Museum, Cinema and Theatre

You can't miss the metal monster that peeks over Hawke's Bay Museum with a corrugated ice-cream cone in his knobbly hand. This is yet another of Napier's fun, eccentric icons, more of which feature inside the art-, culture- and heritage-packed museum. Alongside the museum is The Century Theatre and Cinema, a 330-seater concert venue that stages live music, theatre and film.

Contact: *65 Marine Parade/9 Herschell Street, Napier;* **Tel:** *06-835-7781;* **Fax:** *06-835-9249; info@hbmag.co.nz*

Woolshed Art Workshop

Whether you just want to muse on the creative works of others or dabble your own artistic fingers in a mixture of mediums, the Woolshed Art Workshop offers a unique opportunity to do so. The 100-year-old woolshed has stepped away from its fleece-filled past and now serves as home to Kathy (painter/printmaker) and Adrienne (mosaics), whose expertise makes their art workshop sessions so successful. Phone to find out more about getting arty in Napier's rural and inspiring landscape. Transport provided to and from Napier City if there is a small number of people.

Prices: *Half-day and full-day programmes for groups of up to 10 all year round. Country-style am or pm tea provided & light lunch with full-day programme. $100 for half day to $175.00 full day for 1 or 2 persons (materials included). Special prices available for 3+.* **Contact:** *Kathy Boyle, 360 Seafield Road, Napier;* **Tel:** *06-836-7105; info@woolshedart. com; www.woolshedart.com*

Woolshed Art Workshop

The Orange Tractors of Gannet Beach Adventures

The Art Deco National Tobacco Building

HASTINGS
WINERIES
Ngatarawa Winery
I feel the need to blow the trumpet on behalf of this modest winery, as they seem too nice to blow their own. The picnic-perfect lawn frames a long rectangular lily pond. Great wine and a friendly face at the cellar door sealed the deal for me.
Prices: *$15 - $45.* **Contact:** *Joanne Smith, 305 Ngatarawa Road, Bridge Pa, Hastings West;* **Tel:** *06-879-7603;* **Fax:** *06-879-6675; info@ngatarawa.co.nz; www.ngatarawa.co.nz*

Hatton Estate Vineyard & Winery
Hatton Estate recently won a top New Zealand trophy for its Cabernet Blend, and it exports to international clients including Simpson's-in-the-Strand. But don't expect the rarefied atmosphere of some too-grand-for-its-own-good Old World vineyard. This is New Zealand and they do things differently here. Owner Michael is happy to hold ad hoc wine tastings - he wants to demystify wine and encourage customers to have confidence in their taste buds.
Prices: *Wines from $19.95.* **Contact:** *Michael Daymond-King, 124 Gimblett Rd, Hastings;* **Tel:** *06-870-4777; wine@hattonestate.com; www.hattonestate.com*

HASTINGS
EATING AND DRINKING
Te Awa Winery
If you take the native vineyard-set gardens and match the "head-turning wines of exceptional balance and class" (quaffed and quoth one happy customer) with one of New Zealand's best winery restaurants, you've sketched an image of the not-to-be-missed Te Awa Winery experience. To complete the picture you'd better head down to the Gimblett Gravels wine-growing region of Hawke's Bay and start browsing the menu as soon as you can. With such an array of stunning dishes and wines on offer you may be choosing for some time.
Prices: *Starters range from $16 - $18; mains from $28 - $32; desserts $14.* **Contact:** *Simon Ward, 2375 State Highway 50, Hastings;* **Tel:** *06-879-7602;* **Fax:** *06-879-7756; winery@teawa.com; www.teawa.com*

A Gaggle of Gannets

Cape Kidnappers fits the long pointy bill when it comes to providing a rocky breeding location for gannets. In this particular spot you can get relatively close to them as they have a strange tolerance when it comes to tourists. Sometimes you might even think they were diving for the camera. It is quite something to see the gannets plummet from great heights into the sea and chase their prey underwater. They come to Cape Kidnappers to nest from August to early May.

Vital statistics:
* *They have no external nostrils which means they don't have to purchase a nose-clip for diving.*
* *They have protective air sacks in their face and chest which acts like bubble wrap as they impact with the sea.*
* *They eat a whole lot of fish, and so 'gannet' has become synonymous with a certain type of voracious eater.*
* *At only 13-16 weeks old the chicks make their first solo flight to Australia where they take 5 years to mature.*

Hawke's Bay Farmer's Market

Every Sunday from 8.30am to 12.30pm Hastings A & P Showgrounds parade the Hawke's Bay Farmers' market. Hawke's Bay is a produce-grower's paradise and the Sunday market is bursting with fruit, veg, homemade cheeses, preserves, meats... food basically. Takes place at the A & P Showgrounds, Hastings.

HASTINGS
NATURE AND ACTIVITIES

Tractor Trips, Gannet Beach Adventures

Cape Kidnappers is a world-famous gannet-nesting site. It's practically inaccessible, but this doesn't put Rod and Dayna Heaps off. With the help of their trusty 1949 Minneapolis Molines tractors they take tourists on trailer-rides to see the awesome birds. Incidentally, it is a locally owned and operated family business. The couple have run the business since 1991 after purchasing it from Rod's uncle, the original founder.

Prices: *Adults: $33; children (3 - 15 years): $19; under 2s: free.* **Contact:** *Rod and Dayna Heaps, Hastings, Napier;* **Tel:** *06-875-0898; info@gannets.com; www.gannets.com*

Bridge Pa Golf Course

Follow in the footsteps of Aaron Baddley, James Nitties and Stephen Bowditch at 18-hole Bridge Pa in Hastings. This is one of New Zealand's top golf clubs.

Contact: *1523 Maraekakaho Road, Hastings;* **Tel:** *06 879 7206;* **Fax:** *06 879 7217; gm.hgc@xtra.co.nz*

HAVELOCK NORTH
EATING AND DRINKING

Cuccini Café

Ideal for whiling the morning away with a long-black. The young staff here are genuinely friendly, the cooked breakfast hearty and the pavement tables perfectly positioned for people-watching and enjoying Havelock North's cosmopolitan yet village-like atmosphere.

Prices: *$14.50 for a long-black coffee and fruity muesli.* **Contact:** *9 Middle Rd, Havelock Rd, Napier;* **Tel:** *06-877-8392.*

Te Mata Cheese Company

A speciality cheese manufacturer that excels in everything cheesy. There's a cheese café where you can enjoy cheese, buy cheese, see cheese being made, chomp a cheese dish or sample a wine-escorted cheese platter. Tasty, interesting and perhaps a little fattening but who cares, you're on holiday.

Prices: *Lunches $6 - $12 per person. Cheese $18. Wine $5 - $7 per glass.* **Contact:** *Sonia Sherwood, 393 Te Mata Road, Havelock North;* **Tel:** *06-875-8282;* **Fax:** *06-875-8284; sonia@tematacheese.co.nz; www.tematacheese.co.nz*

HASTINGS   HAVELOCK NORTH   TE AWANGA

🍴 TE AWANGA
EATING AND DRINKING

Clearview Estate Winery and Restaurant

Partial to small places big in atmosphere? Then you'll share the opinion of one of the many delighted Clearview customers who rated the fare of locally-sourced seafood, meat and seasonal produce (and home-grown herbs, olives, citrus and avocados) among the best in the world. A courtyard dining area and the long dapple-shaded tables lounging among the grapevines are perfect for lazy summer afternoons. Rustic barrels, wagon wheels and other hints of the surrounding farm community enforce the relaxed village vibe established in 1989 and continued by the owners. This is a wonderful taste of rural New Zealand. Near to Cape Kidnappers gannet colony.

Prices: *Entrées $10, mains $28, sides $5. All Clearview wines available by the glass from $6.30 - $10.20 and by the bottle from $25 - $45.* **Contact:** *Claire Cameron, 194 Clifton Road, Te Awanga, Hastings;* **Tel:** *06-875-0150;* **Fax:** *06-875-1258; wine@clearviewestate.co.nz; www.clearviewestate.co.nz*

🏔 TE AWANGA
NATURE AND ACTIVITIES

Cape Kidnappers Golf Courses

"If Cape Kidnappers were a book it would be an epic," said Tom Doak, the world-renowned designer of Cape Kidnappers Golf Course. Expect to pay for the privilege of playing here but don't expect ever to find a golf setting quite as spectacular again. The one-off cliff-top course is played high above the ocean on a ridge-and-valley landscape.

Contact: *448 Clifton Road, Te Awanga;* **Tel:** *06-875-1900;* **Fax:** *06-875-1901; proshop@kidnappers.com*

Gannet Beach Adventures

Kids and grown-ups will love this mild and information-packed adventure. A cheery orange true-vintage tractor trundles its comfy trailer along the cliff-lined beach to Cape Kidnappers, the world's largest accessible gannet nesting site. As the longest standing visitor attraction in Hawke's Bay (these guys have been dishing out facts on the intriguing gannets and fantastic local geology for 54 years) their knowledge and experience is inspiring. Run from October to early May. Departure times dependent on tide.

Prices: *Adults $33 ($55 including shuttle transport), children (aged 3-15) $19, pre-schoolers (aged 0-2) free. Enquire about group and family rates.* **Contact:** *Rod and Dayna Heaps, Departure site location - Clifton Beach Reserve, Clifton, Hastings;* **Tel:** *06-875-0898 or freephone 0800-426-638 (within New Zealand);* **Fax:** *06-875-0849; info@gannets.com; www.gannets.com*

Te Awa Winery

Ngatarawa Winery

Wairarapa

North Island

Wairarapa

South Island

Highlights

• Get tipsy at the Martinborough vineyards then wobble your way to The French Bistro for dinner. A popular weekend destination for Wellingtonians, this is a local secret and a lovely drinking and dining experience.

• Make a perfectly timed stop at Greytown for tea and cake, lunch or a whole day. A step down the Victorian Main Street is like a step back in time.

• Watch the birds, the shoreline and the views all along the Wairapapa coastline. Solitude is a rare and wonderful treat and this is where you can find it.

• Venture out at night and visit Mt. Bruce forest and wildlife centre for a tour of its nocturnal residents.

Snow beyond Burnt Spur Vineyard at Martinborough Vineyard

◉ MARTINBOROUGH
EATING AND DRINKING
Coney Wines Ltd

This couple-run winery and café is bursting with character and a must-stop for any wine tour. Tim broke out a bottle of champagne when I popped in and had me giggling between every vine-shaded sip. When he's not happily tending to his current crop he loves bantering with guests and is often known to whip out a guitar. Margaret airs her passion for food in the café where the menu offers a small but scrumptious selection. The setting, food, wine and hosts all score top marks.

Prices: *Pinot noir NZ$32 per bottle. Rieslings NZ$22 per bottle.* **Contact:** *Tim and Margaret Coney, Dry River Road, Martinborough;* **Tel:** *06-306-8345;* **Fax:** *06-306-8344; info@coneywines.co.nz*

The French Bistro

Famous faces don't just beam from the black and white photos on the wall at The French Bistro. "The food and wine were fantastic, but they were the highlight," was how one very happy Oscar-winning customer referred to Wendy and Jim. Chef Wendy hand-writes a much acclaimed French-influenced menu that sits cosily alongside a selection of fine Martinborough wines in this down-to-earth, charming little restaurant.

Prices: *Entrées approx $16, mains $27 - $30, dessert $14.* **Contact:** *Wendy and Jim Campbell, 3 Kitchener Street, Martinborough;* **Tel:** *06-306-8863;* **Fax:** *06-306-8862.*

⚱ MARTINBOROUGH
WINERIES
Martinborough Vineyard

A quest to find a growing area suited to Burgundy-style wines led the pioneers of Martinborough Vineyard to this sunny Mediterranean-like spot. Now they are world famous for their multiple award-winning 'elegant and complex' wines, particularly the pinot noir. Built on a foundation of passion, dedication and great soil, this vineyard offers relaxed tasting from each lovingly filled bottle. The cellar-door staff also have great local knowledge that stretches well beyond the grape. Picnics welcome and certainly worth bringing to this pretty spot.

Prices: *$5 tasting fee applies. Wine prices range from the Martinborough Vineyard Rosé at $19 to an aged magnum of Martinborough Vineyard pinot noir at $225.* **Contact:** *Janine Tulloch, 57 Princess Street, Martinborough;* **Tel:** *06-306-9955;* **Fax:** *06-306-9217; winery@martinborough-vineyard.co.nz; www.martinborough-vineyard.co.nz*

Coney Wines restaurant

Autumn Vines at Martinborough Vineyard

A typical NZ fern

wairarapa

MARTINBOROUGH
NATURE AND ACTIVITIES
Tora Coastal Walk

Only 34km south east of Martinborough, the Tora Coast is an exquisite and very untouristy area of natural beauty. The three-day walk rambles through private hill-country farmland, native bush, dramatic ridges, river valleys and the rugged Tora coastline and its deserted beaches. Comfortable accommodation is provided in each of the three unique farm cottages and hearty, delicious meals come with side-dishes of humour and local knowledge from your hosts.

Prices: *$330 per person incl. 3-nights accommodation, 3-days walking, all meals and luggage transportation.* **Contact:** *Jenny & Chris Bargh and Kiri & Kathryn Elworthy, Martinborough;* **Tel:** *06-307-8115; toracoastalwalk@wise.net.nz; www.toracoastalwalk.co.nz*

GREYTOWN
EATING AND DRINKING
The Main Street Deli

Greytown, the oldest village in Wairarapa, is steadily establishing an identity with a flush of boutique shops, eateries and activities. The Main Street Deli, a two-part café and delicatessen, huddles within a line of classic Victorian building and serves up a range of home-made goodies. I rounded off a hard day on the road with a coffee reviver in the café then tormented myself with their tantalising displays in the deli. Fully licensed and BYO.

Prices: *Meals are $12-$22.* **Contact:** *88 Main Street, Greytown;* **Tel:** *06-304-9022;* **Fax:** *06-304-9022; mainstreetdeli@xtra.co.nz*

MASTERTON
NATURE AND ACTIVITIES
Pukaha Mount Bruce

Ancient trees tower and native birds fly free in the unique environment of Pukaha Mount Bruce. The national wildlife centre offers an assortment of guided tours and will shower you with intriguing information on kaka, kiwi, kokako, kakariki, kereru (mainly birds beginning with 'k' it seems) and tuatara (a native reptile) among other rare and special species. If the monster and glass eel feeding at lunchtime has reminded you of your own rumbling belly, Café Takahe has made a sturdy name for its light, tasty and affordable meals.

Prices: *$10 for adults, $2 for children. Under-5's are free. Guided Tours are available on weekends and public holidays from 10.30am to 12pm and 2pm to 3.30pm. Tours (day and night) are available at other times by arrangement.* **Contact:** *Mount Bruce, Eketahuna, Masterton;* **Tel:** *06-375-8004; www.mtbruce.org.nz*

A stretch of the Tora Coastal Walk

Wellington

North
Island

Welllington

South
Island

Highlights

• Pick up a leaflet from the tourist information centre and head off on one of Wellington's many heritage trails. Wellington is full of classic architecture and notable buildings such as Parliament House and Old St Paul's.

• Take the short, steep and scenic cable-car ride from Lambton Quay to Kelburn and Wellington's scent-filled botanic gardens. Lady Norwood Rose Garden, a spectacular wheel of colour, blooms throughout the summer.

• While in the Botanic Gardens wend your way to the Carter Observatory.

• Shop in Lambton Quay then drag your bag-laden body to the closest café for an ill-earned coffee.

• Get cultural in the capital where the variety of shows, theatres, art and dance is endless. Particularly good theatres are The Circa Theatre and The Downstage Theatre. The New Zealand Film Archive is a great cinema.

• Drive the marine route south of Oriental Bay that weaves from one sandy bay to the next. Precarious wooden villas teeter high above the road and there's a seal colony at Owhiro Bay.

• Apply for a permit to Kapiti Island, a birding hot-spot.

WELLINGTON
EATING AND **DRINKING**

Logan Brown

Steve (Logan) and Al (Brown), perfectionists with 40 years combined restaurant experience, prove exceptional standards don't always have to mean formality. Located in a grand 1920's banking chamber (romantic for those, unlike me, that have a date), the food at Logan Brown is renowned for its generous portions and its focus on striking (yet simple) tastes and textures. Eyes peeled for the bar that's disguised as an aquarium, it serves great drinks and tasting platters for nibblers.

Contact: *Steve Logan and Alister Brown; Cnr of Cuba and Vivian Street, Wellington;* **Tel:** *04-801-5114; deb@loganbrown.co.nz; www.loganbrown.co.nz*

Vista Café

Excellent coffee, delicious home-made muesli and lovely staff who were only too happy to help (an ever-so-slightly lost GG inspector) with directions. All-in-all, a wonderful experience.

Prices: *$6 for a long-black coffee.* **Contact:** *106 Oriental Place, Oriental Bay, Wellington;* **Tel:** *04-385-7724.*

Kai in the City

Traditional Maori hospitality, flavours and music mingle in this wonderful restaurant where authentic dishes and wines are as intriguing as they are tasty. *Ngaa uri a Tangaroa* (gifts from the sea) and *ngaa uri a Tane* (gifts from the land) are all selected for their quality and can be savoured in a number of different ways. Opt for one of their special 'platters to share' or an individual Maori meal. 'Beef eye-fillet on a *hangi* crush with a red wine jus and tamarillo *kinaki*' or 'steamed *kuku, kina kohere, tio repe, hamana, piri piri poaka* and *kawakawa* cakes' certainly tickled my imagination as did the spiced kumara pie (that's sweet potato pie to you and me) for dessert. Open daily 5.30pm - late.

Prices: *Range from $20 - $35 for mains.* **Contact:** *Bill Hamilton, 21 Majoribanks Street, Downtown Wellington;* **Tel:** *04-801-5006;* **Fax:** *04-389-3417; kaiinthecity@xtra.co.nz; www.kaicity.co.nz*

The White House Restaurant

Every long-standing relationship should follow the example set by the White House and its devout following of customers. Head chef Paul's commitment to 'big' flavour combinations and startlingly fresh, seasonal produce has led to 14 years of infallible dishes. Bright harbour views and unfaltering service complete this exceptional eating experience.

Prices: *Mains from $38 - $45, desserts from $18.* **Contact:** *Paul Hoather and Andrew Cameron, 232 Oriental Parade, Oriental Bay, Wellington;* **Tel:** *04-385-8555;* **Fax:** *04-382-9749; info@whr.co.nz; www.whr.co.nz*

Stephan's Restaurant *Logan Brown* *A Matterhorn fish dish*

Matterhorn

Matterhorn's smooth, soft-lit interior, bright tree-spotted courtyard and Swiss-style originality strikes a sophisticated balance between chic and down-to-earth. A broad and colourful clientele, from 'trendies' and businessmen in angular suits to musical bohemian daydreamers, makes for a people-watcher's dream. Three spirit-packed shelves of an 11-metre bar (that's 33 metres of booze) are manned by a host of on-the-pulse bar staff that can throw together cocktails to suit every taste or mood. And there's an all-day-to-late-night food menu to curb every craving. No one puts it better than one regular who said, "go there or go home."

Prices: *Lunch $9 - $21, dinner $26 - $32.* **Contact:** *Sam Chapman, 106 Cuba Street, Marion Square, Wellington;* **Tel:** *04-384-3359;* **Fax:** *04-384-3340; info@matterhorn.co.nz; www.matterhorn.co.nz*

Hummingbird

A number of little birdies told me about this funky café/bar where a continual hum of activity is attracted by fancy cocktails, great music and good food. For feather-weight appetites, those just wishing to curb the afternoon munchies or a late-night emergency alcohol soaker-upper there is a delicious selection of tapas-style 'small plates' to choose from. Heartier 'big plates' are also available.

Contact: *John Coleman, 22 Courtnay Place, Cnr Courtenay Place and Blair Street, Wellington;* **Tel:** *04-801-6336;* **Fax:** *04-801-6339; cafe@hummingbird.net.nz*

Eateria de Manon

Tucked away down a tiny alleyway this rustic French-style eatery is the ideal spot for a romantic rendezvous. The unique menu is small but perfectly formed and certainly won't disappoint. If you're after something a bit different *Eateria de Manon* has that certain *je ne sais quoi*. Vegetarians are catered for but choices are limited.

Contact: *Hannah Fraser, 167 Riddiford Road, Newtown, Wellington;* **Tel:** *04-380-1100; fraserhannah@hotmail.com*

WELLINGTON
NATURE AND ACTIVITIES

Matiu/Somes Island

Matiu/Somes Island was previously used as a human and animal quarantine station, protecting the mainland from its inhabitants. Now the island, a pest-protected wildlife sanctuary and site of cultural heritage, protects its inhabitants from the mainland. It was off-limits to the general public until 1996 when it passed into the care of the DOC. The Dominion Post ferry now does up to nine sailings a day between Queen's Wharf and Matiu/Somes Island. East by West ferries provide a regular service from both central Wellington and Days Bay. Crossings take 20-30 minutes.

Prices: *A small landing fee applies.* **Tel:** *04-472-7356;* **Fax:** *04-471-2075; wellingtonvc@doc. govt.nz; www.doc.govt.nz*

Karori Wildlife Sanctuary

Literally minutes from Wellington city centre Korori Wildlife Sanctuary is a mainland oasis of protected flora and fauna. Natural wetland and native New Zealand bush thrive within the predator-proof fenced area and provide homes for a plethora of species (including the little spotted kiwi). Maps are available for DIY guiding, although I'd recommend one of the day- or night-guided tours for a complete picture.

Prices: *$10 for adults, $4 children.* **Contact:** *Karori Wildlife Sanctuary, 31 Waiapu Road, Karori, Wellington;* **Tel:** *04-920-2222.*

Coffee culture in Wellington

"You can never get a decent coffee in New Zealand!" Americans and Europeans would cry. I remember this from my backpacking days when I worked here as a barista. Well it seems Kiwis have taken the criticism on board. Now it is virtually impossible to get a bad cup of coffee in New Zealand. Every bean is best-quality-organic, every cup a delicately-balanced work of art. Coffee here is savoured sitting down and is an experience in itself.

Nowhere has embraced café culture quite as whole-heartedly as Wellington, which is rumoured to have (though I haven't measured it myself) more cafés per capita than New York. There are certainly an awful lot of them and the majority are wonderfully good and serve a wealth of tasty eats. No doubt you will find a personal favourite among the many that suits your own requirements of sophistication and relaxation.
I have listed a few suggestions just to get you started:

Chocolate Fish Café: family-friendly and relaxed with an unbeatable beachside location, 497 Karaka Bay Road, Scorching Bay, Tel: 04-388-2808.

The Vista Café: superb light fish lunches with a tranquil vibe (loud music omitted), 106 Oriental Parade, Oriental Bay, Tel: 04-385-7724.

Nikau Gallery Café – See 'Wellington City Gallery.'

Midnight Espresso: one of Wellington's original cafés which is open till the wee hours. They have a good selection of vegetarian food and an irresistible cake cabinet. Hot chocolates are bucket-sized and entirely delicious. Young, funky and occasionally loud. 178 Cuba Street. Tel 04-384-7014.

WELLINGTON
CULTURE AND HISTORY
Te Papa Museum of New Zealand

New Zealand's waterfront national museum is both externally and internally impressive. Five floors of art, historical objects, national treasures, Maori stories, re-enactments, interpretations, interactive tasks and visual reproductions focus on the individual components that add up to New Zealand's unique culture and dramatic landscape. The dynamic museum evolves in step with the country it reflects and is kept fresh with a constantly changing programme of entertainment, events and guest displays. My favourite long-standing exhibition is the unassuming 'walk-in' theatre/junk shop at floor level. 'Golden Days' is a vibrant 10-minute visual spin through New Zealand's defining historical moments. You'd need about a week to fully conquer this museum, but, as that's obviously not feasible, be sure you set aside at least half a day. Kids will love the four discovery centres and daily storytelling and will scamper merrily through artificial woodlands, caves and displays. The on-site café stocks great munchies and coffee by the way.

Prices: *Free entry. Tours $10 adult and $5 child.* **Contact:** *Cable Street, Downtown Wellington;* **Tel:** *04-381-7000;* **Fax:** *04-381-7070; mail@tepapa.govt.nz; www.tepapa.govt.nz*

City Gallery and Nikau Café

This is a lovely place to while away an afternoon (although I whizzed round in under an hour and loved what I briefly saw). I was particularly taken by a bizarre alien-inspired exhibition, one of the visiting collections on tour, and the Michael Herschfield Gallery, devoted to Wellington's own pool of artists. Admission is generally free to the majority of exhibitions, although a small entry charge may apply to some. Nikau Gallery Café is on site and perfectly complements its creative contemporary surrounds with an up-beat organic menu. The café is open daily Monday to Sunday 7.30am - 4.00pm for breakfast and lunch, and Friday night for dinner.

Contact: *Civic Square, 101 Wakefield Street, Wellington;* **Tel:** *04-801-3952 (for recorded information) or 04-801-3021 (for general information); citygallery@wmt.org.nz*

Katherine Mansfield's Birthplace

Calling all literary buffs (and those partial to historic houses and a spot of afternoon tea and cake). This wonderfully restored Victorian house and garden pays tribute to Kathleen Mansfield Beauchamp (or Katherine Mansfield to you and I), an iconic female author and one of New Zealand's most famous exports. Stepping back in time to the birthplace of my most admired short-story writer was inspiring.

Prices: *Entry $5.50 adult, $4.00 seniors, $4.00 students, $2.00 children.* **Contact**: *Mary Morris, 25 Tinakori Rd, Thorndon, Wellington;* **Tel:** *04-473-7268;* **Fax:** *04-473-7268; kmbirthplace@xtra.co.nz; www.katherinemansfield.com*

Museum of Wellington City and Sea

From Maui to the Wahine, from Dick to Carmen - this museum has all the stories of Wellington. Housed in a restored heritage building, 9 permanent exhibitions use stunning technology to take you back 1000 years and then lead you to a vibrant present-day Wellington. Feature exhibitions explore social, cultural historical or maritime subjects featuring interesting people, entities, events and places from the capital and beyond. There are events and public programmes throughout the year and in June and July a festival of free performances takes place. Open everyday 10am to 5pm.

Prices: *Free admission. Contact: Queens Wharf, Jevois Quay, Wellington;* **Tel:** *04-472-8904;* **Fax:** *04-496-1949; museum@museumofwellington.co.nz; www.museumofwellington.co.nz*

Museum of Wellington

NORTH ISLAND

UPPER HUTT
NATURE AND ACTIVITIES
Staglands Wildlife Reserve

Spend the whole day here hand-feeding rare and wonderful species of birds, fish and other animals or walking the 10ha of stream and pond-filled landscape and exploring the old bush settlement. At least ensure you stop off for a coffee in the original log-built café as you pass. A few scrubby paddocks, a vision and an awful lot of hard work have transformed this special landscape into an eco-wonderland.

Prices: *Adults $14, senior citizens $12, children $7. Group rates available. Open every day 10am - 5pm (except Christmas Day). Café open 10:30am - 4:30pm. Free use of the BBQ on site.* **Contact:** *Sarah Purdy, Akatarawa Valley, Upper Hutt, Wellington;* **Tel:** *04-526-7529;* **Fax:** *04-526-8529; wildlife@staglands.co.nz; www.staglands.co.nz*

KAPITI COAST
NATURE AND ACTIVITIES
Kapiti Island

Kapiti Island is the summit of a submerged mountain range that was created by an earthquake 200 million years ago. Its more recent history involves a dramatic and highly successful transformation into a predator-free (no cats, dogs, deer, cattle, sheep, rats or possums) nature reserve and one of the nation's most important bird-recovery sites. Many endangered species reside here, including the little spotted kiwi, which is now extinct on the mainland. Visits to the island are limited and you must book ahead to obtain a permit from the Department of Conservation. This is one place however, where a bit of pre-planning is worth the effort. With swimming, snorkelling, a distinct Maori history and walks to the top of the 520m summit that are rewarded with 360° views, ensure you pack swimming-togs, goggles, camera and lunch. Boats depart from Paraparaumu Beach in front of the Kapiti Boating Club. There are two launch operators, Kapiti Marine Charters and Kapiti Tours Ltd to get you there. Apply for permits to the Department of Conservation's visitor information centre in Wellington.

Prices: *The total fees to visit Kapiti Island Nature Reserve are $9.00/adult and $4.50/child plus the cost of launch transport.* **Contact:** *Paraparaumu Beach, Kapiti Coast; kapiti.Island@doc.govt.nz*

KAPITI COAST
CULTURE AND HISTORY
Southward Car Museum

Southward Car Museum has trains, planes and the largest collection of automobiles in the Southern hemisphere. The vintage assembly includes everything from a two-wheeled 1863 bone-shaker to a true gangster's armour-plated, bullet- and bomb-proof Cadillac (previously owned by an employee of Al Capone). Once you've had your fill of automobilia give your legs a spin around the six hectares of surrounding park.

Prices: *Admission costs: adults $10, children $3, family $25 (2 adults and 2 children 5 - 15 yrs).* **Contact:** *Stan Bellamore, The Southward Museum Trust, Paraparaumu, Kapiti Coast;* **Tel:** *04-297-1221;* **Fax:** *04-297-0503; southward@kapiti.co.nz; www.southward.org.nz*

KAPITI COAST
NATURE AND ACTIVITIES
Paraparaumu Golf Course
This is a championship course that has hosted the New Zealand Open on 12 occasions. Try not to get too distracted by the views of Kapiti Island. Visitors are welcome, although it's worth booking a bit in advance.
Contact: *376 Kapiti Road, Paraparaumu Beach, Kapiti Coast;* **Tel:** *04-902-8200;* **Fax:** *04-902 8201; bookings@paraparaumubeachgolfclub.co.nz*

OTAKI
NATURE AND ACTIVITIES
Trinity Farm Living Rose Museum
Forget the usual stuffy old museum with heavy dusty air and a persistently ticking clock: Trinity Living Rose Museum is quite literally a breath of fresh air. One of the country's best collections of old roses cluster and pose throughout three acres of spray-free gardens. Rose aficionados Ann and Lloyd Chapman, the founders of the museum, have passed on everything they know after two decades of collecting, tending, writing and speaking about roses. Blooming lovely.
Prices: *$5 entry fee. Picnics welcome. Coffee and other drinks available.* **Contact:** *Karen and Grant Piercy, 202 Waitohu Valley Road, Otaki;* **Tel:** *06-364-6193 or Freephone within NZ 0800-955-555; roses@trinityfarm.co.za; www.trinityfarm.co.za*

MANAKAU
EATING AND DRINKING
Stephan's Restaurant and Country Café
Songs of praise for this spacious, elegant restaurant can be heard far and wide. European flavours are honest and abundant in the French, Swiss and Italian influenced food. With a devoted staff of locals and a truly lovely country garden this owner-run eatery is homespun with a touch of foreign pizzazz. Located ten minutes drive south of Levin or five minutes north of Otaki.
Prices: *Lunch: mains $12.50 - $23 (most priced between 16.50 - $18.50), dessert $8.50 - $9.50; dinner: entrées $4 - $16, mains around $26, dessert $12.50. Fully licensed.*
Contact: *Brigitte Baumberger, 1164 Main Highway, Manakau Levin;* **Tel:** *06-362-6520;* **Fax:** *06-362-6733; stephans@xtra.co.nz; www.stephans.co.nz*

Te Papa Museum

Staglands

Southward Car Museum

Wanganui and Manawatu

North Island

Wanganui
Manawatu

South Island

Highlights

• Immerse yourself in Whanganui National Park and its grade 2 major river. This key shipping route of the past is now an action zone for canoes, kayaks and jet boats while the park itself is crying out to be walked in.

• Drive the Whanganui River road to Pipiriki. Try not to stop at every scenic photo opportunity or you may be some time.

• Attach yourself to a piece of elastic, take a deep breath and launch yourself off Mokai Bridge. Gravity Canyon's extreme bungy jump and flying fox is found at the end of a brief, picturesque drive just south of Taihape.

• Spend a leisurely morning or afternoon in Kimbolton. It's worth going there just for the drive. If you need extra incentive Hansen's Café and Bar awaits.

• White-water raft at River Valley.

On Horseback with River Valley Adventures

WAIOURU
CULTURE AND HISTORY
Army Museum Waiouru

Highly recommended by GG owners, this army museum 'doesn't glamorise war', focusing instead on soldiers' real-life stories. ANZAC Day is a big deal in New Zealand, so if you really want to get to the heart of the country's identity, you need to know a bit about its military history. Opening every day except for Christmas: 9 am - 4.30 pm.
Prices: *$10 adults, $7 children.* **Contact:** *State Highway 1, Waiouru, Mangaweka.*
Tel: *06-387-6911;* **Fax:** *06-387-6319; www.armymuseum.co.nz*

TAIHAPE
NATURE AND ACTIVITIES
Hikoi ki Paerau, Aorangi Experiences

What, you may ask, is a heli-hike? Well this is New Zealand, where people jump on board a 'copter for a spot of fishing, so why not do the same with hiking? The day starts with the 'scenic' (an understatement, I'm told) flight taking you up to a sub-alpine environment. You then hike through black beech and stands of magnificent podocarp forest. Groups never number more than 10, and the local guides are hugely knowledgeable on everything from indigenous flora to local Maori legend.
Contact: *RD21, Taihape.* **Tel:** *06-388-1444;* **Fax:** *06-388-1859; info@hikoitreks.co.nz; www.hikotreks.co.nz*

Go on, give it some welly!

Try and time a visit to Taihape to coincide with 'Gumboot Day', which is held every Tuesday after Easter. This crazy celebration acknowledges the Gum/Wellington boot in all its rubbery glory – an essential item when embarking on Taihape's rural and often boggy terrain. Bizarre festival activities include a gumboot-tossing contest, which is famed worldwide. The expression go-on-give-it-some-welly might well come from this event.

Wellington citizens are often nicknamed 'Gummies' due to the gum/Wellington boot link.

The Wool Company

Good old-fashioned service and exceptional quality NZ knitwear are both on hand in this relaxed country store. Treat yourself to a New Zealand-made merino jersey and super-soft lingerie and merino possum knitwear, socks and accessories or fabulous ready to knit yarn. Perfect for present-buying dilemmas. If you can't decide while you're there you can check out the online shop and catalogue.
Contact: *Margot Riach, Torea Street, Utiku, South Taihape.* **Tel:** *06-388-0400;*
Fax: *06-388-1873; sales@thewoolcompany.com; www.thewoolcompany.com*

River Valley Adventures   *Hansen's Cafe and Bar*   *The Wool Company*

River Valley

River Valley stands out in my memory as the best white-water rafting experience of my life. Surrounded by 12,000 acres of New Zealand bush on the Rangitikei River, the world-class grade 5 rafting is not the only thing on offer in this stunning and isolated spot. Inflatable kayaking, scenic eco-rafting (for the more serene), horse trekking, guided natural and cultural interpretive bush walks, fly-fishing and even a bit of golf make an appearance. As they say, "like any New Zealand adventure lodge you will find us at the end of the road..." and it's a picturesque road to boot.

Prices: *Half-day Grade 5 white-water rafting $145 pp; full-day scenic eco-rafting, adult $145; 2-hr horse trek $85 pp; half-day horse trek $145; full-day horse trek $189.* **Contact:** *Brian Megaw, Mangahoata Rd, Pukeokahu, Taihape.* **Tel:** *06-388-1444;* **Fax:** *06-388-1859; thelodge@rivervalley.co.nz; www.rivervalley.co.nz*

MANGAWEKA
NATURE AND ACTIVITIES
Mangaweka Adventure Company

A friendly company that runs the full spectrum of rafting trips from hair-raising Grade 5 whitewater rafting on the Upper Rangitikei Gorge section to more sedate family-friendly trips for mum and dad. I like their promise to 'match your boat to your mood'.

Prices: *Day-trips start at $40 for adults and $35 for children.* **Contact:** *Paul and Tricia Eames, State Highway 1, Mangaweka.* **Tel:** *06-382-5744;* **Fax:** *0800-655-747 (freephone within NZ); info@mangaweka.co.nz; www.rra.co.nz*

Whoa Nelly!

Rivers are classified or graded dependent on their rate of flow, turbulence and difficulty. Although this can vary if increased rainfall or a new obstacle (i.e. a tree has toppled into the water) alters the flow, you can still get a general idea of just how challenging your white-water experience will be from its grade.

Grade 1 *– This river is as relaxed as they come. Any rapids are small, regular and pose little difficulty. You'd probably be okay sprawled on a lilo with a cocktail in hand (although don't test that theory... any unexpected obstacles in the water would still need to be negotiated).*

Grade 2 *– Still relatively laid-back and suitable for the more cautious of white-water babies. Waves stay below 1 metre and eddies and bends pose the odd challenge. This is a comfy ride with a bit of a kick.*

Grade 3 *– Okay, now things are hotting up. Broken waves and considerable obstacles make for a fun and thrilling water romp.*

Grade 4 *– Woo hoo! Hold onto your protective helmet people, we're going in! The water is now, most definitely white. Boiling eddies, drops and rocks make for serious buzz-worthy action.*

Grade 5 *– Whoa Nelly! Stomach churning, knuckles white, teeth gritted... determination is what's needed here. There are very few places in the world that raft novice groups on this grade, but it's the biggest adrenaline rush I've ever had. Gather your wits about you and expect a 'big swim' at some point.*

Grade 6 *– Unless you're hardened to the ways of the raft and paddle or the sensation of being in a washing-machine on maximum spin-cycle intrigues you, then forget it. You need some serious skills to even consider Grade 6. Virtually impossible to navigate in a raft and potentially deadly to swimmers... sound like fun? You should leave this one to the few extreme experts.*

Ruahine Adventure Horsetreks

Alan and Liz Rennie run friendly, very personalized horse treks through magnificent beech forest and across their working farm - watch out for the Highland cattle though. Non-riders can go fishing or on eco-walks through the Meersbrooke Reserve. It's best to book in advance.

Prices: *Trips on offer from one-hour long rides to six-day treks. Prices vary accordingly.*
Contact: *Alan and Liz Rennie, RD7, Meersbrooke Farm, Mangaweka.* **Tel:** *06-382-5555, meersbrooke@xnet.co.nz, www.ruahineadventurehorsetreks.co.nz*

MANGAWEKA
CULTURE AND HISTORY
Mangaweka Gallery

The Gallery is set in a fabulous former church that's now painted yellow, red and blue (it shouldn't work but it does) with magnificent, polished wooden floors and natural light streaming in through ornate, mullioned windows. It's the brain-child of British artist Richard Aslett and fits perfectly into tiny Mangaweka's do-it-yourself, bohemian feel. Richard displays his own paintings and photography plus ceramics, sculptures, carvings, and kimonos by NZ favourites including Paul Rayner and Claire Anderson. A café serves Yorkshire tea and dunking biscuits if you're peckish. Open Thursday to Monday from 10am - 5pm.

Prices: *Postcards from 80 cents. Artworks from $10 up to $3,500+.* **Contact:** *Richard Aslett, Yellow Church, State Highway 1, Mangaweka.* **Tel:** *06-382-5447; mangawekagallery@ xtra.co.nz; www.myspace.com/mangawekagallery*

Yes, that's 'Whanganui' National Park with an 'h'

The Maori usually pronounce 'wh' as an 'f' sound but this is not always the case. Wanganui town/region is spelt without out the 'h' as the local Maori pronunciation for harbour (whanga) is spoken as 'wanga' and not 'fanga.' Basically it doesn't matter which way it's spelt, whether you are referring to the national park (Whanganui), town or region (Wanganui) you say 'Wanganui.' Ok?

Rafting with River Valley Adventures

KIMBOLTON
EATING AND DRINKING
Hansen's Café and Bar

Take the stunning scenic drive from Taihape out to the rural village of Kimbolton and reward your view-gazing efforts with a cool beer or crisp New Zealand wine in Hansen's Café and Bar. Actually, you may as well treat yourself to lunch in this vibey place. Feeling almost local in the warm traditional setting I opted for a hearty steak sandwich, which arrived on flour-soft rye bread and was presented with the biggest of smiles. Everything on the New Zealand and café style menu is fresh, tasty and fantastic value.

Prices: *Meals and bar snacks range from $7 - $25. Opening hours dependent on day and time of year (it may be an idea to ring before visiting).* **Contact:***Christine and Steven Easthope, 2900 Kimbolton Road, Kimbolton.* **Tel:** *06-328-5050;* **Fax:** *06-328-5050; hansenscafe@xtra.co.nz*

KIMBOLTON
NATURE AND ACTIVITIES
Cross Hills Gardens and Nursery

Ladies will hanker after a straw hat and floaty dress to breeze around the vibrant park-like gardens of Cross Hills. The virgin bush of 1886 has been developed with seven hectares of rhododendrons and azaleas (over 2,000 varieties!) and still features many old trees and original stone walls. Take a full or magic mini-tour to find out more or enjoy a spot of afternoon tea (in true British country garden style) in the on-site café.

Prices: *Entry fee: adults from $4, children 12 yrs and over $1, children under 12 yrs free. Tours conducted by Rodney or Scott $40 per group. Magic mini-tours $4 per person (minimum 3 people). Booking needed.* **Contact:** *The Wilson Family, RD54, Kimbolton.* **Tel:** *06-328-5797;* **Fax:** *06-328-5773; info@crosshills.co.nz; www.crosshills.co.nz*

MARTON
CULTURE AND HISTORY
John Vickers Homestead Architecture Tours

John Vickers is a font of knowledge on New Zealand's history, and especially its settler architecture. He's a fifth generation New Zealander and former District Mayor, so his interest goes far beyond facts and figures: this is his family's history. His passion was evident when he showed me around his Chapman-Taylor courtyard house, which he restored with his wife Sarah. Book in advance to join one of his day-tours that visits local architectural rarities.

Prices: *Prices vary depending on the group size.* **Contact:** *Vickers, Woodleigh Farm, R.D. 2, Marton.* **Tel:** *06-327-7280;* **Fax:** *06-327-8379; john@historichomes.co.nz*

PALMERSTON NORTH
EATING AND DRINKING

Rydges Boutique Hotel

This ever obliging and consistent restaurant bends over backwards, frontwards and even sideways to keep its guests smiling. When one GG owner visited recently she made a special, off-the-menu request for pan-fried fish. Out it came, "beautifully presented, and beautifully cooked with the wee salad in a ramekin." And if you decide to stick to the menu, the restaurant is great on spices - especially Asian fusion.

Prices: *$29 for a main.* **Contact:** *Leonie Hapeta, 140 Fitzherbert Avenue, Palmerston North.* **Tel:** *06-356-5065; reservations_palmerstonnorth@rydges.com*

PALMERSTON NORTH
CULTURE AND HISTORY

New Zealand Rugby Museum

Rugby union barged its way into New Zealand in the 1870s, grabbing the attention and hearts of the Kiwis who haven't looked back - or passed the ball forward - since. The much-celebrated All Blacks (known for their full black kit and global success) are recognised as heroes throughout the 'egg-chasing' world, but particularly at home. The Black Caps, Tall Blacks and Silver Ferns (cricket, basketball and netball respectively) all wear kit inspired by New Zealand's leading sport and the silver fern (usually stitched on black cotton) has become an internationally accepted symbol for New Zealand. You can find out a whole lot more on the All Blacks at the New Zealand Rugby Museum, which hoards a vast collection of rugby paraphernalia and information.

Prices: *Admission for adults $5 and children $2. Open Mon - Sat 10am - 12pm and 1.30pm - 4pm. Open Sundays from 1.30pm - 4pm. Tour and rugby groups by arrangement.* **Contact:** *87 Cuba Street, Palmerston North.* **Tel:** *06-358-6947;* **Fax:** *06-358-6947; info@rugbymuseum.co.nz; www.rugbymuseum.co.nz*

New Zealand Rugby Museum

Ruahine Adventures

John Vickers Homestead Architecture Tours

Taranaki

North
Island

Taranaki—

South
Island

Highlights

• Walk, climb, ski or just stare in amazement at the splendour of Mt Taranaki. There's a nice driving route that circles the volcano allowing you to photograph it from all angles.
• On your way round, you'll get the opportunity to veer off the road towards the beaches of Oakura and Ounake (both world-class surfing and wind-surfing spots).
• Be entertained by the extensive programme of events, day and night, that take place in New Plymouth's Pukekura Park during its extraordinary Festival of Lights.
• Here's a rare treat for garden-lovers. In the shadow of the mountain is the stunning Pukeiki Garden, home to one of the world's greatest collections of rhododendrons, azaleas and others.

NEW PLYMOUTH
EATING AND DRINKING

André L'Escargot

This traditional French restaurant has a wonderfully glamorous, old-style feel and, appropriately, was a favourite with Tom Cruise when he was filming The Last Samurai in town and around mountain - you'll see him beaming in his snapshot on the wall. Expect fine French cuisine made from hearty fresh New Zealand produce, a great combo that could never disappoint.

Prices: *Starters $13.50 - $21.50, mains $30 - $32.50, desserts $12.50 - $18.*
Contact: *37 - 41 Brougham Street, New Plymouth,* **Tel:** *06-758-4812;*
www.andres.co.nz

Arborio

For those that are a bit peckish after culture-vulturing it through next-door Puke Ariki, glass-fronted Arborio sits right by the ocean and offers great views over to the crashing waves of the Tasman Sea. Breakfast treats such as crisp-fried pillows of bubble and squeak start the day. Lunchtime and dinner menus serve great pizzas and local produce like a lip-smackingly good sirloin steak with beetroot confit and spinach.

Prices: *Breakfasts $9.50 - $17.00. Pizzas $15 - $21. Mains for dinner from $29.50.*
Contact: *Pure Ariki, North Wing, St Aubyn Street, New Plymouth;* **Tel:** *06-759-1241;*
Fax: *06-759-1241; www.macfarlanes.co.nz*

NEW PLYMOUTH
CULTURE AND HISTORY

Govett-Brewster Art Gallery

This contemporary art gallery is renowned throughout New Zealand for its adventurous and original exhibitions. Abstract animation films by 1930s pioneer animator, Len Lye, are a particular highlight among many.

Prices: *Free admission. Opens daily 10.00am - 5pm, except Christmas Day and Good Friday.* **Contact:** *Queen Street, New Plymouth;* **Tel:** *06-759-6060;* **Fax:** *06-758-0390; mail@govettbrewster.com; www.govettbrewster.com*

Puke Ariki

This is Taranaki's knowledge centre, a celebration of the different people and groups who encircle Mount Taranaki. Housing a full public library, museum and information desk, the two-wing glassy complex is situated on the Hill of Chiefs, the most important Maori site in the region and telling location for the artifacts you'll find inside. I particularly liked the giant moa skeleton, a really, really big bird.

Prices: *Entry free. Open 9.30am - 4.30pm weekdays, 1pm - 5pm on weekends.*
Contact: *1 Ariki Street, New Plymouth;* **Tel:** *06-759-6060;* **Fax:** *06-759-6073;*
www.pukeariki.com

NEW PLYMOUTH
CULTURE AND HISTORY
Festival of Lights

The already lovely Pukekura park is transformed into a magical night-time wonderland for two months every summer and is the splendid backdrop for an extensive programme of musical and theatrical entertainment. Amid fluorescent pebble paths, majestically glowing trees and shimmering waterfalls there are romantic, illuminated wooden rowing-boats, thousands of lighting displays, face-painting, a talking giant, fire-poi dancers and parades - more than enough to captivate the young and the not-quite-so-young. Takes place annually from mid-December until early February.

Contact: *Pukekura Park, New Plymouth; www.newplymouthnz.com*

NEW PLYMOUTH
NATURE AND ACTIVITIES
Pukeiti Rhododendron Trust Garden

Set in magnificent rainforest on the lower slopes of Mount Taranaki and looking out to the ocean, this garden is as spectacular as they come. This is New Zealand's premier rhododendron garden and there are more than 20km of bush tracks, mountain streams, old logging lines and plenty upon plenty of plants to keep you well occupied. When I visited, the lady who runs this beautiful garden was deep in China, no doubt researching and finding exotic plant and flower specimens to bring back here to Mount Taranaki.

Contact: *2290 Carrington Road; New Plymouth;* **Tel:** *06-752-4141;* **Fax:** *06-752-4151; pukeiti@pukeiti.org.nz; www.pukeiti.org.nz*

STRATFORD
EATING AND DRINKING
Collage Café

This is a great little café where the contemporary food and ambience satisfy taste buds right up to big city standards. 'Artistic combinations of food' sounds terribly modern, but it matches up to, and even surpasses, its claims.

Prices: *$12 for light meals, mid - $20s for lunch and dinner mains.* **Contact:** *Prospero Place (adjacent to Stratford Information Centre and Percy Thompson Gallery), Stratford.*

Mt. Taranaki or Mt. Egmont

The perfectly shaped 2518m volcanic ash cone of Mt. Taranaki dominates the region with its impressive form. It's a pristine replica of Japan's Mt. Fuji and was used as a backdrop for 'The Last Samurai' (although filming of the Last Samurai became controversial with the Maori who believe the mountain is sacred).

'Taranaki' was the name given to the mountain by the Maori and Captain Cook named it Mount Egmont after John Perceval (2nd Earl of Egmont) who promoted Cook's first voyage. The surrounding Egmont National Park retains the title given by Cook while the mountain continues to be known as both. I rather like 'Taranaki' – 'tara' meaning 'mountain peak' and 'naki' or more likely 'ngaki' meaning 'shining', a reference to the mountains normally snow-capped peak. The lush green fertile slopes can be explored in a whole manner of ways from driving, hiking, climbing (although do be careful) and even skiing.

HAWERA
CULTURE AND HISTORY

Tawhiti Museum

Bruce and Lorrie at Te Popo Gardens send all their guests here, and nobody has ever been disappointed. It comes as no surprise that this is often rated as New Zealand's finest private museum. South Taranaki history is presented in really lively and informative ways, using life-sized figures, scale models, light and sound effects and, of course, artefacts. Displays are constantly being improved, making them more interactive and appealing to younger (and older!) visitors.

Prices: *$10 adults, $2 children. Normally open Friday, Saturday, Sunday and Monday 10 am - 4 pm; winter season June, July and August open Sundays only 10 am - 4pm; summer season January open every day 10 am - 4 pm.* **Contact:** *Nigel Ogle, 401 Ohangai Road, Hawera;* **Tel:** *06-278-6837 or freephone 0800 921 921 within NZ;* **Fax:** *06-278-6837; tawhiti. museum@bitworks.co.nz; www.tawhitimuseum.co.nz*

SOUTH
ISLAND

Flying into New Zealand over the magnificent formation of the South Island, all laid out in miniature below, is an experience I'll never forget. Stretching virtually along the entire western side of the island, the impressive Southern Alps dominate the scene, rising to form a craggy spine that separates the wet, wild Tasman coast from the drier eastern planes that lead to the great Pacific. Only a quarter of the country's population live on the South Island and much of its scenic diversity that make it so popular with visitors - glaciers, lakes, fiords, rivers and tussock plains – remain untouched.

The island and its roads lend themselves most helpfully to be travelled in a figure-of-eight-ish loop, hugging both coasts and traversing the snowy peaks twice. Obviously you can jump in wherever you like, but seeing as most journeys start where the ferries come in from the North Island at Picton, then it's here that I'll begin too. Though this is terrific driving country, do be aware that journey times will take quite a bit longer than anticipated, expect frequent hops out of the car to take yet another panoramic photo. The natural scenes are like a bottomless visual feasting pot. This is the kind of place that will make your eyes ache.

From the ferry into Picton, you'll see the high hills of the Marlborough Sounds, a series of flooded valleys with islands splattered upon the calm waters of the Cook Strait. Travel across their waterways and through the Blenheim vineyards and along the east coast to Kaikoura where high mountains preside over a rugged, rocky coast. Famed for its sea-mammals, this is home to a year-round sperm whale population, masses of friendly dolphins and blubbery seals that bask right near the road.

From here the Canterbury Plains sweep down from the Alps like a patchwork quilt that's interspersed with braided rivers. Christchurch is at the centre of all this. Flat, green and really quite English, this is the largest city on the island and definitely worth a visit before driving over to the stunning Banks Peninsula. Formed by volcanic activity, there is a lot of Maori and, surprisingly, French history in and around Akaroa and its wildlife- and boat-filled harbour.

From here, take the Tranzscenic railway (it's a shame to be the one behind the wheel) across Arthur's Pass. This is the highest and most jaw-droppingly spectacular route over the Alps. At the top tussock-covered basins are hemmed in by mountains and beech forest envelops the steep descent down to the western shore. This should be good preparation for the topographical drama that awaits you on the narrow strip of the West Coast. Expect a coastal drive of big-budget cinematic proportions. This route is renowned for its unsurpassed array of glaciers, dense

rainforest, coastal lagoons, mirrored lakes and wild beaches pounded by the Tasman waves.

Continue south for even more crane-necking action as you drive through the Haast Pass – many people's favourite – and onto the plains of Otago to the lakeside village of Wanaka, guarded by Mt Aspiring National Park. Just over the ski fields are picturesque Arrowtown, buzzy and adrenaline-fuelled Queenstown and, a little further on and definitely not to be missed, the Dart River Valley and sleepy Glenorchy. Venture inland to explore the gold-mining history, Cromwell orchard-country and Bannockburn vineyards in this rich-yellow-tinted region.

It hardly needs saying, but a trip to the South Island is not complete without a dip into Southland's Fiordland National Park. As wild and remote as New Zealand gets, the fiords and forests here are enduring remnants of the land's natural history. Te Anau and Lake Manupouri are quiet places to potter for a few days and make far better starting points for trips into Milford than trekking all the way by bus from Queenstown like most tourists tend to do.

Highly underrated, in fact thankfully so, is the Southern Scenic Route that follows the south coast and takes you from Te Anau to Dunedin. Passing by spectacular mountains (again), through tiny rural townships and rolling farmland and along the superb Catlins coast up to the Otago Peninsula and the old Scottish town of Dunedin. Birds (most notably penguins and albatrosses) and other wildlife are prolific in this isolated and unspoilt part of the country. To truly get away from it all, catch a ferry over to Stewart Island, one of my favourite places in NZ, from Bluff.

From Dunedin you can follow the coast north to Christchurch or take the inland route through the Mt Cook National Park, not forgetting to stop and stare in amazement (actually this is not really an option, even on a rainy day) into the bright blue waters of Lake Tekapo and over to views of Mt Cook/Aoraki, the tallest peak in Australasia.

Once you reach the Canterbury Plains, head to the hills around Hanmer and bubble away in its natural thermal springs before crossing the Lewis Pass over towards the West Coast again. This time bear right through the Nelson Lakes Park and on to see the Abel Tasman National Park in Nelson. Here, gloriously golden sandy beaches and thick forest make for ideal walking and relaxing country, the perfect place to park up the car, put down your camera and rest before heading back to Picton.

Nelson

Highlights

- Hop from café to café in central Nelson making sure you leave room for the odd art gallery and museum break. The World of WearableArt and Classic Car museum and the Nelson Provincial Museum are both fantastic.
- Time your visit with the weekend to catch the eclectic Nelson market.
- Hop over to Rabbit Island for a picnic.
- Potter around Mapua Wharf and take a boat trip out into the estuary where wonderful birdlife abounds.
- Shuttle by sea taxi to Abel Tasman National Park or settle into a sea kayak and navigate your way through clear waters, around intriguing granite outcrops and into secluded sandy bays. Eyes peeled for seals and split apple rock (a giant round rock that's split like a freshly-chopped apple).
- Dig out some hippy threads and immerse yourself in Golden Bay's laid-back alternative vibe. The inspiring area, filled with artists, sculptures and musicians, is a honey-pot for creative types.
- Ramble around the excellent walking tracks in Kahurangi, New Zealand's 2nd largest national park, and, if you're feeling energetic, trek the Heaphy Track to Karamea on the West Coast.
- Spot wildlife, jump off sand-dunes and check out the lighthouse on a Farewell Spit eco-tour. The gargantuan sand bar is a designated wetland of national importance.
- Pick up a paddle/fishing rod in Murchison and kayak, raft or fish the rapid waterways of Nelson Lakes National Park.

GOLDEN BAY
EATING AND DRINKING

The Mussel Inn

Just a great country pub. The Mussel Inn doesn't aspire to be anything more that its laid-back, spirited self. Within the NZ-woolshed-Aussie-farmhouse setting they serve good pub food, locally-brewed booze and home-made lemonade or ginger beer for those abstaining from the hard stuff. Live music features regularly on a Friday or Saturday night and all original artists, whether they're big, small, local, international, folk, jazz, blues, reggae, pop or world, are presented in the same chilled-out manner. There are no pokies, TVs or pool tables here: "when you come to enjoy the music - you come to enjoy the music."

Prices: *Food $3 - $14.* **Contact:** *Andrew and Jane Dixon, Onekaka, Takaka;* **Tel:** *03-525-9241; haveabeer@musselinn.co.nz; www.musselinn.co.nz*

The Courthouse Café

Set in Collingwood's original courthouse building this unique little café radiates historic charm. Mostly fresh organic and GM-free ingredients are used in the extensive and tasty menu. With dishes such as Moroccan vegetable tajine for dinner and a beautiful selection of fish, vegetarians will be well fed. Meat munchers will go for venison medallions or the courthouse meaty breakfast with tamarind chutney. The café is fully licensed and serves excellent coffee.

Prices: *Breakfast $4.50 - $18, lunch $5 - $20, dinner (small plates) $4 - $17, (large plates) $18 - $28.* **Contact:** *Bindia and David Kolff, Collingwood, Golden Bay;* **Tel:** *03-524-8025;* **Fax:** *03-524-8026; bindia.mariana@gmail.com*

The Naked Possum!

Possums are a pest in New Zealand, so the eco-tannery at 'The Naked Possum!' has no qualms about turning them into leather lampshades and cushions. Jocelyn and Grant's unique eco-tourism venture began with their passion to protect the rata trees from being destroyed by possums. Now you can browse the multitude of fur and leather products in the possum shop, treat yourself to a potted rata tree from the native nursery and enjoy a hearty meal in the smoky atmosphere of the bushman's fire. The café (handily found at the start of the Kaituna walking track) specialises in wild game meats with fresh garden salads, but there are great vegetarian and gluten-free options available too. Open 7 days a week: 9am till 10pm in summer and 10am till 5pm in winter.

Prices: *Meals between $10 and $35 in the café/restaurant. Possum leather products - $10 - $2,000.* **Contact:** *Jocelyn Rae and Grant Fitz-William, Kaituna River, Collingwood, Golden Bay;* **Tel:** *03-524-8433; info@nakedpossum.com; www.nakedpossum.com*

The Monza Gallery

Rata Forest surrounding the Kaituna Walking Track

The Naked Possum! Shop

Totally Roasted Coffeehouse, Roastery and Café

Jo's passion is coffee. We're talking single origin, fair-trade, hand-roasted (currently from East Timor) coffee - the sort that slips down like silk and perks you up for hours. Chris's passion is food. He aims to "create food that makes you feel good when you eat it" using simple, clean and sharp flavours. Mix all this with an on-site gallery, sculpture-stocked garden and funky atmosphere and you have a unique café experience that's totally worth a visit.

Contact: *Jo McLean and Chris Falconer, Abel Tasman Drive (just before Pohara Beach), Golden Bay;* **Tel:** *03-525-0396;* **Fax:** *03-525-9833; totallyroasted@totallyroasted.com; www.totallyroasted.co.nz*

Godwits in flight, Mapua Adventures

Farewell Spit

Farewell Spit sweeps from the northernmost tip of the South Island forming a protective shield to the curve of Golden Bay. It was the last part of New Zealand watched by Captain Cook as he drifted out to sea – hence the 'Farewell' (although Maori know it as Tuhuroa). The spit stretches for roughly 26km above sea level and a further 6 km underwater and is made of fine, mineral-packed golden sand. Strong currents running through Cook Straight whip up material and deposit it on the stable southern side (that faces Golden Bay) while the northern side is continually stroked by high winds and the Tasman Sea, causing it to lick round into a thin arc. The sand bar is constantly dynamic and is expected to grow a further 2km in the next 5 years! It seems that most bizarre and anomalous land formations are usually rife with wonderful wildlife and Farewell Spit is no exception. Designated a wetland of national importance, the restricted access wildlife reserve is teeming with black swans, Canada geese, Australian gannets, oystercatchers, Caspian terns and an umpteen-thousand strong squad of migratory waders. It has also been occasionally problematic for the odd whale.

The only way to visit the actual spit is via a guided tour with one of Collingwood's licensed tour operators. Farewell Spit Safaris run a good selection of eco tours. Allow a whole day as trips are between 3 and 6 1/2 unforgettable hours. Expect to jump off dunes, drop in on the gannet colony and visit the lighthouse.

If you don't have time to go the whole hog it is possible to drive yourself as far as the Farewell Spit visitor centre. The scenic route passes through rural farmland and ends at the visitor centre, Paddle Crab Kitchen (incidentally a great spot to refill while pondering views of the world's biggest sand bar) and Puponga Farm Park, which is crisscrossed with walking tracks and dotted with view-points.

GOLDEN BAY
NATURE AND ACTIVITIES
Bencarri Nature Park

Perfect for family expeditions, Bencarri Nature Park offers a gold blend of animals, history, nature and eats. They do a ripping gourmet burger and home-made soups and cater brilliantly for kids with child-friendly healthy snacks.
Contact: *McCallum Road, Kotinga, Takaka;* **Tel:** *03-525-8261;* **Fax:** *03-525-9741;*
leithal@xtra.co.nz

GOLDEN BAY
CULTURE AND HISTORY
Monza Gallery

The MONZA or 'More Outstanding New Zealand Art' gallery encapsulates this unique, creative corner of New Zealand with a spectrum of fine works by artists, jewellers, potters, weavers and sculptors. Perfect to get a one-stop taste of Golden Bay's quirky art scene and find that 'little bit different' something to take home.
Prices: *Art prices range from $15 - $6,000.* **Contact:** *Philly Hall, 25 Commercial Street, Takaka, Golden Bay;* **Tel:** *3-525-8510; phillyhall@xtra.co.nz; www.monza.co.nz*

ABEL TASMAN
NATURE AND ACTIVITIES
The Sea Kayak Company

World-roaming Kiwis Pete and Maureen have spent their lives living and working in stunning locations. And now, with picture-perfect Abel Tasman on their doorstep, they feel it's their duty to share it with you. Your guide will put together the best paddling adventure with their knowledge of all the secret cove-like nooks and rocky crannies that protrude in splendour from the iridescent waters.

Prices: *A range of trips are available at varying prices. Opt from single or multi-day guided tours (fully catered) or select and independent kayaking options where you pay by the day. Kayak hire and kayak/hiking options also available.* **Contact:** *Peter and Maureen Clinton-Baker, 506 High Street, Motueka;* **Tel:** *03-528-7251;* **Fax:** *03-528-7221; info@seakayaknz.co.nz; www.seakayaknz.co.nz*

The Sea Kayak Company

SOUTH ISLAND

 nelson

 MAPUA
EATING AND DRINKING
Flax Restaurant and Bar

Everybody raves about the pork belly at Flax; in fact, everybody raves about Flax full stop. I was in Mapua too early in the day to sample the delights of the restaurant and bar myself, but with countless recommendations and graphic descriptions of their fabulous dishes ringing in my ears, I felt as if I'd personally savoured each one. To torment myself further I explored their waterside location, browsed the delicious-sounding menu, pressed my nose up against their glass front and peered in at the swish interior. Plan your schedule better than mine to include dinner here.

Contact: *Marie, Shed 1, Mapua Wharf, Mapua;* **Tel:** *03-540-2028;* **Fax:** *03-540-2029; flax@flax.co.nz*

 MAPUA
NATURE AND ACTIVITIES
Touch the Sea Aquarium

'Touch the Sea' brings you eye to goggly eye with some of New Zealand's sea and shoreline critters. Watch octopus, eels, sharks, rays and sea-horses do their thing in watery confinement and learn just how bizarre some creatures can be. This place is brilliant for kids.

Prices: *Child $4.50, adult $7.50 and family entry $16.* **Contact:** *Murray & Jenny Goss, 8 Aranui Rd, Mapua Wharf, Mapua;* **Tel:** *03-540-3557;* **Fax:** *03-540-3557; info@seatouchaquarium.co.nz*

 NELSON
EATING AND DRINKING
Boat Shed Café

Paddling on stilts in the harbour this traditional boatshed has become a Nelson landmark for both its heritage and legendary seafood. Treat yourself to the full-on 'Boat Shed Seafood Experience', something live from the tank or pick from the extensive food and wine menu. Fresh and friendly, this is fine dining in a relaxed atmosphere.

Prices: *Breakfast $10 - $20, lunch $12 - $30, dinner $20 - $35, dessert $10 - $35, wine $35 - $250 a bottle. Seafood extravaganza experience $85 - $300. BYO for $10 corkage.* **Contacts:** *Aaron McCorkindale, 350 Wakefield Quay, Nelson;* **Tel:** *03-546-9785; aaron@boatshedcafe.co.nz*

Spoonbills - Mapua Adventures

Hopgoods Restaurant and Bar

The Boat Shed Café

Hopgoods Restaurant and Bar

I was uncontrollably drawn into this little restaurant. My morning attempt to stroll past was halted by a sun-shaded street table, flat white and a healthy bowl of home-made muesli, yoghurt and honey. It's all about quality and taste at Hopgood's and I savoured every mouthful while watching Nelson life amble by. Kevin Hopgood, a fellow pom, projects the cheer of his surroundings into the European, contemporary food and atmosphere. I just wish I'd had time to stop for dinner as well.

Prices: *Brunch/lunch $7 - $19.50, dinner: starters from $7, mains from $21.50 - $31.50.*
Contact: *Kevin Hopgood, 284 Trafalgar Street, Nelson;* **Tel:** *03-545-7191;* **Fax:** *03-545-7151; hopgoods@xtra.co.nz*

Morrison Street Café

Morrison Street Café's outdoor munching area feels like a little oasis in the centre of town. These guys' recipes are so good that they've brought out their own cookbook and you can expect everything from the freshly-baked counter food or the table-service menu to be unusual and divine. They use Atomic Coffee, which has won them a number of awards, and they display local art, which you can buy if the urge takes you.

Prices: *Mains $8 - $16.* **Contact:** *244 Hardy Street,* **Nelson;** *Tel: 03-548-8110;*
Fax: *03-548-8113; mail@morrisonstreetcafe.co.nz; www.morrisonstreetcafe.co.nz*

Café Affair of Nelson

My steak arrived sizzling upon a hot rock at this exciting eatery. Surrounded by landscape-inspired décor and eclectic Kiwi memorabilia I was tempted to complete the atmosphere with one of the carefully selected wines, but a lone inspector shouldn't drink (ahem, well...). Families are welcome here and children entertained leaving parents to grab some lunch or just a fragment of peace and a civilised coffee.

Prices: *Anything between $6 and $30.* **Contact:** *Derrick Harding, 295 Trafalgar Street, Nelson;* **Tel:** *03-548-8295;* **Fax:** *03-548-8295; cafe.affair@xtra.co.nz*

Rabbit Island

NELSON
WINERIES
Woollaston Estate

Philip and Chan teamed up with Glenn and Renee in 2000 to form Woollaston Estates, three separate, beautifully set and special wineries. Their shared love of the Nelson area, and of course good wine, has led to quality wine-making that continues to develop. You can sample the wines from Burke's Bank and Kelling Road at Mahana, a deceptively tall building (you'll see) with a garden on the roof. Keep an eye out for the summer events held here. Cellar door is open for tasting from Labour Weekend till Easter and by appointment at other times if you have a larger group.

Prices: *Summer tasting fees $1 per wine tasted (this is waived if the wine is purchased). Full tasting for groups is $6 pp.* **Contact:** *Philip and Chan Woollaston, 243 Old Coach Road, Upper Moutere, Nelson;* **Tel:** *03-543-2817;* **Fax:** *03-543-2317; mail@woolaston.co.nz; www.woolaston.co.nz*

NELSON
CULTURE AND HISTORY
The Nelson Provincial Museum

New Zealand's oldest museum, founded in 1841, is home to over 1.4 million local treasures. It is a complete pleasure to breeze around the immaculate displays, soaking up the ambience of past days and marvelling at the collections and local art. The museum started with a request for a number of books 'of useful character' to be shipped from British shores. It's now an astoundingly diverse portrayal of Nelson and Tasman history, grown from those early boat-bound days, the heritage of a proud community. This is a great place to get an insight into local history and identity.

Prices: *Free to residents and children and by $5 donation for other visitors.*
Contact: *Bob Dickinson, Cnr Hardy and Trafalgar Streets, Nelson;* **Tel:** *03-548-9588;*
Fax: *03-548-9589; enquiries@museumnp.org.nz; www.nelsonmuseum.co.nz*

World of WearableArt and Classic Cars Museum

Extravagant outfits, bizarre bras and mint-condition classic cars... the usual combo. The World of Wearable Art and Classic Car Museum is a little like a firework display in its tendency to wrench unplanned exclamations from your lips. This is an exhibition where art is taken off the wall to adorn the body. It began as a modest promotion for a rural Nelson art gallery and has since become a high-water mark looked up to by artists throughout New Zealand. The Classic Car Gallery adds an extra dimension to the museum with 50 classic and modern vehicles flaunting their own glinting bodywork. See Wellington section for details on the annual World of Wearable Art Annual Awards Show (WOW).

Prices: *$18 adult. Family and senior concessions available. Open 10am – 5pm daily.* **Contact:** *95 Quarantine Road, Annesbrook, Nelson;* **Tel:** *03-547-4573;* **Fax:** *03-547-0856; info@wowcars. co.nz; www.wowcars.co.nz*

The Nelson Provincial Museum

nelson

RICHMOND
EATING AND DRINKING
Te Mania and Richmond Plains Cellar Door and The Grape Escape

The cellar door for Te Mania and Richmond Plains wines is set in a delightful 130-year-old settlers' cottage that forms part of 'The Grape Escape'. The wide balcony, sweeping lawns and cottage gardens, complete with children's playground (and Rosie the old tractor), spell fun for all, particularly those supping the various award-winning wines. Browse the arts, crafts and local labels then indulge in one of the Grape Escape café's 'exceedingly good cakes'. The café and wine bar offer morning and afternoon tea and lunch (which have all been known to blend seamlessly together in the past).

Prices: *Wine prices range from $16 - $30 a bottle. There's a small fee for tasting refundable upon purchase.* **Contact:** *Cheryl Harrey, Mc Shane Road, Richmond;* **Tel:** *03-544-4054; cellardoor@temania.co.nz; www.grapeescape.co.nz*

RICHMOND
CULTURE AND HISTORY

Höglund Art Glass Studio and Gallery

There is something truly mesmerizing about watching a glassblower at work. I was hooked. Years of delicatley honed skills go into producing stunning works of handblown art glass and jewellery. Learn about the history of glass and the tricks of the trade on the fascinating guided tour and in the Glass Museum, or simply stroll around the gardens and admire the finished objects in the gallery and shop (entry free), with their striking colours and bold designs. Closed Good Friday, Boxing Day and Christmas Day.

Prices: *Glass gallery: admission free. Glass centre: $15 (children under 14 years free with paying adult).* **Contact:** *Ola Höglund and Marie Simberg-Höglund, Lansdowne Road, Richmond;* **Tel:** *03-544-6500;* **Fax:** *03-544-9935; artglass@hoglund.co.nz; www.nelson.hoglund.co.nz*

MURCHISON
EATING AND DRINKING
Rivers Café

Settled neatly at the heart of river-laced Murchison, Rivers Café has come a long way since its days as a petrol station. Although the original pumps still stand proud outside, re-fuelling now comes in the form of fine-quality coffee and fresh, healthy meals. Stop off for a lunchtime nibble while flumped in a sofa or fill your tank with a superb meal and wine at dinner. Gluten-free options available.

Prices: *Lunch $7 - $22. Evening dining: entrées $15 - $17, mains $22 - $36.* **Contact:** *Jude Alfeld, 51 Fairfax Street, Murchison;* **Tel:** *03-523-9009;* **Fax:** *03-523-9933; jude_rivers@xtra.co.nz*

The Nelson Provincial Museum

MURCHISON
NATURE AND ACTIVITIES

New Zealand Kayak School

Mick Hopkinson, the kayaking guru of New Zealand (watch his BBC-documented first descent from Everest on the Dudh Khosi in Nepal and his 'big swim' if in any doubt), runs brilliant multi-day courses for those wishing to learn the art of paddling. Aided by a skilled and enthusiastic team of instructors you'll be rolling and taking on Murchison's white water in a matter of days. Courses are tailored to varying skill levels and price includes top-quality bunkroom accommodation.

Prices: *4-day courses of varying levels $795 (cost includes instruction, accommodation, video analysis, swimming pool sessions and transport around Murchison). Equipment hire $60 - $100. A 2-day refresher course is $395.* **Contact:** *Mick Hopkinson, 22 Grey Street, Murchison;* **Tel:** *03-352-5786 or 03-523-9611 (Sept - April);* **Fax:** *03-352-5786; mick@nzkayakschool.com; www.nzkayakschool.com*

Ultimate Descents New Zealand

Based in one of the wettest and most beautiful areas of the world, Ultimate Descents New Zealand can select any level of white-water to suit a variety of rafting and kayaking trips. Your highly-trained, multi-talented guides will share their passion for this unique river-woven location and ensure that you're not only safe but clued up on the watery environment.

Prices: *Buller Gorge rafting: $105 pp. Family rafting: adults $95, kids under 14 $75. Kayaking: $115. Karmea heli-rafting: 1 day $350, 3 days $1,050.* **Contact:** *Tim Marshall, 51 Fairfax Street, Murchison;* **Tel:** *03-523-9899;* **Fax:** *03-523-9811; ultimate@rivers.co.nz; www.rivers.co.nz*

Ariki Falls - Ultimate Descents

 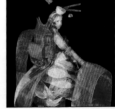

World of WearableArt and Classic Car Museum

Marlborough

North Island

South Island

Marlborough

Highlights

- Exert your taste buds touring Marlborough's many wineries which are concentrated around Blenheim and Renwick.
- Tug on your walking boots or cycling shorts and step/wheel out onto the 71km Queen Charlotte Sound track. 3-5 days of scenic tramping heaven.
- Allow a little extra time to drive the dramatic (and slightly hairy) Queen Charlotte Drive between Picton and Havelock. The bush-fringed 40km road winds past numerous bays and is dotted with art and craft studios.
- Explore the sunken valleys of The Sounds by boat trip, ferry or kayak. Rolling bush and native forested hills rise from crystal waters and are inhabited by incredible sea life, birds, and classic Kiwi baches.
- Clip clop through Pelorus Nature Reserve on horseback or pack a lunch and meander by foot.
- Go mussel mad in Havelock, the home of New Zealand's green-lipped species. The Sounds produce exquisite seafood and perfect wine to match.

KEKERENGU
EATING AND DRINKING

The Store Kekerengu

The tiny town of Kekerengu ultimately is 'The Store' and you should devote a good chunk of your day to a leisurely lunch and exploration of this coastal find. Equidistant from Kaikoura and Blenheim the café-restaurant (and still functioning post-office) forms a naturally perfect stop along the striking and rugged coastal drive. Whether you make a laid-back gourmet meal of it (crayfish seems to be the order of the day) or opt for a briefer coffee and delectable cake stop, the position is astounding. Inspired by the rustic, nautical décor I took the opportunity to write a few postcards home and sent them on their way.

Prices: *Cabinet food $3 - $8, blackboard menu $11 - $90, average blackboard price $16.50.*
Contacts: *Clive Macfarlane, SH1, Kekerengu;* **Tel:** *03-575-8600;* **Fax:** *03-575-8620; the_store@xtra.co.nz*

BLENHEIM
GUIDES

Marlborough Travel

Family-owned and operated by fifth-generation Marlburians these guys have won awards for their vast knowledge of the area. They offer a range of landlubber and seafarer tours: freshly-steamed mussels served with local sauvignon blanc on the Greenshell Mussel Cruise, a uniquely insightful private wine tour or a day of luxury touring in their BMW 7 series vehicle...on their trips they will happily tailor to and organise whatever tickles your fancy.

Prices: *There are a range of different tours, boat cruises and prices.* **Contact:** *Scott Mckenzie, Blenheim;* **Tel:** *03-577-9997;* **Fax:** *03-577-9979; info@marlboroughtravel.co.nz; www.marlboroughtravel.co.nz*

BLENHEIM
WINERIES

Seresin Estate

Visit the cellar door to sample Seresin's subtle wines, its fine quality, occasionally fruity, olive oils and the new selection of seasonal preserves and local manuka honey. I felt a bit like Charlie in a sophisticated (non-chocolate) factory on the mini-tour I was given where the gigantic vats of wine dwarf even the tallest of wine-makers. Seresin's vines are operated under organic and biodynamic principles.

Prices: *There is a small tasting charge, fully redeemable on purchases.* **Contact:** *MJ Loza, Bedford Rd, Blenheim;* **Tel:** *03-572-9408;* **Fax:** *03-572-9850; www.seresin.co.nz*

Gibb's Vineyard Restaurant

Grove Mill Winery

Herzog Winery

marlborough

BLENHEIM
EATING AND DRINKING

Herzog Winery and Luxury Restaurant

Already renowned at home for their restaurants and winery, Swiss imports Thérèse and Hans Herzog and their team of top European chefs uprooted and packed their fantastic reputations to replant them here in Blenheim's perfect soil. Recently voted the 'best restaurant' in New Zealand, Herzog is undisputedly fine on all counts. A very cheery Nicola showed me around the vineyard whose position is absolutely idyllic, food divine and wine meanwhile, ah the wine.... Bistro is open for casual lunches and restaurant for fine dining in the evening, both from Oct - May only.

Prices: *Cellar door bistro mains $18-$28. Restaurant degustation menu: 3-courses from $89, 5-courses from $119. A la carte options available. Winery open all year. Master cooking classes and kitchen 'confidentials' also highly recommended - enquire for further details.*
Contact: *Therese and Hans Herzog, 81 Jeffries Rd, Blenheim;* **Tel:** *03-572-8770;*
Fax: *03-572-8730; info@herzog.co.nz; www.herzog.co.nz*

Highfield Estate

Worth a wine tasting and view-gazing stop. The distinctive salmon-pink building sits high on the Brookby Ridge appreciating an unsurpassed spread of Wairau Valley views. Skip up the castle-style turret to make the most of the view and eat inside or outside.
Contact: *Naomi Galvin, Brookby Road, Blenheim;* **Tel:** *03-572-9244;*
Fax: *03-572-9257; www.highfield.co.nz*

Gibbs Vineyard Restaurant

Locals and wine-makers alike are found relaxing at Chris and Heidi's restaurant. It could be the excellent wine list, the taste-charged European food or the prosperous garden that draws them in. Whichever it may be, you'll almost feel local yourself at this homely establishment where the warm welcome makes you feel as if you've come to a friend's for dinner.
Prices: *Starters $12.50 - 18.50, mains $31.50 - $38.50, desserts $11.50 - $15.50.*
Contact: *Chris and Heidi Gibb, 258 Jacksons Road, Blenheim;* **Tel:** *03-572-8048;*
heidichrisgibb@xtra.co.nz; www.gibbs-restaurant.co.nz

BLENHEIM
NATURE AND ACTIVITIES

Wine Tours by Bike

The cycling oenophile is in their element amongst the flat vineyards of Marlborough country: virtually no hills, beautiful scenery, and boutique vineyards by the dozen. There are over 30 vineyards that can be explored by bike within a 10km radius of Blenheim, reached by quiet back roads and vineyard tracks, and ranging from the big names to the family affair. Fortunately, along with all the usual cycle-gear, Nigel and Helen supply wine panniers for you to stow away that odd cellar-door purchase. They also will pick you up and drop you off from your local accommodation and replace or repair your bike should you breakdown during the tour.

Prices: *Up to 4 hours bike rental $40 per person; over 4 hours and up to 8 hours NZ $55 per person.* **Contact:** *Nigel and Helen Hart, Argrove Lodge, 191 Bells Road, Blenheim;* **Tel:** *03-577-6954; info@winetoursbybike.co.nz; www.winetoursbybike.co.nz*

RENWICK
WINERIES

Bladen Estate

A tiny and utterly charming owner-run winery where 100% Kiwi wines are sipped in the jovial company of the hosts. This is the kind of place that hangs an apologetic 'sold out' sign on the door when the supply of pinot gris and sauvignon blanc have been a bit too popular (always a hazard when you produce such great wine).

Prices: *Wine prices range from $18 - $30 a bottle.* **Contact:** *Dave Macdonald, Conders Bend Road, Renwick;* **Tel:** *03-572-9417;* **Fax:** *03-572-9217; dave@bladen.co.nz*

Grove Mill Winery

Grove Mill's philosophy is to produce the highest quality wine in a way that results in minimum impact on the environment. Native gardens and a wetlands sanctuary both feature on site and are home to a clatter of birds and the southern bell frog (Grove Mill's green-limbed mascot and symbol). Indulge in a cheeseboard from the cellar door, taste and learn from the unique vine library and browse the New Zealand contemporary artworks on sale at the Diversion Gallery (also at the cellar door).

Prices: *Wine tastings free of charge.* **Contact:** *Karen Walshe, Waihopai Valley Road, Renwick;* **Tel:** *03-572-8200;* **Fax:** *03-572-8211; info@grovemill.co.nz; www.grovemill.co.nz*

PICTON
EATING AND DRINKING

Le Café

Le Café has come a long way since introducing the first real coffee machine to Picton and sparking a local addiction to the brown stuff. The café, now twinned with a fun and refined restaurant, boasts a full bar, interesting wine list, a great menu (try the fresh locally-landed fish), local art, regular live music, cracking views of the sounds and great carrot cake.

Prices: *Breakfast $6.50 - $17; lunch $13.50 - $21; dinner, starters $10.50 - $12.50, mains $17.50 - $30, desserts $7.50 - $9.50.* **Contact:** *Peter, 12-14 London Quay, Picton;* **Tel:** *03-573-5588; lecafe@xtra.co.nz; www.lecafepicton.co.nz*

The Marlborough Sounds - Wilderness Guides

PICTON
NATURE AND ACTIVITIES

Wilderness Guides

If a day is all you have, these guys can more than fill it for you. In fact, I would recommend allowing a number of days to play with Wilderness Guides. Steve and Juliet have grown up in the Marlborough Sound, living and working in the giant natural adventure park they call home. The Gibbonses have the know-how to wring maximum enjoyment out of any track, kayak or mountain bike trail in the Sound (they also cover the Heaphy Track and Nelson Lakes). They look after your packs, lunch, gear, accommodation and anything else you may need. Great fun and great value: "I got more than my value for money. Put your prices up!" demanded one disgruntled guest.

Prices: *Dependent on type and length of trip. Guided and independent, single and multi-day trips are available for walks and kayaking. Mountain bike hire $45 per day. Kayak rental $40 per day (discount rates available for a number of days).* **Contact:** *Steve and Juliet Gibbons, Picton Railway Station, 3 Auckland Street, Picton;* **Tel:** *03-520-3095 or 0800 266 266;* **Fax:** *03-520-3096; admin@ wildernessguidesnz.com; www.wildernessguidesnz.com*

Marlborough Sounds Adventure Company

Whether you want to paddle, mountain bike, trek or dabble in all three, Marlborough Sounds Adventure Co makes it happen in safe, enlightening and pleasurable style. Due to Marlborough's temperate climate the Queen Charlotte walk (a coastal panoramic feast of a track that's not steep but relatively long) can be tackled all year round and takes 4 - 5 days. These wise and long-standing chiefs of the sea-kayaking world are more than qualified to help you navigate yourself in the Sounds and will create a trip to suit your time-frame.

Prices: *Vary depending on length of trip and type of activity. Luggage transportation is included in all walking packages. Kayak and mountain bike rental available. Mountain bike rental price doesn't include luggage transfers.* **Contact:** *Sara Archdale and David Watson, London Quay, Picton;* **Tel:** *03-573-6078;* **Fax:** *03-573-8827; adventure@marlboroughsounds.co.nz; www.marlboroughsounds.co.nz*

Myths and Legends Eco-Tours

The old Maoris believe that stories stimulate dreams and if we were to lose the ability to dream our spirits would die. Pete and Takutai keep the art of story-telling alive on board Tutanekai, their 75-year-old kauri boat. They visit remote bays, islands and inlets and guide you on bush walks through native forest. I left time and inhibitions ashore and relaxed completely in the company of this fascinating couple, who are wise in all things Maori and environmental. Propped on pillows, wrapped in a blanket, the Marlborough Sounds - dolphins, seals, bird colonies, beach and the sea itself - unfurled around me. The pulse of tourism beats very slow here. You will step lightly away from the experience with a head packed with knowledge and wonder how it got there.

Prices: *Dependent on type of tour. Trips can be tailored to individuals.* **Contact:** *Peter, Takutai and Tane Beech, Picton;* **Tel:** *03-573-6901; info@eco-tours.co.nz; www.eco-tours.co.nz*

Wine Tours by Bike

Marlborough Sounds Adventure Company

Another pot of mussels at Havelock's Mussel Pot

 **PICTON**
CULTURE AND HISTORY
The Edwin Fox

The Edwin Fox, one of the world's oldest surviving ships, has retired to Picton's foreshore. Before her (or should I say his?) days as a symbol of historical interest The Edwin Fox saw service in the Crimean War, shuttled convicts to Australia and immigrant settlers to New Zealand, transported meat, coal and other goods, was sold for a shilling and then was finally attacked by vandals and scavengers. You can learn more about these colourful stories and explore the rare teak Bengal-built remains of the ship at the Maritime Centre.

Prices: *Admission for adults $8 and children $2.50. Open daily 9am - 5pm summer or 9am - 3pm winter.* **Contact:** *Edwin Fox Maritime Centre, 100 metres from the rail ferry terminal on the Picton foreshore, Picton;* **Tel:** *03-573 6868; edwinfoxsoc@xtra.co.nz*

HAVELOCK
EATING AND DRINKING
The Mussel Pot Restaurant

With its iconic, giant pot of mussels on the roof, you can't miss the Mussel Pot in Havelock, 'mussel capital of the world'. Here, these tasty little critters are cooked up in a multitude of ways and matched with top-quality Marlborough wines. An idyllic garden sets the scene in summer while the warmth emitted from friendly staff and an atmospheric fire keeps things cosy in winter.

Prices: *Mussel dishes $17, starters from $2.50, mains from $14 - $24 and desserts from $8.50.* **Contact:** *Paul and Carla Suisted, 73 Main Road, Havelock;* **Tel:** *03-574-2824;* **Fax:** *03-574-2878; musselpot@xtra.co.nz; www.themusselpot.co.nz*

Slip Inn Café, Restaurant and Wine Bar

You can't get any closer to the sea than the Slip Inn. Make the most of this marina location with a bottle of wine and some of Havelock's famous mussels. If you're not a *fruits de mer* fan the home-made pizzas, breads and cakes are also superb.

Prices: *Breakfast $4.90 - $18.50 (mega breakfast!); lunch $9.50 - $20, pizza menu $14 - $21, mussel menu approx $16; dinner $10.50 - $29.50.* **Contact:** *Katrina Hodel, Havelock Marina, Havelock;* **Tel:** *03-574-2345;* **Fax:** *03-574-2247; slipinn@slingshot.co.nz*

Green Lip Mussels

New Zealand green lip mussels, named for their green-tinged shells, love the pure, clean waters of Havelock and grow there in abundance. Not only are they good to eat, but it seems they are also good for your health. Regular mussel eating can reduce joint pain, improve flexibility and rebuild lost cartilage. So they say.

Hooked on seafood? Then rock up for Havelock's mussel festival in March.

Here's a vaguely interesting fact: male mussel meat is creamy white, while female mussel meat is orange. They are, however, as plump, sweet and tender as each other. Just one more major difference between mussels and human beings.

Marlborough Travel, the Greenshell Mussel Cruise

Canterbury

Highlights

- Pick your jaw up from the floor after driving the rugged Kaikoura and Canterbury coast, then savour Kaikoura's sea life from land, sea, air or restaurant.
- Get steamy in Hanmer open-air hot springs, which are particularly special in the snow – there's nothing quite like experiencing a winter wonderland in your swimming costume.
- Christchurch is not known as the 'most English' or the 'garden' city for no reason. Take a long stroll through huge Hagley Park, visit its botanical gardens and the fascinating Canterbury Museum, and then collapse on the banks of the River Avon to have a picnic and watch the punts glide past.
- In season (June – Sept) head to the snowy peaks of Mt Hutt (there are other fields but this is the closest) for a day of skiing or snowboarding. Crowds here are small and the location a stunner, looking out over the Southern Alps, Canterbury Plains and the Pacific coast.
- Spend a few days away from the city in the pastures of the Banks Peninsula. The walking track here is superb and French-obsessed Akaroa is a fascinating, pretty little township.
- Take to the water in Akaroa Harbour for a day spent sailing, or better swim with the adorable endemic Hector dolphins that call it home.
- Experience the highlands of Mackenzie country by foot or car, or take off from Mt Cook settlement and see the region's turquoise lakes and the country's highest peak Mt Aoraki/Cook from the air. To cruise over the South Island's snowy spine, the Southern Alps, is an unsurpassable adventure.

AKAROA
EATING AND DRINKING

C'est La Vie

Rave reviews abound about C'est La Vie, a Banks Peninsula institution. Host and owner Magdalena serves typically delicious French fare in copper cooking pans in her tiny, warmly-lit and homely restaurant. An eclectic combination of hanging Christmas lights, stuffed toy rabbits and guests' comments are scrawled on its walls for decoration. Not that any is needed for the food here is so fabulous that it shouts for itself. The *duck à l'orange* is legendary and the venison in red wine sauce with poached pear is fast becoming so. Seafood from the harbour, including large green-lipped mussels and gurnard, are gathered in a creamy medley and local fruits are employed in yummy desserts like pear tart and a chocolate sauce with fresh kiwi and feijoas. Do book ahead, there are only two sittings each night and seats fill fast.

Prices: *Main courses $28 - $30. There is a wine list but you can also BYO.* **Contact:** *Magdalena Lau-Nelles, 33 Rue Lavaud, Akaroa;* **Tel:** *03-304-7314; cestlavie@xtra.co.nz*

Lake Tekapo

Whatever the weather, the turquoise waters of Lake Tekapo are startling. Its remarkable blueness is caused by 'rock flour', which is made up of finely ground rock particles held in suspension in melt water that is brought down from the glaciers at the head of the lake. It is worth stopping off at the Church of the Good Shepherd, a peaceful spot despite the tourists, and a lovely place to take a picture....

Treecrop Farm

This is the perfect place to spend a lazy afternoon. A lovely 20-minute walk from the town centre, you'll enter Lynne's wonderful wild wilderness gardens, criss-crossed with walking tracks that lead to historic beech forests, waterfalls and even the ocean at Otanerito Bay. Included in the entrance fee to the gardens is a cappuccino, hot or iced chocolate drink or a berry juice with fresh herbs best enjoyed from the sheepskin-strewn verandah overlooking the greenery. For a little extra edible 'treats' are served from the orchards.

Prices: *Entrance to gardens and verandahs is $12 pp, includes drink. Access to farm tracks is free of charge.* **Contact:** *Lynne Alexander, Grehan Valley Road, Akaroa;* **Tel:** *03-304-7158; lynne@treecropfarm.com; www.treecropfarm.com*

French Frolics in the 'long harbour' of Akaroa

In 1838, French whaler Jean François Langlois negotiated the sale of the Banks Peninsula from the local Maori tribe, and later returned to France to gain support for his colonising plan and to form a trading company that was to become the vehicle for his ambitions.

With the backing of the French government, around 60 settlers emigrated in 1840, escorted by navy captain Charles Lavaud and the warship L'Aube. However, upon hearing of their plans just days before their arrival, the British thwarted the French by rushing to Akaroa in their own warship to quickly raise the British flag and claim their sovereignty of the area under the (recently signed) Treaty of Waitangi.

Pipped to the post, if only the French had arrived a couple of years earlier, this may well have become a French-speaking colony after all. Nonetheless, despite the assertion of British sovereignty, the settlers remained and have clearly stamped their mark on Akaroa. Streets and houses have French names and many of their descendents still live in town. Akaroa is very proud of its French history and heritage, and each year the famous Akaroa French Festival is held in April celebrating all things French through films, music, family entertainment and, of course, delicious local food and wine.

Ma Maison Restaurant

Wonderfully positioned right on the harbour waters, this busy restaurant has a lovely garden and a warm open fire inside for chillier wintery days. On the menu when I visited were roast chicken with pecorino dauphinoise, NZ beef fillet with horseradish rosti and, of course, fresh Akaroa salmon, rounded off (and I think I do mean rounded) with scrumptious sticky toffee pudding and brandy snaps or a decadent chocolate fondue with strawberries for dipping.
Prices: *Starters $10 - $15, mains $25.50 - $30, desserts $10.50 - $14.50.* **Contact:** *6 Rue de Balguerie, Akaroa;* **Tel:** *03-304-7668; mamaison@ihug.co.nz*

French Farm Winery

This lovely winery has a distinct feel of provincial France with its terracotta buildings, rose-filled garden terraces, lavender bushes and vines that sweep down to the azure blue waters of the harbour. The main restaurant serves local favourites like Akaroa salmon and lamb and there's a pizzeria that specializes in proper thin and crispy-based pizzas. All of which are great washed down with a glass of chardonnay or pinot noir from their barrels.
Contact: *French Farm Valley Road, Akaroa;* **Tel:** *03-304-5784;* **Fax:** *03-304-5785; frenchfarmwinery@xtra.co.nz; www.frenchfarmwinery.co.nz*

Akaroa Fish 'n' Chips

This is a great, proper NZ chippy where locals come for spot-on lunchtime treats of freshly battered fish and perfectly salted chips. Sit outside and feel the breeze come straight off the harbour waters as you munch away on its produce.
Prices: *Lunch for one is about $4. Contact: 59 Beach Road, Akaroa;* **Tel:** *03-304-7464.*

AKAROA
NATURE AND ACTIVITES

Pohatu Penguin Habitat

Breeding season amongst the white-flippered penguins in the small Pohatu-Flea Bay is a busy time for Francis and Shireen. For the last decade they have monitored the lives of their old friends, witnessing such a number of divorces, births and deaths that would make most TV soaps seem tame. This is the largest of the littlest penguin's colony on the mainland and one that needs constant protection from introduced predators. Small, guided groups are taken on fascinating tours into the colony enabling you to observe the penguins unobtrusively. You can also take out a kayak to explore the spectacular scenery and wildlife of Pohatu Marine Reserve. The best time for penguin viewing is the breeding season between September and January.

Prices: *Penguin evening tours: $55 adult, $40 children under 12. $16 pp without pick-up from Akaroa though 4WD needed to access the bay. Book through Akaroa Information Centre.* **Contact:** *Francis and Shireen Helps, Pohatu-Flea Bay, Akaroa;* **Tel:** *03-304-8552; fshelpspohatu@xtra.co.nz; www.pohatu.co.nz*

Onuku Heights Horse Treks

Riding is a great way to appreciate the countryside, whether you are looking over the hedge into your neighbour's garden (one of my mother's favourite pursuits) or gazing open-mouthed at stupendous vistas. Thankfully, horse-treks at Onuku Heights focus on the latter, showcasing the wild Banks Peninsula landscape at its best, with not a topiary hedge in sight! You will ride out on the 309-hectare sheep and cattle farm through native bushland and under ancient matai trees. The pure bred Quarter Horses are all well trained and a dream come true for experienced riders.

Prices: *From $140.* **Contact:** *Eckhard Keppler, 166 Haylocks Road, RD 1, Akaroa;* **Tel:** *03-304-7112 or Freephone within NZ 0800-748-732;* **Fax:** *03-304-7116; onuku.heights@paradise.net.nz; www.onuku-heights.co.nz*

Dolphin Experience

Dolphin Experience in Akaroa take small groups out into the sheltered harbour waters for the opportunity of swimming close to the dolphins. This is not the dolphin-touching, 'flipper' type experience many hope for.

Happily, as well as being sweet as pie, Hector dolphins are completely wild so these tours are carried out strictly on the dolphins' terms.

Prices: *Swimming: adults $98, children $80. Watching: adults $48, children $25. Children under 5 can't swim but can go out on the boat and watch for free.* **Contact:** *61 Beach Road, Akaroa;* **Tel:** *03-304-7726; dolphins.akaroa@xtra.co.nz; www.dolphinsakaroa.co.nz*

Hectors Dolphin and Calf

Akaroa Dolphins

Hector dolphins, blue penguins, fur seals and fascinating sea birds are just a few of the creatures that call Akaroa Harbour home. Pip's family in Akaroa dates back to 1838 (interestingly they were some of the original French settlers from Normandy) so guests get a really personal insight into the history, geology (the harbour waters fill what is actually a massive volcano crater), ecology and Maori traditions of the region. Small groups allow for more personal cruises on their wonderfully stylish, yet discreet and quiet vessel. Guests also receive a complimentary drink of NZ award-winning wine, beer or organic juice and some delicious, fresh home-baking.

Prices: $60 per adult, $30 per child (5 - 15yrs), 4 yrs and under $20. **Contact:** Michelle Lake and Pip Waghorn, 65 Beach Road, Akaroa; **Tel:** 03-304-7866; cruise@akaroadolphins.co.nz; www.akaroadolphins.co.nz

Hector's Dolphins

Endemic to the coast of New Zealand, not only are these rounded little chaps the smallest sea-living dolphins in the world, but sadly they also happen to be the rarest of all oceanic species. Threatened by set nets and a low birth rate, there are only 2,000-2,500 individuals within two distinct populations off the South Island coast
and another tiny group of 100 dolphins off North Island shores.

Much smaller than other species, Hector's dolphin adults grow to a length of 1.2m to 1.4m and their calves are like little sea-faring rugby balls at just 50-60cm at birth. With foreheads that curve down to the mouth's tip, small rounded dorsal fins and a well defined colour scheme it is not just their petiteness that makes them distinctive. Their bellies are white, bodies grey, flippers, fins and tails black and they are all marked by a jazzy swoosh of white that extends from the belly along the flanks towards the tail.

Hector's dolphins are really sociable types and usually swim in groups of 2 – 12. They are particularly friendly towards humans and will often swim to investigate you, your kayak or your boat. See Dolphin Experience.

For a real dolphin experience try swimming with them...

The Antarctic Experience

The Giant's House Garden

SOUTH ISLAND

AKAROA
NATURE AND ACTIVITIES
Banks Peninsula Track

Millions of years ago a fiery volcano poured layer upon layer of its molten lava fingers seaward where they were reshaped by the mighty Pacific Ocean to form the Banks Peninsula. This new 2 - 4 day walking track was created by eight local families and traverses the area's old volcanic valleys and ridges, all worn with time and covered now in a patchwork of verdant pastures, freshwater streams and waterfalls. Accommodation along the way is very comfortable, quirky and full of character. This is a magical setting to walk in and a splendid contrast to the usual Great Walks for which NZ is famed.

Prices: *4-day option is $225 pp, 2-day option $150 pp.* **Contact:** *Sonia Armstrong, Akaroa;* **Tel:** *03-304-7612;* **Fax:** *03-304-7612; bankstrack@xtra.co.nz; www.bankstrack.co.nz*

Akaroa Fox Sail

Sailing on this classic 85-year-old, 50ft ketch is a really special way to experience the beauty and wildlife of Akaroa Harbour, one of two drowned volcanoes that form the Banks Peninsula and home to dolphins, seals and penguins. Sailing these protected waters is hugely popular with locals and you can see what the fuss is about on the Fox II, where you're most welcome to join the crew in a hands-on, eco-friendly sailing experience. Alternatively, let others do the thinking and sit back, relax and enjoy the sun, sea and hills.

Prices: *$50 per adult, $25 for school-age children, children under 5 go free. Private charters by arrangement. Leaving from Daly's Wharf in Akaroa 10:30am and 1:30pm from mid-Dec - May. You can book on board or at the Akaroa Information Centre.* **Contact:** *Roy and Sarah Borrelli, Akaroa Information Centre, 41 Muter Street, Akaroa;* **Tel:** *03-304-7024 or 0800 FOX SAIL (369 7245); info@akaroafoxsail.co.nz; www.akaroafoxsail.co.nz*

AKAROA
CULTURE AND HISTORY
Akaroa Guided Walks

Suky is a great guide. She's entertaining, passionate about her subject and is always dressed for the part (quite literally in her 19th-century costumes). Walk through the streets of Akaroa and study their names and buildings for clues to its past and unique French history. You'll hear tales of early whalers, Captain Langlois and many other colourful characters from whom many locals descend today. Suky also offers longer walks to the town's interesting cemeteries or half-day hiking trips into the largely open, pastoral landscape of the peninsula where the hard work of climbing all those hills is constantly rewarded with truly magnificent views.

Prices: *Guided historic walks: $30 pp for a personally-guided, one-hour walk in town streets, but make sure you pre-book. Her tour on audio guide can be hired for $10 pp from the information centre in town (open daily) without pre-booking.* **C** **ontact:** *Suky Thompson, 59 Tizzards Road, Robinsons Bay, Akaroa;* **Tel:** *03-304-7733; suky@akaroawalks.co.nz; www.akaroawalks.co.nz*

Akaroa Fox II at Sail

Akaroa Farm Tours

Spend the afternoon meeting Murray, the sixth generation of Johnses at Paua Bay, and more sheep than you can shake your wellies at. This is the place to experience real rural NZ life and to get to know the creatures that are such a big part of it. You'll watch Murray work the sheepdogs who'll work the sheep who'll then be worked upon by the sheep-shearers. Afterwards there's tea and scones in the beautiful homestead garden delightfully topping off this personal, interactive and refreshingly authentic tour.

Prices: *Adults $55 and children $35 for a two and a half hour tour, includes tea and scones.*
Contact: *Murray Johns, Paua Bay Hillcountry Farm, 113 Beach Road, Akaroa;* **Tel:** *03-304-7170;*
Fax: *03-304-7170; info@akaroafarmtours.com; www.akaroafarmtours.com*

The Giant's House and Sculpture Garden

Linton was christened 'the giant's house' when a small child, gazing up at the imposing home from the valley below, declared it must belong to a giant because it was so big. Today, surprises abound in its glorious garden. Artist Josie's elegant, abstract sculptures are a seriously playful, whimsical and flamboyant celebration of life. Welded steel sculptures and extraordinary mosaics on steps and a sculptural wall sit comfortably amongst colourful terraces of roses, vegetables, citrus fruits and flowers. This is a unique and an all-round creative feast of an experience! Come between 2pm - 4pm for a tour.

Prices: *$12 pp, $6 per child under 12.* **Contact:** *Josie Martin, 68 Rue Balguerie, Akaroa;*
Tel: *03-304-7501; info@linton.co.nz; www.linton.co.nz*

OKAINS BAY
CULTURE AND HISTORY

Okains Bay Maori and Colonial Museum

Maori and colonial history come together in this extensive and fascinating museum. The Maori artefact building houses some of its rarest objects including a sacred god stick that dates back to 1400, an 1867 war canoe and a valuable greenstone hei tiki (neck garment) recovered in England and brought back to Okains Bay by the museum''s founder. The displays of early pioneering life are great for kids, who can visit a working blacksmith''s shop, a print shop, a slab cottage and try out traditional horse-drawn gigs and carts. This really is an amazing exhibition of life in early New Zealand. Each year on the 6th February, Okains Bay commemorates the signing of Waitangi Treaty with a traditional Maori welcome and the arrival of the museum waka (or canoe).

Prices: *Adult $6, child $2. Open 10am - 5pm daily (except Christmas Day).*
Contact: *Murray Thacker, Main Road, Okains Bay, Banks Peninsula;* **Tel:** *03-304-8611;*
okains.museum@xtra.co.nz; www.bankspeninsula.com

The Banks Peninsula Shoreline

Akaroa Guided Walks

Okains Bay Museum

SOUTH ISLAND

CHRISTCHURCH
GUIDES

Meet New Zealand Vacations

Jeanette is wired with the same predilections as GG for the natural, unstuffy, humorous and unusual. Her tailor-made holidays extract the stress from having to fine-plan your trip. A New Zealander with years of tourism experience, she will discuss your likes, dislikes and holiday aims and then present you with a hassle-free, pre-booked and logistically achievable self-drive itinerary. (A lot of people need some advice on what they can comfortably do in two weeks!) To truly tap into the heart of local Kiwi hospitality there is no better person to direct you off the beaten track.

Prices: *Cost entirely dependent on each tailored tour.* **Contact:** *Jeanette Elliott, Sumner, Christchurch;* **Tel:** *021-790-054 or 03-326-7196; jeanette@meetnewzealand.co.nz; www.meetnewzealand.co.nz*

Graeme Williams Guiding

Graeme Williams, photography and birding aficionado, knows the roaming Canterbury high country, plains and coastline dale-side up and hillside down. He offers a range of photography, birding, eco-based, farm and scenic tours depending on the season and your specific interests. With Graeme's store of knowledge and a maximum group size of 4, all your exploration goals will be personally met.

Prices: *Dependent on the tour. All include a personal guide, 4WD transport, pick-up, drop-off, morning and afternoon teas and lunch.* **Contact:** *Graeme Williams, Waianiwaniwa Road, Darfield;* **Tel:** *03-318-3685;* **Fax:** *03-318-3711; graemesguiding@xtra.co.nz; www.graemesguiding.co.nz*

Jack Tregear New Zealand Tours

Tour-guide, author and historian extraordinaire Jack Tregear, is a dyed-in-the-wool Christchurch resident and direct descendant from some of Canterbury's original settlers. "What he doesn't know hasn't been done," or so say GG stalwarts Leonard and Stephanie from The Weston House. His tours cover most of the region, focusing on what life would have been like for the European settlers. And yes, there are even a couple of battlefields. Well skirmish-fields, actually.

Prices: *Dependent on the tour. E-mail for more details.* **Contact:** *Jack Tregear, 20 Birchwood Close, Prebbleton, Christchurch;* **Tel:** *03-344-5588;* **Fax:** *03-344-5588; jt@jtnztours.co.nz; www.jtnztours.co.nz*

John Morton Fishing Tours

John Morton is 'Lord of the Flies'. If fishing with bugs floats your boat, John is the most comprehensive guide to the South Island (Stewart Island included) and will compile the best fishing schedule possible. Trips dabble in both fresh and salt-water fly-fishing and span a variety of great locations. It's best to contact John direct and talk fish with him.

Prices: *$600 per day. Maximum two anglers. Angler must have own licence. All gear provided except rainwear. Fishing season runs from October - May.* **Contact:** *John Morton, Christchurch;* **Tel:** *03-332-2284; johnmorton1@clear.net.nz; www.tieaflyvideos.com*

CHRISTCHURCH
EATING AND DRINKING

Simo's Moroccan Restaurant

A Kiwi friend in the know divulged Simo's secret high-street location (which I had walked past countless times and never noticed) when he escorted our GG team to dinner. True to the Moroccan way "eating is never done alone or in a rush" so we shared the pleasure of Moroccan Simo's exquisite food for the entire evening. I ate so much I became one with my chair. Be sure to say a friendly *salaam* to chef Simo, a man whose character spreads as wide as his smile.

Prices: *Tapas $10, entrée $13 - $18, mains $29 - $34, dessert $7.50 - $12.50. Vegetarian and gluten free options available. Set menus available $55 or $65 a head.* **Contact:** *Simo Mohamed Abbari, 114 City Mall, Cashel Street, Christchurch;* **Tel:** *03-377-5001; chef@simos.co.nz; www.simos.co.nz*

Le Bon Bolli Brasserie and Restaurant

The feel of this great restaurant is of Paris at the turn of the last century. Or so I imagined as I made myself comfy in the cosy, red brasserie downstairs and ordered *coq au vin* (the best I've had - even in France) and a decadently garlicy fondue with baguette, so utterly delicious that you won't mind sleeping alone for the night. There is a fine dining restaurant upstairs too, also very French and very wonderful. This is the kind of restaurant that gets almost embarrassingly showered with awards, and justifiably so.

Prices: *Various salads, mussel dishes, bruschettas, entrements and mains from $14.50 - $32. Amazing desserts $9.50. Opening hours: Brasserie opens daily from 10am - 11pm.* **Contact:** *Cnr Worcester Boulevard & Montreal Street, Christchurch;* **Tel:** *03-374-9444; lebonbolli@xtra.co.nz; www.lebonbolli.co.nz*

Annie's Wine Bar and Restaurant

Good eclectic New Zealand food and a whole lot of wine. Annie's wine list has 50 Canterbury and hard-foraged-for New Zealand wines, all excellent and available by the glass, as well as a vast local and international cellar. The restaurant is set in an old Victorian building that now forms part of the Arts Centre. Casual yet classy, this is a place where you could relax all afternoon with a couple of chums and a few bottles of wine.

Prices: *Starters $6 - $17, entrées $15.50 - $32, mains $22 - $34, desserts $7 - $15.* **Contact:** *South Quad of the Arts Centre, Christchurch;* **Tel:** *03-365-0566;* **Fax:** *03-365-9821; annieswinebar2@ihug.co.nz*

Patch and I admire the views on one of Kate Tapley's horse treks

C'est La Vie

Simo's Moroccan Restaurant

SOUTH ISLAND

CHRISTCHURCH
EATING AND DRINKING

Curator's House Restaurant and Café

It's not just the flowers and trees that fill the air with floating aromas in Christchurch's botanical gardens. The black-beamed original Curator's House, now transformed into a charming restaurant, serves fresh-from-the-garden New Zealand food. A hint of Spain wafts from the tapas menu, which is the perfect choice for al-fresco, afternoon nibblers. These guys are dedicated to the principles of environmental sustainability, which in short, means they grow most of their own fruit and veg - you don't get much fresher than that.

Contact: *7 Rolleston Avenue, Botanic Gardens, Christchurch;* **Tel:** *03-379-2252;* **Fax:** *03-379-2258; info@curatorshouse.co.nz; www.curatorshouse.com*

Hay's Restaurant

Celia and Allan Hay do lamb like no other. They farm their own sheep at their Pigeon Bay family property and use fresh produce from local suppliers. This is innovative New Zealand cuisine spiced with a sprinkle of Asia and a dash of the Mediterranean. Trust these guys and go for the lamb special served medium rare. It may come chargrilled with a green pea coulis, white truffle oil and glazed Jersey bennies or with apricot-chutney-infused jus, roast Portobello mushrooms, mint jelly and dauphinoise potatoes... the possibilities are endless and scrumptious.

Prices: *Starters $10 - $20, mains $32 - $38, dessert approx $13.* **Contact:** *Celia Hay, 63 Victoria St, Christchurch;* **Tel:** *03-379-7501;* **Fax:** *03-366-2302; eat@foodandwine.co.nz; www.foodandwine.co.nz/hays_restaurant_christchurch_nz.htm*

Rossendale Restaurant and Winery

Set in a restored gatekeeper's lodge and within 15 minutes of Christchurch's city centre, Rossendale comes highly recommended. Pop in to quaff some of their fine Chardonnay and Pinot Noir before sampling the restaurant's extensive menu that ranges from seafood chowder to red Thai prawns. The Devonshire teas sound pretty tempting too, after all this is more English-than-England-itself Christchurch.

Prices: *Set menu from $55.* **Contact:** *168 Old Tai Tapu Road, Christchurch;* **Tel:** *03-322-9684 or 03-322-7780;* **Fax:** *03-322-9272; office@rossendale.co.nz; www.rossendale.co.nz*

The Raspberry Café

This quaint Christchurch café is a big favourite with GG owner Merrilees. You can sit outside in the sun or, if its chilly, warm your tootsies by the fire whilst sampling fresh berries, puddings and yummy cakes.

Contact: *Jane Scott, Rhodes Rd, RD2, Christchurch;* **Tel:** *03-3269-979.*

Pegasus Bay Winery

The Curator's House

Graeme Williams Guiding

Strawberry Fare

This is it... I've found it... heaven in a diner! Strawberry Fare's substantial menu spans breakfast, lunch, dinner and supper but the reason you really go there is for the desserts. Don't get me wrong, the savoury options are terrific, but the sweets... oh, the sweets will melt the heart of even the most austere pudding fanatic. It's the chocolate that got me. In fact 'the ultimate chocolate dessert' consisting of chocolate fudge brownie, chocolate mousse, chocolate ice cream, dark chocolate pâté and berry compôte. It's too wicked to eat on your own but the retro-romantic setting means two is perfect company.

Prices: *Dessert prices range from $14.50 - $17.50. Breakfast prices range from $6.50 - $17.50, lunch from $5.50 - $31.50 and evening from $5.50 - $32.50.* **Contact:** *Liz, 114 Peterborough Street, Christchurch;* **Tel:** *03-365-4897;* **Fax:** *03-377-4665; info@strawberryfare.com; www.strawberryfare.com*

CHRISTCHURCH
NATURE AND ACTIVITIES
Horse Connection NZ

Get to know your horse and let it get to know you during your pre-ride 'partnering up' session. For riders of all experience, the Natural Horsemanship (learning your horse's own language) principles by which Kate runs her horse-treks are both fascinating and rewarding to learn and apply. Though by no means fluent in horse, by the end of my ride, I did feel that we were connecting on a level more complex than simply 'you, me, go... stop!' At least, we definitely connected in appreciation for the natural beauty of the Canterbury countryside - me with my camera, my new friend Patch with his mouth. Kate has just inaugurated overnight treks, 5 days to Hanmer Springs, or overnight trips over Port Hills to Governors Bay.

Prices: *Half-day session (2.5 hrs) $90 and $40 per hour thereafter. All day (up to 6 hrs) $200. Groups of up to 6 riders. One-hour session is $50 pp. Prices double for exclusive rides with own personal guide. All equipment, tea, photos, lunch (for longer rides) provided.* **Contact:** *Kate Tapley, 543 Armagh, Christchurch;* **Tel:** *03-329-0160;* **Fax:** *03-377-1207; kate@katetapley.co.nz; www.katetapley.co.nz*

Balloon Adventures - Up Up and Away

Chris and Hal are passionate about ballooning and with 15 years experience, their enthusiasm is still on the rise. Watch as the parks, rivers and buildings fade into the distance and make way for the patchwork farmland of the Canterbury Plains. You'll be in full and stunning view of the Southern Alps to the west and the endless blue of the ocean to the east. Be prepared for a very early start, obligatory glasses of champagne and please, just don't forget your camera!

Prices: *$280 pp, $240 for children (5 - 11 yrs).*
Contact: *Chris Johnston and Hal Tapley, Unit 6, 31 Stevens Street, Christchurch;* **Tel:** *03-381-4600;* **Fax:** *03-381-4611; info@ballooning.co.nz; www.ballooning.co.nz*

Ballooning with Balloon Adventures

Christchurch Bike Tours

New Zealand's only guided city bike tour has been operating for six years in Christchurch, a (thankfully) flat and attractive city. This tour, on trusty retro-style Bauer bikes, takes you to all the highlights of the city, making the most of the abundant green spaces and cycleways. It's a great way to begin to map out the town if you are planning a longer stay, or to visit all the must-see places in the fresh air and sunshine if you're more pressed for time. Tours depart daily at 2pm (minimum of two people). November till March.

Prices: *$30 per person.* **Contact:** *Stephanie and Ben Fitts, 24a Achilles Street, Dallington, Christchurch;* **Tel:** *03-366-0337;* **Fax:** *03-366-0337; chchbiketours@yahoo.co.nz; www.chchbiketours.co.nz*

Willowbank Wildlife Reserve

You're guaranteed to see a kiwi here (I'm talking about the bird of course) - no small promise in these parts. Open till 10pm each night there are several other oddities that you might find too; wekas (unusual, famed NZ wood hen), blue ducks (rare), throat tassled kune kune pigs (one-off, origin unknown), tuataras (one of the world's closest living relatives of the dinosaurs), a pond of eels (not that rare but yucky) and most bizarrely of all 'pakehas' (Maori for white men) doing the haka and dancing with poi. The latter is explained by the interactive cultural performances that are put on each evening teaching you about the South Island's Maori, their customs and their history. Combine all this with an evening buffet for a great night out.

Prices: *Entry price to reserve children $10.50, adult $21. Ko Tane Maori Cultural Performance and Guided Tour $49 adults, $42.50 concessions, $23.70 under 15, under 5 free. Taste New Zealand evening buffet $59.* **Contact:** *Kathy Rangiwananga, 60 Hussey Road, Christchurch;* **Tel:** *03-359-6226;* **Fax:** *03-359-6212; info@willowbank.co.nz; www.willowbank.co.nz*

Christchurch Botanic Gardens

These gardens are just so pretty you could happily spend hours wandering in and out of the different sections. In fact I ran around it most days and never got bored. The jungly glasshouse is wonderful, as are the delightful aromas that float from the walled rose garden. There are loads of shaded spots under trees and several paths around the river. Floral shows and houses are open from 10.15am to 4pm daily.

Prices: *Free entry.* **Contact:** *Information Centre, Rolleston Avenue, Christchurch;* **Tel:** *03-941-7590;* **Fax:** *03-941-8267; christchurchbotanicgardens@ccc.govt.nz; www.ccc.govt.nz*

Christchurch Bike Tours

The Tranz Scenic Rail Journey

Maori Basket-weaving at Willowbank

Tranz Scenic Rail Journeys

Tranz Scenic operate two scenic spectacles of train journeys in and out of Christchurch. Widely considered one of the world's greatest rail journeys, the TranzAlpine traverses the mighty Southern Alps between Christchurch and Greymouth, beginning at the Pacific Ocean and ending by the Tasman Sea. On the way, you'll pass through a truly bewildering variety of scenery. The journey begins by crossing the flat, alluvial plains of Canterbury that end at the foothills of the mountains. From here, a system of tunnels and three huge viaducts aid your ascent up through massive gorges and valleys to reach the broad Waimakariri and Bealey river valleys high above where beech forest eventually gives way to the snowcapped peaks of the Arthur's Pass National Park. Huge skies and even bigger mountains fill the surrounding panorama and are utterly astounding. From here you'll pass through the 8.5km tunnel at the small alpine village of Arthur's Pass before making the descent down the western side past yet more valley's, lakes and rivers into Greymouth. This journey is so spectacular that it really is a shame to a) forget you camera or b) do it when the weather and thus visibility is really bad, though chances are that if it's raining on one coast, it's probably fine on the other. Another spectacularly scenic rail journey travels up the east coast from Christchurch to the port of Picton and vice versa. The journey travels through some of New Zealand's finest horticultural areas and farmland pastures. With impressive mountains to one side and the rough and rugged Pacific coastline on the other, the train passes through the seaside village of Kaikoura. If you have the time it is well worth a stop to go out onto the water and see the famous whales and dolphins close up. If time is short, chug on and you might see some of the amazing wildlife from the comfort of your own carriage. This journey is a brilliant way to cut out time on the road when arriving at or departing from ferries crossing over to the North Island.

Prices: *TranzsAlpine Christchurch - Greymouth from $109 pp rtn. Tranzcoastal Christchurch - Picton from $99 pp rtn, (from $109 for single Christchurch - Wellington which includes Interislander ferry crossings).* **Tel:** *04-495-0775;* **Fax:** *04-472-8903; bookings@tranzscenic.co.nz; www.tranzscenic.co.nz*

CHRISTCHURCH
CULTURE AND HISTORY

Canterbury Museum

Antarctic exploration, early colonial settlements, Maori life and ancient fauna are all well exhibited within this beautiful, elderly, garden-set building. Although I'm not a huge fan of taxidermy I was quite astounded to see a giant moa among other incredible stuffed creatures and insects.

Prices: *Free entry, voluntary donations are welcome.* **Contact:** *Rolleston Ave, Botanic Gardens, Christchurch;* **Tel:** *03-366-5000; www.canterburymuseum.com*

View at Hammer Springs

CHRISTCHURCH
CULTURE AND HISTORY

International Antarctic Centre

From Scott to Shackleton, explorers have long used Christchurch as a gateway to the 'Great White South'. Re-creating its atmosphere and environment, this attraction provides people with the opportunity to experience the awesome Antarctic continent in a fun, interactive way without the need for all that cold, dangerous travel and disgusting powdered food. Wander through Scott's base, peer into the eyes of crazy-looking Antarctic fish in the aquarium, see Little Blue penguins in NZ's first indoor/outdoor penguin viewing area, ride over crevices in a Hagglund amphibious vehicle, dress up in survival clothing and sit astride a skidoo or, best of all, get 'exchillerated' (their word not mine!) in the 'Antarctic Storm', a snow and ice extravaganza with stunning lightning, authentic storm audio and 40km/h winds. Blows every 30 mins, coats and over-shoe boots provided, hairbrushes afterwards are not.

Prices: *$30 adult, $25 child. Concessions and family rates apply, under 5's go free. Hagglund Ride and snow audio phone extra. Winter: April - Sept 9am - 5.30pm; $25 adult, $15 child. Summer hours: Oct - Mar 9am - 7pm.* **Contact:** *Wendy Smith, 38 Orchard Road, Christchurch;* **Tel:** *03-353-7798;* **Fax:** *03-353-7799; info@iceberg.co.nz; www.iceberg.co.nz*

Sperm Whales in Kaikoura

The nutrient-rich waters of Kaikoura are a thriving marine playground full of whales, dolphins and seals. In fact nearly half of the world's 76 species of whales and dolphins have been spotted frolicking offshore. Hector and dusky dolphins are the most common to skim the water's surface while sperm whales haunt the depths, surfacing intermittently for air and to wave a friendly flipper or tail. Feeding on a seafood cocktail of groper, shark and squid, the sperm whale is the largest toothed creature in the sea (they are HUGE!) and a year-round feature in Kaikoura's waters.

Vital Statistics

- *Its unusual box-like head contains the largest brain in the world and accounts for over a third of its body weight.*
- *They store a liquid called spermaceti in their heads which helps control their buoyancy. When the liquid cools it becomes denser and creates negative buoyancy. allowing the whale to dive down and vice versa.*
- *They can dive up to 2500m but only head to depths of 1000m in Kaikoura (still mighty impressive considering I laboured at 35m).*
- *Their steel-grey skin is ribbed and shrivelled with white patches around the lips, tail and flank that grow as they get older.*
- *Their flippers are 1.5m long and are used for breaking and steering.*
- *3 tonnes of blood pump through their massive veins.*

Marine conservation is so strict in Kaikoura that only one company is permitted to run whale-watching tours and the numbers of boats are very limited. Due to this you should try and book up well in advance and perhaps allow a couple of days leeway in case your trip is cancelled due to bad weather. Call 03-319-6767 to book a boat trip or opt for a bird's-eye viewing from a helicopter or plane. If you're extra lucky you may very well catch a glimpse of them from the shore. I was lucky enough to catch a cheeky whale-burst plume of water through a pair of binos.

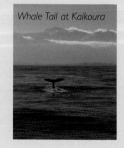

Whale Tail at Kaikoura

Christchurch Arts Centre

Every Saturday and Sunday this place comes alive when artistic types descend here to sell their wares, though the Galleria inside has open workshops daily and has a reputation as one of the best craft centres in NZ. You'll find a tremendous variety of lovely things: hand-crafted jewellery made from paua shells and greenstone, gorgeous sheepskin rugs, local artists' work and so on... all very genuine and home-grown. There are several food stalls on site at the weekends with every Asian cuisine you can imagine. One sells terrific Bavarian sausages and another Belgian waffles. The old-fashioned art-house cinema here shows a great selection of interesting films (as art-house cinemas are supposed to). Opening hours: Retail shops and galleries are open 10am - 5pm, 7 days a week. Arts and crafts market is every weekend from 10am until about 4pm.
Contact: *Worcester Boulevard, Christchurch;* **Tel:** *03-366-0989;* **Fax:** *03-379-7576; info@artscentre.org.nz; www.artscentre.org.nz*

Kaikoura Seals

I was amazed by just how close you can get to these sleek creatures at the Kaikoura seal colony. Just follow the signs from the town, wander out onto the rocks and you're there. Be aware, however, that the seals are also there and they have teeth. I almost tripped over a snoozing rock-shaped one. I narrowly avoided getting bitten - or was it yawning?

WAIPARA VALLEY
EATING AND DRINKING
Athena Olive Groves

In Greek mythology, the Goddess Athena struck the bare soil with her spear and caused an olive tree to spring up; her useful gift to the people of a city. The people were so delighted with the tree that Zeus gave Athena the city and named it after her (Athens). Equally taken with this godly fruit are the Gunn family who farm and traditionally cold-press it into some of the world's best (and Canterbury's first) extra-virgin olive oil. Book in for one of Roger's unique tours or pop in to taste and buy.
Contact: *Roger and Bronwen Gunn, 164 Mackenzies Road, Waipara Valley;* **Tel:** *03-314-6774;* **Fax:** *03-314-6074; athenaolives@ihug.co.nz; www.athenaolives.co.nz*

Pohatu Penguin Habitat - penguins in sea cave

Pegasus Bay Winery and Restaurant

After living, breathing, making, tasting, studying, writing about and judging wine since the early 1970's the Donaldson family seriously know their stuff and have the credentials to prove it. You can sample the juice borne of the fruits of their labour at their winery in Pegasus Bay. Better still, indulge in the total food and wine experience at their restaurant. The delicious menu is created around the wine list with each dish perfectly matched to a suggested wine.

Contact: *The Donaldson Family, Stockgrove Road, Amberley, Waipara;* **Tel:** *03-314-6869;* **Fax:** *03-314-6861; info@pegasusbay.com; www.pegasusbay.com*

HAWARDEN
EATING AND DRINKING

Hurunui River Wines

Trundling off the track is well worth it for this small-scale winery. The vineyard is part of a larger sheep and cattle farm so you can drink up the true Canterbury countryside whilst swigging free samples of home-brewed wine. The dinky café serves a superb antipasto platter and cheese or breadboards, a perfect accompaniment to a sunny afternoon and a bottle of wine. If a cold beer or coffee and cake is more your thing you won't be disappointed. A playground, sandpit and pétanque pitch provide entertainment for under-age younglings and young-at-heart grown-ups.

Contact: *Wendy Alabaster and Mark Hassall, 110 Costellos Road, Hawarden;* **Tel:** *03-314-4495;* **Fax:** *03-314-4496; sales@hurunuiriver.co.nz; www.hurunuiriver.co.nz*

Kaikoura

The Maori named kai (to eat) koura (crayfish) because its waters were filled with rock lobster that were particularly good to eat. This crustaceous delicacy still tastes just as good today and can be enjoyed from most eateries in Kaikoura. A few small establishments dotted along the coastal drive between Kaikoura and Kekerengu literally cook crayfish fresh from the boat. Nin's Bin, a small takeaway, boil them in natural mineral water - no preservatives, additives or flavour enhancers, just fresh, organic crayfish.

HANMER
EATING AND DRINKING

The Old Post Office Restaurant

Gone are the days when brown paper packages tied up with string used to pass through the hands of the post office staff. Now the fully-converted restaurant ensures that food (one of my favourite things) is signed, sealed and delivered to your place mat. The classic New Zealand cuisine, specialising in lamb and beef, remains in tune with the historic surroundings and is excellent.

Contact: *Michael, 2 Jacks Pass Rd, Hanmer Springs;* **Tel:** *03-315-7461.*

Hapuku Lodge Restaurant

Dolphins at Kaikoura

French Farm Winery

Malabar Restaurant

Entirely unique and renowned for its impeccable service and quality, the Malabar is primarily distinguished by its traditional-twist dishes. A team of chefs from across the world bring together the best of Europe, India, South-East Asia and the Middle East to form a taste-sensational menu. Asian fusion/Indian dining is how they describe it.

Prices: *Entrées from $14 - $17 and mains from $24 - $34.* **Contact:** *Sudip Misra and Christina Tseng, 5 Conical Hill Road, Alpine Pacific Centre, Hanmer Springs;* **Tel:** *03-315-7745;* **Fax:** *03-315-7745; malabarltd@xtra.co.nz*

Rustic Café and Tapas Bar

A family-run café that excels in coffee, cakes and nibbly eats. Perch outside on wooden tables and plough your way through a multitude of tapas-style dishes while enjoying Hanmer's unique alpine village vibe. Well, that's what I used to do each time I took a break from driving the Lewis Pass (which equated to quite a few times after 4 months). Even if you're just passing by it's worth the 10-minute drive from the main highway. Go on... we all need a coffee break sometimes (that was my excuse anyway).

Contact: *Stacey Stewart, 8 Conical Hill Road, Hanmer Springs;* **Tel:** *03-315-7274; rustic2005@xtra.co.nz*

HANMER
NATURE AND ACTIVITIES

Hanmer Springs Thermal Pools and Spa

Visitors have been soaking in the thermal waters in this alpine village for 125 years, and in recent years they have received plaudits after plaudits. The hot spring water mixes with freshwater to produce pools of varying temperature (32°C - 42°C), so you can pick the perfect pool for soaking that old war wound, or just for relaxing. Your watery options are endless: landscaped rock pools, sulphur pools, a 25m freshwater lap pool, family activity area and more. Splash away as long as you can!

Prices: *Adult $12, child $6. 10am - 9pm daily. Health and beauty treatments are offered, prices vary according to treatment.* **Contact:** *Scott Callaway, Amuri Avenue, Hanmer Springs;* **Tel:** *03-315-0000; info@hanmersprings. co.nz; www.hanmersprings.co.nz*

The View from a Hanmer Springs Pool

SOUTH ISLAND

HANMER
NATURE AND ACTIVITIES

Hanmer Air

Why walk when you can fly? Jackie Frame offers an aerial perspective over some of the South Island's most dramatic scenery. With over 14 years piloting experience and a passion for New Zealand's natural beauty, Jackie will tailor a trip that treats you to the best mountain-filled views.

Prices: *20-minute flights, adult $95, child $80; 50 - 60 minutes, adult $185, child $155.* **Contact:** *Jackie Frame, Culverden, Hanmer Springs;* **Tel:** *027-435-9810;* **Fax:** *03-315-8143; hanmerair@xtra.co.nz; www.hanmerair.co.nz*

Hanmer Springs Adventure Centre

Hanmer Springs can be a relaxing spa town for a gentle weekend break - or it can be a bit of an adventure capital. These guys will help you out with the latter. They have information on and can organise bookings for various outdoor pursuits that people like to thrill themselves with. They rent out equipment for mountain biking, fishing, skiing and snowboard gear (the nearest slope is 17km away). Open 9am - 5pm.

Contact: *20 Conical Hill Road, Hanmer Springs;* **Tel:** *03-315-7233; info@ hanmeradventure.co.nz; www.hanmeradventure.co.nz*

KAIKOURA
GUIDES

Maori Tours Kaikoura

I heard so much praise and received so many recommendations for these guys it was no surprise, on meeting Heather and Maurice, to find they are truly lovely. This is an unpretentious experience that gives a rare insight into modern-day Maori living. Big on information, revelations and fun, but small on numbers, this cultural exchange is personal and completely individual.

Prices: *Adult $99, child (up to and including 15 yrs) $55.* **Contact:** *Heather and Maurice Manawatu;* **Contact:** *10 Churchill Street, Kaikoura;* **Tel:** *03-319-5567;* **Fax:** *03-319-5573; info@maoritours.co.nz; www.maoritours.co.nz*

KAIKOURA
EATING AND DRINKING

Hapuku Lodge Restaurant

Looking up from the rustic wooden tables in Hapuku Lodge's native garden, the view of Kaikoura's spectacular mountains is stunning. With its coastal position and deer-mown grassy surround it's not surprising that the restaurant at Hapuku Lodge specialises in venison and local seafood (including live crayfish). Formerly an award-winning cafe, this restaurant continues to use the finest local and organic produce and the result is pure and simple - a great meal in a beautiful place.

Prices: *3- to 4- course set menu: $75 per person.* **Contact:** *Rod and Belinda Ramsay; State Highway 1 at Station Road, 12 km north of Kaikoura;* **Tel:** *03-319-6559;* **Fax:** *03-319-6557; info@hapukulodge.com; www.hapukulodge.com*

Hislops Café

So it is possible for healthy to be tasty! Hislops Café excels in everything wholesome: home-made soup of the day arrives steaming alongside a slice of Hislops' wholemeal bread (made with the finest, fresh-milled flour), while warm wood-roasted salmon reclines on a bed of pumpkin and kumara rosti. The list of fresh, organic flavours and produce goes on. I stopped here every single time I passed through Kaikoura, not because I'm particularly healthy, quite the contrary in fact - I couldn't resist the fab coffee and cakes.

Prices: *Breakfast $5.50 - $18; lunch $14.90 - $22.50; dinner, entrées $5 - $15.50, mains $16.50 - $39, desserts $10.50 - $13.50. Prices an indication only.* **Contact:** *Paul Hislop, 33 Beach Road, Kaikoura;* **Tel:** *03-319-6971;* **Fax:** *03-319-7516; cafe@hislops-wholefoods.co.nz; www.hislops-wholefoods.co.nz*

Niaroo Café

Set in a lush garden centre, Niaroo Café is quite a find in the farming town of Levin. I sat in the sun and lapped up some tasty 'Eggs Montreal': poached eggs and salmon on sourdough bread washed down with a strong long-black. The waitresses were friendly and owner Mark Cohen's menu extensive. The chocolate cake looked especially gooey and tempting... if only I'd had room.

Prices: *$14.50 for coffee and 'Eggs Montreal'.* **Contact:** *Mark Cohen, 4 Buller Rd, Levin, Kaikoura;* **Tel:** *06-368-0187; marioworldwide@hotmail.com*

Sheep-shearer in action

Green Dolphin Restaurant and Bar

Matt has inherited Mum (and chef) Faye's special recipes and refined them with his own food-loving stamp. The Green Dolphin looks out over the rocky bay of Kaikoura and is always aglow with cheerful customers and staff. The unfalteringly fine seafood is an obvious choice here with famous Kaikoura crayfish picked fresh from the sea. Matt cooks it to perfection and you'll eat it to perfection after a briefing on how to dismantle it with perfection from a bubbly waiter. Happiness breeds happiness at the Green Dolphin and you will eat each lovingly-prepared mouthful with a smile on your lips.

Contact: *Matt Marshall, 12 Avoca Street, Kaikoura;* **Tel:** *03-319-6666; greendolphinkaikoura@xtra.co.nz*

Nins Bin

Sea-fresh crayfish served from a caravan by the side of the road, overlooking the wild Pacific Ocean. You don't get much more real than this. Carry on the State Highway One north of Kaikoura that hugs the rugged coast. After a 15-minute drive, you'll come to a lay-by on your right-hand side. Stop, enjoy the scenery and wolf down some rich, fleshy crayfish. Delicious.

KAIKOURA
NATURE AND ACTIVITIES

The Kaikoura Coast Track

All you need is a good pair of boots and a reasonable degree of fitness. Sally and David have covered everything else. Whilst you tramp the 3 days of bush, beach and remote farmland you'll only worry about whether your camera will have enough view-capturing memory. At each farm-stay a smiling, knowledgeable host will greet you with your pre-delivered bags while a hot shower awaits. By offering such an insight into rural Kiwi life, the Kaikoura Coast Track is full-on tramping with a twist.

Price: *3-day tramp $160 pp includes bag transport, guide booklet and map, safe car park and farm stay accommodation with self-catering facilities. 2-day mountain biking: $70 pp. Bring your own food and sleeping bag. Meals and linen available by prior arrangement.* **Contact:** *Sally and David Handyside, Medina, Cheviot, Kaikoura;* **Tel:** *03-319-2715; sally@kaikouratrack.co.nz; www.kaikouratrack.co.nz*

Encounter Kaikoura

You must book well in advance to bag yourself a space on one of these very special and emotionally charged tours. Strict conservation regulations are in place to protect Kaikoura's dusky dolphin colony but, with exclusive rights to these dazzling creatures, 'Dolphin Encounter' will boat you right up to the action. Whether you watch from on board or snorkel up, jump in and join them, is up to you. For the more bird-brained 'Albatross Encounter' focuses on the rugged Kaikoura coastline and its spirited society of feathered, and often endangered, friends. Coming face to face with an albatross is an experience you certainly won't forget in a hurry. Also, there's a café on site for pre/post-trip nibbles.

Prices: *Dolphin Encounter: watching $65 (child $55), swimming $130 (child $120). Albatross Encounter: adult $80, child $40.* **Contact:** *Lynette Buurman, 96 Esplanade, Kaikoura;* **Tel:** *03-319-6777;* **Fax:** *03-319-6534; info@encounterkaikoura.co.nz; www.encounterkaikoura.co.nz*

Glenstrae Farm 4-Wheeler Adventures

Alastair and Anita have spiced up the Kaikoura coast with a good dash of adrenaline. All safety gear, full instruction, tremendous location and, of course, your own set of wheels are provided. You just have to put it all together, hang on tight and keep your eyes open. The trip is eco-conscious too and you will learn about the dramatic coastline, rugged reef, beaches and seal colony - all of which you get to see (eyes open remember...). The 8-wheel Argo Tour (a bit like a mini, open-top tank) is also available and is suitable for kids.

Prices: *Guided ATV tour $110 per adult (departs 8:30am and 1pm). Argo tour $60 per adult, $25 per child (departs 9:30 am and 1:30pm).* **Contact:** *Alastair and Anita, Glenstrae Farm, SH1, Kaikoura;* **Tel:** *03-319-7021 or freephone 0800-004-009 (within New Zealand);* **Fax:** *03-319-7023; info@4wheeladventures.co.nz; www.4wheeladventures.co.nz*

The Kaikoura Coast Track

Otago

North Island

South Island

Otago

Highlights

• Spend an afternoon on the Otago Penisula outside Dunedin where you'll come across royal albatrosses, rare yellow-eyed penguins and noisy (and rather stinky) sea lions.

• Wander through the streets of architecturally rich Dunedin and, after noting its uncanny resemblance to parts of Edinburgh, grab a great cup of coffee in one of the many cafés for which it is now famed.

• Walk, bike or ride the Otago Rail Trail following old train-tracks through historic mining towns over vast tussock plains and under widescreen skies.

• Escape the kerfuffle of Queenstown and take the stunning 40-minute drive to the head of Lake Wakatipu to the tiny, picturesque hamlet of Glenorchy. Here you can be tranquil, ride horses, jet-boat or walk in the Dart Valley amid spectacular mountain scenery. If you've time for a proper tramp, the Routeburn and Rees-Dart Tracks are truly excellent.

• Pick your favourite bottle of pinot noir, Central Otago's speciality grape, from among the many at vineyards in and around Bannockburn, Queenstown and Wanaka.

• Make the most of the ridiculously beautiful scenery around Lake Wanaka. Get a 'lakeside tracks' map, hire a bike, pack a picnic and get peddling.

• Queenstown and Wanaka act as a great base for some of the best skiing/boarding in the Southern Alps. If you ever needed a reason to visit NZ in winter (June-Sept) this is it.

otago

MOERAKI
EATING AND DRINKING
Fleur's Place

There is no place like Fleur's. Praised by locals and foodies alike (Cuisine magazine recently voted the restaurant in the top 100 'things' in NZ), this is a fantastic owner-run seafood restaurant where all pretence is firmly left at the door and the food is left to speak for itself. The freshest ingredients are caught, picked, baked and smoked from the premises and people travel miles for naturally great food and Fleur's warm and generous hospitality. Sitting on the harbour's jetty with the sea to three sides, I sat tickled by my find, refreshed by the sea air and nourished by the best bouillabaisse south of Marseille... my favourite restaurant in NZ by a long nautical mile.

Prices: *Entrée soups from $12 through to mains from $22.50 to $34. Desserts are around $10.50 and coffee $3.50.* **Contact:** *Fleur Sullivan, 169 Haven Street, Moeraki;* **Tel:** *03-439-4480;* **Fax:** *03-439-4481; mail@fleursplace.com; www.fleursplace.com*

Moeraki Boulders

Moeraki is renowned for the intriguing, spherical boulders found strewn along its beach. They can be seen emerging from cliffs and slowly disappearing into the sand and the sea, the most perfect examples of their kind found anywhere in the world. Scientific history says the boulders were formed over many, many years, somewhere in the region of 65 million in fact. Starting off as lime crystals underground, they attracted other minerals around them eventually to form the boulder shape. Then, crystallisation of calcium and carbonates changed particles in the muddy undersea sediments gradually forcing the rounded boulders upwards and onto the surface, where you'll find them now.

But they also have a human history that is only a few hundred years old. Some 1,000 years ago, whilst searching for precious stones, the great voyaging Arai-te-uru canoe and its crew were shipwrecked. The boulders represent the traditional food baskets onboard containing kumara, gourds and calabashes (traditional Maori food) that were washed ashore. Some of the crew reached safety, but others were overtaken by dawn and turned into hills nearby that bear their names.

Whichever is your chosen version, do stop off to break up your journey, walk along the beach to have a look and, most importantly, work up a hearty appetite for lunch at the fabulous Fleur's Place, five minutes away in the village's harbour.

SOUTH ISLAND

DUNEDIN
EATING AND DRINKING

Bisztro In the Villa

Set in a turn-of-the-century villa this is the kind of restaurant you might hope to find in a small French or Italian town. Karl and Darlene specialize in 'slow-cooking', old-world-style food and Bisztro has quickly become a local favourite. Rich and creamy smoked pork cheeks with kumara and moi-moi mash is quite notoriously wicked (in a very good way), as too is the lemon tart with star-anise praline crumbs. There's a big fire inside and a bar nicely set in the quiet backdrop of native trees and ferns.

Prices: *Starters $9.50 - $14, mains $21 - $29, desserts $10.50. Closed on Sunday and Monday.* **Contact:** *Karl and Darlene Toth, 95 Filluel Street, Dunedin;* **Tel:** *03-471-9265; adrema.bisztro@xtra.co.nz*

Tandoori Palace

It's hard to find a decent curry in New Zealand. Happily Kirit and his team of top Indian chefs serve up some of the best tandooris, jalfrezis, pasandas et al in the country. Try one of the non-traditional dishes such as a 'chicken anarkali', especially tangy with chopped onion, tomato and pomegranate. Saucy.

Prices: *Mains from $11 - $22.* **Contact:** *Kirit Gandhi, 18 Mailer Street, Mornington, Dunedin;* **Tel:** *03-453-1132; info@tandooripalace.co.nz; www.tandooripalace.co.nz*

The Rush for Gold

The Otago Gold Rush began in 1861 with the discovery of the precious metal by the banks of the Tuapeka River near present-day Lawrence. Though gold had been found previously on the Coromandel Peninsula and in Nelson, and later on the West Coast, Otago was the site of New Zealand's biggest strike. A trickle of prospectors from Europe, Australia and China and beyond fast became a flood, and soon thousands were braving hot, dry summers, cold, harsh winters and starvation in search of a quick fortune. This led to the rapid expansion and commercialisation of the new settlement of Dunedin, which for a time became the country's largest and most prosperous city.

Nova Café

Sometimes all you need is a nice, casual café with good, wholesome comfort food. Enter Nova Café, right next to the art gallery; it serves up really good nosh day and night. There's no need to pre-book so you can be as spontaneous as you wish.

Contact: *29 The Octagon, Dunedin;* **Tel:** *03-479-0808; novacafe@extra.co.nz*

Plato

Firstly, hats off to whoever came up with the name - I'm still chuckling! The Plato building once played host to seafarers around the world, so it's fitting that nowadays it lays on some of the best seafood in Dunedin. A quick skim down the menu leaves any self-respecting foodie drooling: baby flounder grenobloise, king prawns with a mizuna salad and local clams steamed in their shells. Plus there's the prerequisite freshly-baked ciabattas to dip in all those lovely seafood juices. I loved the 1950's crockery as well, a perfect fit with the retro surroundings. Dinner: Monday to Sunday from 6pm; brunch / lunch on Sundays from 11am.

Prices: *Main courses between $23 and $29.* **Contact:** *Nigel Broad, 2 Birch Street, Dunedin;* **Tel:** *03-477-4235; plato@platocafe.co.nz; www.platocafe.co.nz*

Table Se7en Restaurant & Bar

The atmosphere is buzzing and funky and the food is excellent, bang up-to-date, Pacific Rim-meets-Mediterranean: chilli prawns, pork belly and, according to one GG owner, the presentation is "amazing". Monday - Saturday: lunch 12 - 3pm; dinner from 6pm.

Prices: *Around $100 for a three-course dinner and wine.* **Contact:** *Michael Wilson, Cnr George & Hanover Streets, Dunedin;* **Tel:** *03-477-6877; tableseven@xtra.co.nz*

The birds of Otago Peninsula

Royal albatrosses

The sight of a soaring albatross is unforgettable. With wings up to 3m across these majestic birds can swoop to speeds of more than 70 mph. Usually albatrosses breed on remote, storm-bound islands, but the mainland colony on the Otago Peninsula at Taiaroa Head is the only one of its kind in the world.

Though graceful on the wing, albatrosses are distinctly clumsy on the ground. The social and family life of the breeding colony is fascinating. From the moment the eggs, weighing up to 500 grams, are laid during the first few weeks of November, a pair of albatrosses will nurture the egg and chick for a period lasting some 300 days. Despite long separations at sea, these 'marriages' normally last for life, and they are long ones too. One bird was known to lay its egg at the grand age of 62! It is not until the following September that the young albatross wanders from its nesting ground to test its outstretched wings and eventually take off with the aid of a strong wind.

The Royal Albatross Centre at Taiaroa is a great place to learn more about these intriguing birds and to see the colony in action from the observatory. The centre is open daily all year except Christmas Day. Prior bookings for tours are essential. Contact them on 09-478-0499 or email reservations@albatross.org.nz.

And yellow-eyed penguins...

"The birds made a wet day sunny," says one happy visitor to the albatrosses' neighbours on the peninsula, the world's rarest penguin. The Yellow-Eyed Penguin Reserve offers the best viewing in New Zealand with over 1km of tracks and underground walkways that link 15 viewing hides. Professional guides with the very popular Twilight Wildlife Tours in Dunedin will explain the scenic beauty and wildlife of the area and get you in the right places at the right time for photographic opportunities. Contact Wild South on 03-474-3300 or at wildsouth@clear. net.nz. www.wilddunedin.co.nz.

DUNEDIN
NATURE AND ACTIVITIES

College of Natural Therapies

I like to think of myself as a well-maintained woman. But why is it that every time I walk into my local beautician's I feel like the progeny of an unfortunate liaison between Cruella De Ville and Worzel Gummidge? Well ladies, help is at hand with The College of Natural Therapies. The antithesis of a clinical therapist's over-chromed shop, this happy, friendly company set in a rustic cottage easily fits into that overused marketing term: 'off the beaten track'. But more importantly, anyone and everyone will feel at home.

Prices: *From $30.* **Contact:** *Sandra Poole, 40 Clyde St, Roseneath, Dunedin;* **Tel:** *03-472-7347; lotuscollege@paradise.net*

St Clair Beach

Yes, yes, we know... Dunedin is the Edinburgh of the south, and so on and so forth. But the beaches really are quite pleasant during summer or so I've heard, St Clair especially. Apparently a lot of people don't realise there's a beach there, which is good for those of us who do! And to make matters even better, there's a saltwater pool that's heated throughout summer. And when you get peckish, there's a café with the most munch-able pizzas in Dunedin.

DUNEDIN
CULTURE AND HISTORY

Olveston

"Olveston is an eloquent expression of one man's dream," says the flyer. Recommended by all locals I came by, this historic house offers an intimate glimpse of the life-style of a privileged family in the early 1900's. It reflects a way of life enjoyed by just a few, but that represents a most important piece in the mosaic of early New Zealand life as a whole. Wander through the gardens before exploring the decorative detail of its Jacobean style, grace and grandeur.

Prices: *One-hour tours are $15 for adults and $6 for school-age children.* **Contact:** *Grant Barron, 42 Royal Terrace, Dunedin;* **Tel:** *03-477-3320;* **Fax:** *03-479-2094; olveston@xtra.co.nz; www.olveston.co.nz*

Larnach Castle

If I tell you that this is New Zealand's only castle, built in 1871, you probably won't be that impressed. (Although it is old enough, I am told, to house a resident ghost). And yes, you will have seen older and more authentic castles elsewhere, but not many will have boasted such a beautiful setting as this one, right on the stunning Otago Peninsula just outside town. This is a great place to stop by for tea while exploring the peninsula and there is always something worth seeing in its renowned and beautiful garden.

Prices: *Castle including grounds: $20 adult, $10 children (5 - 14). Gardens and grounds: $10 adult, $3 children.* **Contact:** *Sophie Barker, 145 Camp Road, Otago Peninsula, Dunedin;* **Tel:** *03-476-1616;* **Fax:** *03-476-1574; larnach@larnachcastle.co.nz; www.larnachcastle.co.nz*

Larnach Castle

otago

ALEXANDRA
EATING AND DRINKING
Blues Lounge

The Blues Lounge is everything a café should be with a wonderfully warm and friendly atmosphere, funky orange retro furniture and a menu that serves up the best gumbo stew this side of New Orleans. The kumara and chicken soup was pretty memorable as well, especially when eaten during one of the worst snowstorms in living memory! The artwork and wine is local and the staff double-up as musicians during the evening jamming sessions. Definitely worth a stop if you're passing through this sleepy, rural town.

Prices: *Soup of the day: $9.50.* **Contact:** *49 Centennial Drive, Alexandra;* **Tel:** *03-448-5959; booking@blues-lounge.co.nz; www.blues-lounge.co.nz*

ALEXANDRA
NATURE AND ACTIVITIES
Altitude Adventures

Alexandra is the unofficial capital of South Island mountain biking and if you're looking for a guide Altitude Adventures take groups along the track and trails etched into the hills by the hardy 1860 pioneers. Unfortunately, the temperature was below zero when I visited so no bicycle clips for me. But from spring onwards this really is the best way to see the wild, mountainous landscape of Central Otago.

Prices: *From $85.* **Contact:** *88 Centennial Avenue, Alexandra;* **Tel:** *03-448-8917; phil@altitudeadventures.co.nz; http://www.tourism.net.nz/listings/jump/attractions-and-activities*

ALEXANDRA
CULTURE AND HISTORY
Clutha River Cruises

Whispers of gold, greed and hard times permeate through the Roxburgh Gorge. Aussie Steve has a passion that will keep you enthralled as he presents the rocky dwellings, Chinese wild thyme and the most ancient orchid known to man that all bear witness to the gold-mining rush that once ripped through these parts. The setting is spectacular, the boat super-swish and the wine fully flowing as you cruise through the history and isolation of mining life. Fascinating stuff.

Prices: *$95 pp. Includes refreshments midway through tour.* **Contact:** *Steve Toyer, Alexandra;* **Tel:** *021-355-489; clutharivercruises@xtra.co.nz*

Dux de Lux

Mediterranean Market

Olveston

CLYDE
NATURE AND ACTIVITIES

Otago Central Rail Trail

Tie up your boats, saddle up your horse or pump up those bicycle tyres to retrace the route of the former Otago Central Branch railway line from Middlemarch to historic Clyde. Fairly new to the tramping 'scene', those in the know rave about this 3-7 (depending on speed and mode) day journey that's steeped in a sense of history and remoteness allowing you to gaze at scenery the highways never reach. To top this, it has also preserved, largely intact, the railway line - an important part of the area's heritage. For information on accommodation, facilities and services contact an i-site branch in the area.
Contact: *Alexandra Visitor Centre, Centennial Avenue, Clyde;* **Tel:** *03-448-9515;*
Fax: *03-440-2061; alexandra@centralotagonz.com; www.otagocentralrailtrail.co.nz*

The Bungy

It all started with the people of Vanuatu in the Pacific who have been throwing themselves from huge towers for centuries, with nothing more than a few vines tied to their feet. It was this ancient ritual that inspired the Oxford University Dangerous Sports Club to try a few experimental jumps in the late 1970s. And then, seeing the club's video, New Zealander AJ Hackett teamed up with fellow speed skier (and adrenaline-junkie) Henry van Asch to develop the bungy into the ritual it is today. Kawarau Bridge outside Queenstown was the world's first full-time site.

When AJ Hackett dived off the Eiffel Tower back in 1987, suspended by a rubber cord strapped to his ankles, the bungy legend was born, and has been going strong ever since.

So, go ahead if you've the stomach for it. It is very safe, I'm told. And you will not regret it... I'm told. I, for one, am just too busy to quite get round to fitting one in... shame. But even if you don't get to do the jump you can still find out what happens behind the scenes. A 45-minute interactive 'Secrets of Bungy Tour' at the original Kawarau Bridge will take you on a fascinating cinematic adventure and then give you exclusive access to the bungy viewing deck.

And if this is ample time to justify the decision that taking the leap is maybe not for you, you can head over to the lovely Winehouse & Kitchen Restaurant and Wine Cellar down the way for some far more refined tippling, followed by lunch. A morning's 'bungying' never sounded so pleasant.

Secrets of Bungy Tour: $40 pp, includes transport from Queenstown. Off State Highway 6, Gibbston. Tel: 0800-286-493; www.bungy.co.nz.

The Secrets of Bungy Tour

CROMWELL
EATING AND DRINKING

Freeway Orchard

Just off the highway into Cromwell, this is the largest fruit stall in 'orchard country' Central Otago. An extensive array of local produce from apples and pears to peaches and persimmons are piled high, ripe for picking. There are ice creams, juices and wheatgrass shots as well as a few more local delights - fresh tamarillos, dried kiwi fruit, fancy scroggin' and feijoa jam to name but a few - that must be tried.

Contact: *Jill Checketts, Highway 8b, Cromwell;* **Tel:** *03-445-1500;* **Fax:** *03-445-1508; freewayorchard@ihug.co.nz; www.freewayorchard.co.nz*

The Big Picture

No other wine-tasting experience is quite like this. Catch a virtual flight in the auditorium to take in the wineries of Otago in one fell, drive-free swoop. Soar across the Otago landscape, its grassy plains, surging rivers and rugged hills before banking up past ridged vines as you fly over Bannockburn's vineyards. Touch down at the wine-makers' and view the stunning scenery that makes this region so geographically unique, with, thankfully, five real glasses of world-renowned local wines to sample along the way. And then there's the aroma room, lined with silver stoppers coated in scents relating to different wines, the object being to identify each one. Finally, to complete your sensory journey, enjoy a delicious post-flight meal in the next-door restaurant, choosing wine from your favourite vineyard to go with it.

Contact: *Phil and Cath Parker, Cnr Sandflat Road and State Highway 6, Cromwell;* **Tel:** *03-445-4052;* **Fax:** *03-445-4053; info@wineadventures.co.nz; www.wineadventures.co.nz*

Central Otago Farmers' Market

The market wasn't running when I visited in deepest, snow-covered winter, but as it comes highly recommended, it really should be mentioned. Set in the fertile heartland of Central Otago, you could spend a happy day here under the South Island's wide blue skies; buying, and eating, local cherries and apricots, and gossiping with locals over the lunchtime BBQ before taking some fresh fish home for a slap-up supper. Takes place on the 1st and 3rd Sunday of the month (Sept to Easter) 9 am - 1 pm; every Sunday in January.

Contact: *Jane Shaw, Cromwell Old Town, info@provisions.co.nz*

QUEENSTOWN
EATING AND DRINKING

Wine Tastes Central Otago

Connoisseurs, quaffers and teetotal gadget geeks will all love this brilliant, state-of-the-art 'try before you buy' wine tasting innovation. Simply put credit on your wine card and work the room, bottle to bottle to bottle to bottle... sipping, sampling or sloshing your way through the 80 wines (including 24 specialty pinot noirs) on display. You should be a veritable wine buff (in theory) by the time you've exhausted your card. If not I'd suggest redoubling your efforts with a top-up.

Prices: *purchases can be made at any value the customer wishes to load on their card.*
Contact: *Chrissy Schreiber, 14 Beach Street, Queenstown;* **Tel:** *03-409-2226;* **Fax:** *03-409-2290; queenstown@winetastes.com; www.winetastes.co.nz*

SOUTH ISLAND

Queenstown Wine Trail

Yes, yes, we all know that Queenstown is a party town full of raucous twenty-one year-olds. But for the more refined amongst us, it is also home to some of the best small-scale wineries in Central Otago - you just need to look at the indecently ruby roadside berries to know that there is fire in that soil. Under the tutelage of Kevin and the young, resolutely non-snooty vineyard staff, we visited Gibbston Valley, Peregrine, Watiri Creek and Amisfield, tasting their well-marinated pinot noirs (Central Otago's grape of choice) as well as a host of other goodies from the cellar. Queenstown Wine Trail operate daily wine tours and also organise private tours.

Prices: *$99 - $285 pp.* **Contact:** *Heather McDonald, Queenstown;* **Tel:** *03-442-3799;* **Fax:** *03-442-3796; info@queenstownwinetrail.co.nz; www.queenstownwinetrail.co.nz*

QUEENSTOWN
EATING AND DRINKING

Wai Waterfront Restaurant

Under the watchful gaze of the Remarkables mountain range, this elegant seafood restaurant by the lake is perfect for both alfresco summer lunches and après-ski cosy suppers by the fire. Their famous Bluff Oyster menu is Wai's trump card but chef Martin's philosophy for well-prepared, simple food, make all dishes hugely popular with locals, Greenwood Guides and critics alike.

Prices: *Entrées $16 - $25, mains $29 - $41. Chef's 7-course degustation menu with wine is $155, without $100. Oysters are market price.* **Contact:** *Jan Rae-Robertson, Absolute Waterfront, Steamer Wharf, Beach Street, Queenstown;* **Tel:** *03-442-1405;* **Fax:** *03-442-1405; info@wai.net.nz; www.wai.net.nz*

Amisfield Winery & Bistro

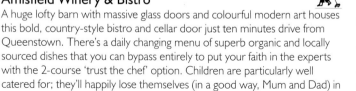

A huge lofty barn with massive glass doors and colourful modern art houses this bold, country-style bistro and cellar door just ten minutes drive from Queenstown. There's a daily changing menu of superb organic and locally sourced dishes that you can bypass entirely to put your faith in the experts with the 2-course 'trust the chef' option. Children are particularly well catered for; they'll happily lose themselves (in a good way, Mum and Dad) in the big box of toys and nice garden.

Prices: *Lunches between $9.50 and $27 a dish, desserts $12.50. 'Trust the chef' menu $45 per person, minimum 2 people.* **Contact:** *10 Lake Hayes Road, Queenstown;* **Tel:** *03-442-0556;* **Fax:** *03-442-0553; bistro@amisfield.co.nz; www.amisfield.co.nz*

The Winehouse & Kitchen

Peering over a gorge, the setting of this farmhouse style restaurant and cellar door is sensational. Find your sunny spot in the garden and share one of their delicious 'platters for two' washed down with its suggested wine companion. Between courses, venture further down the gorge to watch brave souls jump off the NZ's original bungy bridge.

Prices: *Food (something light to platters for two): $13 - $48. Wine: glass $6 - $15; bottle $20 - $50.* **Contact:** *Rapid No 1963 (Kawarau Bungy Centre car park), State Highway 6, Gibbston, Queenstown;* **Tel:** *03-442-7310;* **Fax:** *03-442-7317; kirsten@winehouse.co.nz; www.winehouse.co.nz*

Vudu Cafe

Vudu was my spiritual home in Queenstown. When they closed for a refurb on my last day, I felt a genuine sense of loss. This wonderfully friendly and relaxed café made the best porridge with stewed fruit and molasses, and the house pinot noir wasn't bad either (porridge and wine were not consumed together, I hasten to add). The décor was funky, the music chilled, and I loved the neighbourhood noticeboard full of yoga classes and organic food markets.

Prices: *$9.50 for soup of the day.* **Contact:** *23 Beach St, Queenstown;* **Tel:** *03-442-5347;*
Fax: *03-442-5357; admin@vudu.co.nz; www.vudu.co.nz*

Mediterranean Market

The freshest, the finest and the most diverse are attributes that keenly describe products in this wonderful market shop, deli and café. Everything is in-store here from piles and piles of just-picked fruit and veg, obscure 'what's that?' Japanese products to more familiar local pinots and imported Italians. The best markets are sourced, the finest meats and cheeses are imported, breads are baked and salads and their condiments are prepared daily to kit out the most cosmopolitan of picnic hampers and platters. Deli-icious!

Contact: *53 Robins Road, Queenstown;* **Tel:** *03-442-4161;* **Fax:** *033-442-4162;*
shop@mediterranean.co.nz; www.mediterranean.co.nz

Walk to the Skyline Gondola and Restaurant

This is a steep but hassle-free walk that's guaranteed to turn your cheeks rosy red - just don't get lost like yours truly! From Shotover St, turn right onto Brecon St and you will come to the gondola station. There is a walking track on the left-hand side that takes you on a steep incline through pine forest. The views across Queenstown and Lake Wakatipu are pretty special and I'm told the gondola ride down is fun, though unfortunately I never made it! The restaurant was closed when I visited as well, but I'm inclined to believe the website's boast that this is 'the best spot in Queenstown to watch the sun go down!'

Prices: *Gondola Price: $20.* **Contact:** *Brecon Street, Queenstown;* **Tel:** *03-441-0101;*
Fax: *03-442-6391; gondola@skyline.co.nz; www.skyline.co.nz*

Dux de Lux Restaurant, Bar and Brewery

After a day on the slopes there's no better venue to pull off the boots, have a couple of beers and start tapping those toes. No less than an institution on the NZ music scene, musicians come from far and wide playing jazz to rock and everything in between. Alpine Ale and Ginger Tom are just two of their award-winning and seasonally home-brewed beers. Famed for its vegetarian and seafood dishes, the restaurant is just next-door.

Prices: *Beers from $5 - $7, starters/light meals $6 - $12, mains $10 - $38, pizzas $18 - $24. Kids meals $8.* **Contact:** *14-16 Church Street, Queenstown;* **Tel:** *03-442-9688;* **Fax:** *03-442-9608;*
info@thedux.co.nz; www.thedux.co.nz

Wine tastes

Amisfield Winery

The Winehouse and Kitchen

otago

QUEENSTOWN

QUEENSTOWN
NATURE AND ACTIVITIES
Queenstown Garden Tours

Vibrant spring, long hot summer or golden autumn - whatever the prefix, all these days provide a perfect backdrop to showcase the gardens on Heather's tours. Enjoy a restful respite from a hectic holiday schedule to meet, chat and swap green-fingerly tips with some great personalities and their stunning rural gardens, all in the surrounding beauty of Queenstown. If you get the chance, don't miss spring's blaze of colour where blossoms, peonies, natives and perennials combine in a riot of flowery hues.

Prices: *Adults: $96 pp incl GST. Tours run daily from 10th October to 31st March. Morning tea is included in the price.* **Contact:** *Heather McDonald;* **Tel:** *03-442-3799;* **Fax:** *03-442-3796; info@queenstowngardentours.co.nz; www.queenstowngardentours.co.nz*

Golf-Cross

Trust New Zealanders to come up with another opportunity to play rugby; this time whilst playing golf. Golf-Cross, otherwise known as 'the game played with the oval golf ball,' is not just a gimmick. Conceived back in 1989 by New Zealander Burton Silver, this game is great for those who can't quite decide where their sporting allegiances lie. It's basically golf played with goals instead of holes, and with an oval instead of a round ball. You use the same rules as golf and the same clubs - though you won't need your putter. It's simply that the target is now suspended in mid-air and every shot is pretty much going where you want it to, or so one hopes. There are currently four courses in New Zealand, one of them at Rippon Vineyard in Wanaka. Another is being constructed at Nokomai Station on the highway between Queenstown and Te Anau.

Air Milford

The strange thing about flying in a tiny Cessna 185 'sports car' is that, although you're speeding along at around 200kph, it feels like floating. We crossed the Southern Alps from Queenstown to Milford Sound over rocky pinnacles and freshly fallen gullies of snow flecked with blue glacier ice. The vista was massive, and breathtaking, and very Peter Jackson. I half-expected to see Gimli wheezing away on the mountainside. In true Kiwi style, Air Milford is a friendly and relaxed company and this trip comes highly recommended. Weather permitting of course.

Prices: *From $405.* **Contact:** *Hank Sproull, 1 Tex Smith Lane, Queenstown Airport, Queenstown;* **Tel:** *03-442-2351;* **Fax:** *03-442-3249; info@airmilford.co.nz; www.airmilford.co.nz*

Dart Stables

Queenstown Guided Walks

Air Milford

Adventure Junkies

Adventure Junkies is for people who want, yes you guessed it, adventure, and lots of it. A variety of ways to achieve this are on offer: jet-boating, rafting, heli-biking, bungy-jumping, canyon swinging... the list, my friends, is endless. The difference here is that unlike your average gap-year student, with too much time and too little cash, Adrenalin Junkies is designed for those of us who can't go gallivanting off for months at a time, and who might appreciate decent accommodation of an evening. Under the watchful eye of Russ, a Brit and long-term NZ resident, you will travel with a small, like-minded group of people. Trips last for ten days picking up in Christchurch and dropping off in Queenstown.

Prices: *From $3795.* **Contact:** *Russ Johnston, Queenstown;* **Tel:** *03-442-5325; info@adventure-junkies.com; www.adventurejunkies.com*

Info & Track

Slap-bang in the middle of Queenstown, this is a booking office/tourism info/ski-hire shop all rolled into one. They have a huge selection of equipment including gloves and goggles, they don't charge a booking fee and they do offer a wealth of information on anything and everything from local walking tracks to snow reports. I went on a day's snowboarding package - all my equipment, lessons, ski-pass and transport to and from Coronet Peak for $145.

Prices: *$145 for a one-day snowboarding package.* **Contact:** *Russ Johnstone, 37 Shotover Street, Queenstown;* **Tel:** *03-442-9708; adventure@infotrack.co.nz; www.infotrack.co.nz*

Kelvin Heights Golf Course

This has to be one of the most picturesque and highly photographed courses in the world. Surrounded by Queenstown's Lake Wakatipu on three sides, its backdrop is the craggy, towering and magnificent Remarkables. The course is not long, but the undulating, tree-lined fairways are tight with greens of a good size and speed.

Prices: *Non-affiliated players $60. Cart hire $35.* **Contact:** *Queenstown Golf Club Kelvin Heights, Queenstown;* **Tel:** *03-442-9169;* **Fax:** *03-442-8061; info@queenstowngolf.co.nz; www.queenstowngolf.co.nz*

Adventure Junkies

ARROWTOWN
EATING AND **DRINKING**

The Postmaster's House Restaurant

'Designed for the adventurous' the tasting menu here is meant to tantalize the most epicurean of palettes. Neither starter size nor main the one-size-fits-all dishes are somewhere in-between so it's best to pick a few and share. Quite a relief when there's so much yumminess (Ottoman steak tartare, citrus, pistachio and pecorino salad, sticky glazed quail) on offer.... For those that know their minds, there are also starter and main sizes on offer as well. The stunning greenstone slab of a bar is great for pre-dinner drinks at this award-winning, 'almost perfect' (so says the NY Times) eatery.

Prices: *Everything comes in both starters size $16 and main size $30. Shut Mon in summer and Mon/Tues in winter.* **Contact:** *Peter Waters, 54 Buckingham Street, Arrowtown;* **Tel:** *03-442-0991;* **Fax:** *03-442-0983; bookings@postmastershouse.com; www.postmastershouse.com*

 GLENORCHY
NATURE AND **ACTIVITIES**

Dart Stables

The Glenorchy Valley really feels like Lord of the Rings country (and indeed is), and to gallop through it on horseback is to steal onto its set and experience it for yourself without all those funny costumes and pointy ears. With over 50 happy horses, all levels of experience from complete beginner to lifelong rider can find a steed to suit. Beginners are tutored and encouraged whilst old hands are offered the opportunity to ride to their experience with at least one knowledgeable and enthusiastic guide for every five riders.

Prices: *River Wild: 2 hrs riding from $115 pp; Ride of the Rings: 5-hr trip (1.5 hrs riding) from $155 pp; River & Rings: (combo of both) from $245 pp; Day in Paradise: (5-6 hrs riding) from $245pp; Overnight in Paradise: 2-day ride (5-6 hrs riding/day) from $525 pp.* **Contact:** *Peter and Jenny Davies, Glenorchy;* **Tel:** *03-442-5688;* **Fax:** *03-442-6045; dartstables@glenorchy. co.nz; www.dartstables.com*

Mountainland Rovers

'Must be the most intrepid and magical off-road adventure in NZ.' Recommendations don't come better than this. A fifth generation descendent of the founder of Queenstown, Dick has this whole area not only in his blood but also under the wheels of his landy. Traverse open plains, glaciers, mountain ranges and sheep stations on one of his hugely entertaining trips. Comfort is supreme through wind, rain or shine and there's a billy in the back for cuppas and some famous 'mountain' cake.

Prices: *Rees Valley tour: ex Queenstown, adult $159, child $80, allow 5 hrs; ex Glenorchy, adult $139, child $65, allow 3 hrs. Film location tour: ex Queenstown, adult $139, child $69, allow 4 hrs; ex Glenorchy, adult $109, child $59, allow 3 hrs.* **Contact:** *Dick Watson, Glenorchy;* **Tel:** *03-441-1323;* **Fax:** *03-441-1321; info@mountainlandrovers.co.nz; www.mountainlandrovers.co.nz*

The Postmaster's House Restaurant

Dublin Bay Pottery

Dart Wilderness Jet

Dart Wilderness Jet

Tucker up with a complimentary Kiwi BBQ lunch, in the company of your very own Southern Man, before being taken on your way to the original back country jet boating adventure that's made the Dart Valley world-famous. You'll weave leisurely through the magnificent alpine valley along the braided course of the river at the foot of the Mt Aspiring National Park. On the way you''ll hear tales of Maori legends and yarns of early pioneers before halting at a secluded beach to walk through an enchanted beech forest.

Prices: *Ex Queenstown: adults $209, children $105. Ex Glenorchy: adults $188, children $94. Family pack: 2 adults, 2 children, 2nd child goes free. Child rate 5 to 15 yrs old, under 5's go free.* **Contact:** *Susan Miller, Glenorchy Information Centre, Oban Street, Glenorchy;* **Tel:** *03-441-0303;* **Fax:** *03-442-9940; info@glenorchyinfocentre.co.nz; www.glenorchyinfocentre.co.nz*

WANAKA
EATING AND DRINKING

Missy's Kitchen

Lip-smackingly tasty food, cosy red interiors, big open fires and a terrace with sensational views over Lake Wanaka and the snowy peaks beyond make Missy's an unforgettable feast for the soul. Brenda, Tony and sons Alfred and Otis offer up the freshest ingredients in a zesty, Pacific Rim/tapas-style menu, sloshed down with exotic cocktails and over 70 wines, and all served with lively bonhomie.

Prices: *Entrées from $15, mains from $29.50 and desserts from $12.* **Contact:** *Brenda Jessup and Tony Lynch, Level 1, 80 Ardmore Street, Wanaka;* **Tel:** *03-443-5099;* **Fax:** *03-443-5098; dine@missyskitchen.co.nz; www.missyskitchen.co.nz*

Café Fe

Named after the famous Mt Iron, Café Fe rests high above Wanaka and is a great place to sit and ponder town, lake and mountains over lazy long lunches or weekend brunch. The menu's a line up of breakfasting favourites and fresh seasonal mains such as peppered venison with blackcurrant and apple vinaigrette or Aoraki salmon. Children score big here with their own menu, sandpit and toys.

Prices: *Breakfasts and lunches from $9.50 to $17.50.* **Contact:** *Heritage Park, Cnr Cardrona Valley & Orchard Roads, Wanaka;* **Tel:** *03-443-4683;* **Fax:** *03-443-4412; cafefe@xtra.co.nz*

Te Táwara o Wanaka

Café Fe's older brother gets to stay up late, sleep all day and test its (and your) taste buds with fancier, more grown-up fare. With windows onto mountains and a courtyard under the stars Te Táwara o Wanaka is a fun venue where dishes like spiced beetroot and mascarpone bavarois, roast Moroccan spatchcock and an 'intermezze' of green apple sorbet set the culinary scene for a really special night out.

Prices: *Entrées from $15, mains from $27.* **Contact:** *Heritage Park, Cnr Cardrona Valley & Orchard Roads, Wanaka;* **Tel:** *03-443-4411;* **Fax:** *03-443-4412; info@tawara.co.nz; www.tawara.co.nz*

Te Tawara

Missy's Kitchen

Café Fe

The Ardmore Street Food Company

Tucked away behind the main drag yet just across from the lake, Mark and Cris's newest café and deli is the kind of place that makes tourists and locals alike come in and feel right at home. I certainly did when I dropped by for an excellent coffee and some rocky road kill (immeasurably more pleasurable than it sounds!). Artisan breads, specialty mains, mighty burgers and decadent cakes join over 30 innovative deli concoctions to set your taste buds a-singing.

Prices: *Breakfasts from $9.50 - $15.50, burgers and mains $15 - $16.50. Rocky road kill and other desserts from $6.50.* **Contact:** *155 Ardmore Street, Wanaka;* **Tel:** *03-442-2230;* **Fax:** *03-443-2240; wanakapie@xtra.co.nz*

WANAKA
NATURE AND ACTIVITIES
Siberia Experience

Fly, walk and jet-boat your way through Mt Aspiring National Park. Oggle-friendly window seats are guaranteed on stage one as you fly over miles and miles of mountain. 25 minutes later you'll be on a nature walk through the Siberia Valley reaching the Wilkin River in time to catch your (jet boat) ride back to where you started. This is one of those 'best-kept secrets' that people rave about - a real extravaganza of a trip, great value for money and suitable for all ages and fitness levels. Not to be missed. There is also a helicopter option which is far less weather dependent.

Prices: *Adult $275, child $213 (3 - 13 yrs), under 3s travel free.* **Contact:** *48 Helwick Street, Wanaka;* **Tel:** *03-443-4385;* **Fax:** *03-443-8666; action@siberiaexperience.co.nz; www. wilkenriverjets.co.nz; www.siberiaexperience.co.nz*

Southern Alps Air, Scenic Flights Wanaka

Skip the traffic and visit Milford Sound by air. On the way there, it's a wild wilderness of glaciers, snow, rugged mountains, acres of rain forest - an undiscovered wonder-world that can only be appreciated from above. Take in vast chunks of Mt Aspiring and Fiordland World Heritage Parks and the 3030m-high Mt Aspiring en route to the Sound. Here, you can catch a cruise or just soak up the grandeur before heading back via a different route past the Sutherland Falls. First-class in every way, the scenic route is the only route worth taking. All passengers get a window seat.

Prices: *Milford Sound: adults $380 - $420, children $230 - $270. Mt Cook and glaciers: adults $370, children $145. Mt Aspiring and glaciers: adults $210, children $92.* **Contact:** *48 Helwick Street, Wanaka;* **Tel:** *03-443-4385; flights@lakewanaka.co.nz; www.southernalpsair.co.nz*

Frogz

"Like a giant hydro slide through the mountains" this is the biggest day out on white water, on sledges! Invented by some crazy French men in the '70s this has become a recognized sport and is great, great fun. Spend the day careering down 15km of the spectacular Kawarau River from the infamous 'Chinese Dogleg' rapid right through to the final portage at the cavernous ''Natural Bridge'. This trip has it all with big grade 4 rapids, big grade 6 portages, big gourmet lunch and small group sizes - you'll leave as a fully qualified frog with a big, wide grin.

Prices: *Roaring Meg trip: half day, grade 3+, 4.5 - 5 hrs, $135 pp, min age 12. The Gorge trip: full day, grade 4, 9 - 10 hrs, $285 pp, min age 16. Pick up from Queenstown, Wanaka or Cromwell.* **Tel:** *0800-443-8244;* **Fax:** *03-443-8244; reservations@frogz.co.nz; www.frogz.co.nz*

Puzzling World

Specializing in puzzling eccentricity, a visit to Stuart Landsborough's Puzzling World should only be attempted before wine tasting in the nearby vineyards. Offering the world's first 'modern-style' Great Maze, incredible illusion rooms, tumbling towers and a puzzle centre and café, this remarkable business has entertained and amazed visitors of all ages for over 30 years. I particularly enjoyed the tilted house where the displays are normal but your mind is tricked and straightens up the room at the expense of the displays that seem to hang at impossible angles... weird stuff, I left utterly confused.

Prices: *The leaning towers, puzzle centre/café and Roman toilets are free to enter. The Great Maze and the Illusion rooms are $7 adult, $5 child per attraction or $10 adult, $7 child for both.* **Contact:** *Main Highway, 2km north of Wanaka;* **Tel:** *03-443-7489;* **Fax:** *03-443-7486; info@puzzlingworld.co.nz; www.puzzlingworld.co.nz*

WANAKA
CULTURE AND HISTORY

Dublin Bay Pottery

"My life is my pottery," Joy told me as she wrapped up my purchases in newspaper. She's been a potter for thirty years now based in her country barn in tranquil Dublin Bay. I brought a beautiful pastel-green, clay tile with flowers imprinted from a wooden stamp that Joy picked up in India. There's a good selection of functional and decorative ware including her kiln-fired art glass jewellery. All are one-offs, hand-made by Joy, so it's well worth a stop-off on the road to the West Coast. Take the road to Dublin Bay off State Highway 6. The Pottery is signposted.

Contact: *Joy Paterson, 190 Dublin Bay Rd, Wanaka;* **Tel:** *03-443-1158;* **Fax:** *03-443-1158; joydublinbay@ihug.co.nz*

Artisans' Co-operative Studio

Wanaka is known for its artsy community and there's no better place to meet local artists or find out about art in the area than here. Ten local artists work from this co-operative arts and crafts studio and shop and you'll see their work in the pottery, photography, woodwork, textiles, glass and jewellery on display.

Prices: *Pieces of varying prices.* **Contact:** *54 Ardmore Street, Wanaka;* **Tel:** *03-443-7578;* **Fax:** *03-443-7960; artisans-studio@hotmail.com*

Frogz

Southern Alps Air

Puzzling World

Southland

North Island

South Island

Southland

Highlights

• Cross over to complete and utter wilderness in Doubtful Sound. Skim over its still waters in a kayak amongst bottle-nosed and dusky dolphins, Fiordland penguins and furry seals.
• Stock up on mint cake, get yourself a compass, buckle up your tramping boots and head out on the 3 - 4 day walking extravaganza that is the world-famous Milford Track. Alternatively, for another walk in the Fiordland National Park that's big on scenery yet low on crowds, try the 4-day Kepler Track from Te Anau.
• Hover in a helicopter over the dramatic (much photographed and world's tallest) cliff face of Mitre Peak, watching it drop steeply down into Milford Sound.
• Visit the world's most southerly town in April and join in the oyster-slurping fun at the annual Bluff Oyster (a true NZ speciality) and Seafood Festival.
• Go midnight kiwi spotting on Stewart Island and see other rare birds on neighbouring, predator-free Ulva Island.
• For a really remote hiking experience, walk part or all of Stewart Island's Rakiura Track. From here there's not much between you and, well... an awful lot of cold, deep sea, and eventually the Antarctic.
• Explore the rugged and largely undisturbed coastline of the Catlins. Sea, estuary and forest birds will delight ornithologists whilst the amazing wave-like pinnacles at The Nuggets and an incredible fossilised forest at Curio Bay are geology-dreamy.

Trips'n'Tramps

southland

Redcliff Café and Bar

Simple but oh-so-tantalizing dinners are served at this great restaurant. The building is a replica of an old European settlers' cottage and comes replete with big wood fires, an old creaky wooden bar and a huge outdoor patio and garden. A meal of local crayfish followed by Fiordland wild venison cannot fail to impress and is best finished off with a riesling-poached pear glazed with manuka honey and then a while spent listening to some live music in the front bar. This is a real local meeting place with live music, good cheer and popular poetry nights.

Prices: *Starters from $5 - $14.50 (crayfish is $22). Mains $19.50 - $32. Desserts $9.50 - $12.* **Contact:** *Megan Houghton, 12 Mokonui Street, Te Anau;* **Tel:** *03-249-7431; kurt-moggy@xtra.co.nz*

Sandfly Café

I liked this cosy corner café (and more) so much that it quite literally became my office for the couple of days I was based in Te Anau. Shaun and Fiona have successfully lined up the right ingredients to create an absolute local favourite; great food, superb coffee, comfy chairs, internet facilities, lazy tunes and sunny mountain views inside and out. Relax, plan or reflect on your Fiordland adventures over the pancake stack (for the hungry) or mountain muesli bowl (for the hungry, but sensible).

Prices: *Breakfasts from $5 - $13. Salads, sandwiches and sweet treats varying prices according to selection that day.* **Contact:** *Shaun and Fiona, No 9, The Lane, Te Anau;* **Tel:** *03-249-9529;* **Fax:** *03-249-9529; shaunfi@xtra.co.nz*

La Toscana

For the true taste of Tuscany in er... Te Anau, head no further than this friendly, family-run establishment. Though now run by the Sheppards, previous owners Justine and Antonio still provide authentic recipes from Italy. La Toscana is a favourite with locals who return time after time for its casual café feel, but especially for its really big bowls of pasta and scrumptious desserts. *Buon appetito!*

Prices: *Starters $3 - $14, medium pastas (a meal in itself with dessert) are $11.50 - $14.50 and large ones are $13.50 - $17.50. Pizzas from $10.50. Desserts come in large portions and are from $6 - $8. Good selection Italian and NZ wines and beers or BYO.* **Contact:** *Margaret and Brian Sheppard, 108 Milford Road, Te Anau;* **Tel:** *03-249-7756;* **Fax:** *03-249-7760; latoscana@xtra.co.nz; www.latoscana.co.nz*

Trips'n'Tramps

These guys are brilliant. They operate small-group trips to Fiordland including hiking, cruising on Milford Sound and meeting up with one of the most amazing helicopter rides around. With their laid-back style, hugely personalized approach and wonderfully informative nature guides, Trips'n'Tramps stand miles apart from the typical megalith operators transporting tourists to Milford daily by the bus-load. This way, you can stop where you want (nicely avoiding the big buses), do what you want (within reason) and importantly have a good laugh while you're at it... huge and contented sighs of relief all round.

Prices: *Scheduled day trips Te Anau - Milford Sound up to $148 pp, includes nature cruise. Private transfers and charters anywhere on South Island up to $800 day rate/late model Landcruiser.* **Contact:** *Kakapo Road, Te Anau, Fiordland;* **Tel:** *03-249-7081;* **Fax:** *03-249-7089; trips@teanau.co.nz; www.milfordtourswalks.co.nz*

TE ANAU
NATURE AND ACTIVITIES
Tawaki Dive

You can stop re-reading your depth guage. Though these waters are less than 18m deep you can expect to come face to face with other-waterworldly creatures that normally live to depths of 50m to 200m! Both the diving and the marine life here in Milford Sound are truly remarkable and it's all due to a small layer of tannin-stained fresh water that floats on the surface of its relatively clear, denser seawater. Make this much more than just interesting dinner-party chat by doing the diving deed and seeing it for yourselves. Dave and Sarah run the only diving operation in these waters, and their trips are informative, safe and importantly, really good fun.

Prices: *Milford Sound day trips: 5 hr cruise and 2 guided dives, ex Te Anau $199, ex Milford $169, full scuba gear $75; non-divers and snorkellers is $100 less pp, snorkel hire $35. PADI courses: open-water $525, advanced $399, rescue diver $399.* **Contact:** *Sarah Stirrup and Dave Johnson, 44 Caswell Road, Te Anau, Fiordland;* **Tel:** *03-249-9006;* **Fax:** *03-249-9009; sarahdave@tawakidive.co.nz; www.tawakidive.co.nz*

TE ANAU
CULTURE AND HISTORY
Fiordland Cinema

Sit in your large, plush seat, order a cheese-board and enjoy a glass of wine as you rise up from the sea to 8,000ft and look down over some of the most awe-inspiring landscapes on earth. Mysterious, evocative, exhilarating and utterly, utterly spectacular, Ata Whenua (Shadowlands) takes you on a journey through extremes of season, climate and terrain, all filmed within the nearby Fiordland World Heritage National Park. This is truly unforgettable stuff, so good in fact that it's probably the first film ever to have its own cinema built just for its viewing.

Prices: *$10 adult, $5 child for Ata Whenua. Feature movies prices vary.* **Contact:** *Grant Chapman, 7 The Lane, Te Anau, Fiordland;* **Tel:** *03-249-8844;* **Fax:** *03-249-8850; info@ fiordlandcinema.co.nz; www.fiordlandcinema.co.nz*

A typical day in the 'office' for Trips'n'Tramps

southland

Curiosity at Curio Bay's petrified forest

Deep in the South Island, along the Catlins coast, hidden under the waves at high tide, lies a clue to New Zealand's birth - a petrified sub-tropical forest of stumps and trunks dating back 160 million years (give or take 20 million). This is one of the most extensive fossil forests in the world and the cycads, tree ferns and kauri here are similar to South American species, evidence of New Zealand's place in the ancient super-continent, Gondwanaland. Try as I might, I couldn't quite fathom just how geologically ancient the tree-like swirls in rocks before me were. It is quite extraordinary and definitely worth a visit.

MANAPOURI
NATURE AND ACTIVITIES
Doubtful Sound Adventure Kayak and Cruises

Experience the mystery, moods and isolation of one of New Zealand's deepest and least disturbed fiords from the cockpit of your very own kayak. Enjoy a refreshing cuppa and cookies before gearing up to paddle this remote geological monument. Towering cliffs, sheltered coves, wooded islands, sandy beaches and crashing waterfalls, an area renowned for its dolphins and birdlife - in a word, awesome.

Prices: *Doubtful Sound: full day tour $205 pp, two day tour $315 pp. Lake Manapouri kayak rentals from $45 pp per day.* **Contact:** *Reg Calder and Jo Wilson, 33 Waiau Street, Manapouri;* **Tel:** *03-249-6626;* **Fax:** *03-249-6923; information@fiordlandadventure.co.nz; www.fiordlandadventure.co.nz*

Sandflies

Sandflies, for those lucky enough not to have made their acquaintance, are nasty little biting insects with the dubious distinction of being New Zealand's only pest. Smaller than mosquitoes but with a similar (though actually slightly worse) bite, they appear in clouds around Milford Sound and along the West Coast's wild beaches. In fact, they are generally plentiful in most wilderness areas below 900m. They have a particular talent for driving you mad. Besides hoping for rain, frost or their early extinction, it is best to avoid hanging around in shady forests, their favoured domain.

In the olden days drinking paraffin was the preferred tonic, but nowadays a good insecticide should suffice as well as covering up... prevention always being the best cure. (Top tip: Avon's 'So-So Soft' moisture lotion has proven its worth midge-busting in Scotland, and works a treat on keeping sandflies at bay too. Bird's Ferry Lodge swear by the stuff and even keep supplies for grateful guests.)

Luckily, even sandflies have their weaknesses. Learn them. Firstly, they are slow; even when walking at a slow pace they cannot keep up and you will not notice them. This works even better if there is a wind. And lastly (obviously not that many weaknesses then) they go away at night. As soon as it gets dark they will disappear, only to return at first light. This can be a trial in summer when it stays light until 10pm, but cover up and there will always be relief ahead if you can wait until dark.

SOUTH ISLAND

What sounds like a sound is a fiord...

Contrary to their names, Milford Sound, Doubtful Sound, Dusky Sound et cetera are, in fact, fiords. Sounds are flooded river valleys whereas fiords are valleys carved by the tremendous power and pressure of glaciers during successive ice ages and then, later, as the ice melts and the water-levels rise, they are flooded.

Fiordland Ecology Holidays

A huge map of the southern seas covers the entire ceiling of Ruth and Lance's 45° South bookshop. Below it, over cups of tea, true natural history, eco-tourism experiences are hatched. Voyages combine nature, conservation and research and cover all of Fiordland, Stewart Island and sub-Antarctic Islands. It is all very exciting. With 28 years' worth of experience Lance's knowledge of these areas is as broad as its waters are deep. "The best 6 days wilderness adventuring I ever spent was a trip in the safe hands of Lance Shaw." So said David Bellamy. Trips, taken on the 'Breaksea Girl' (the only chartered eco-tourism boat operating in the remote and otherwise inaccessible Dusky Sound) are totally unique and offer fascinating opportunities to explore for dolphin, seals and penguins and to walk in forests to learn about eco-systems. 45° South Bookshop has an amazing selection of books on anything that deals with 45° South and below.

Prices: *3 - 7 day scheduled cruises for groups of 10, diving &/or research trips, available for private charter to Doubtful & Dusky Sounds, Preservation Inlet & Stewart Island from $250 per day per person.* **Contact:** *Ruth and Lance Shaw, 5 Waiau Street, Manapouri;* **Tel:** *03-249-6600;* **Fax:** *03-249-6600; info@fiordland.gen.nz; www.fiordland.gen.nz*

MANDEVILLE
EATING AND DRINKING
The Moth Restaurant and Bar

This well-loved Mandeville institution is situated on the old airfield just 10 minutes' drive from Gore. Judy has cultivated a great reputation for fresh, simply presented food that's served down nostalgia runway in a restaurant full of wartime aviation memorabilia. Best of all, there's an air museum here too and lucky visitors can take flights in the beautiful old Tiger Moth aircraft.

Prices: *Light daytime meals $8.50 - $16.50, starters $8.50 - $16.95, mains $26.50 - $29.95, desserts $9.50. Closed on Mondays (and Tues in winter). Ask for details on joy flights in the Tiger Moth.* **Contact:** *Judy Taylor, Old Mandeville Airfield, State Highway 94, 15km from Gore on the Queenstown Highway;* **Tel:** *03-208-9662;* **Fax:** *03-208-8488; themoth@xtra.co.nz; www.themoth.co.nz*

Fiordland Ecology Holidays

Ruggedy Range Tours on Stewart Island

Encountering the locals on one of Ulva's guided walks

Fiordland National Park

Fiordland is a region dominated by forest and water. Its fourteen fiords and five major lakes are flanked by steep mountains clad with thick, temperate forest, making the interior virtually impenetrable except along its 500km of tracks. The isolation, variety of habitats and the incredible annual rainfall (ranging from a paltry 1m in the east to a massive 8m in the west) of the area allow a diverse flora and fauna to thrive and there are over 700 plants endemic to it.

Some of the best examples of plants that were once found on the ancient super-continent of Gondwana still exist here. The most prominent of these are the evergreen beech trees that make up about 80 - 90% of the forest. The two main types you'll see are the silver and the red varieties, though the mountain beech is pretty common too. The other main forest type is the mixed podocarp. This is a gorgeous mix of trees from beeches to a good collection of native pines such as rimu, kahikatea, matai, miro and other leafy trees like the kamahi and the beautiful rata, which produces lovely red flowers around Christmas.

Incredibly, much of the forest grows on virtually sheer, rock cliff-faces, especially noticeable on the sides of the fiords. These trees survive with next to no soil and it is only moss that holds the moisture and the nutrients around their shallow roots that cling to the rock. On some of theses cliff-faces only 5 - 10% of the trees will actully be anchored into cracks in the rock. All the other trees rely on those anchor trees for their very existence. Unfortunately this means that if one of the anchor trees lets go, then the rest all avalanche to the valley floor or into the waters of the fiord and leave huge, treeless scars on the mountainside that take many years to regenerate.

The National Park is also known for its wildlife and is, or was, home to some of New Zealand's strangest birds. The takahe, for example, is a large flightless rail related to the more populous pukeko, more commonly known throughout Australasia as the purple moorhen. The bird is of ancient lineage and was thought to be extinct until it was rediscovered in 1948. Fiordland was also the final refuge for the world's only flightless parrot, the nocturnal kakapo. There are now a number of recovery projects for these unique birds on pest-free offshore islands. In the absence of human activity, marine wildlife flourishes here as well. Bottlenose dolphins, New Zealand fur seals, little blue penguins and Fiordland crested penguins or tawaki are happy residents in the waters of the fiords.

The environment below the water is as fascinating and unique as its acclaimed landscape above. Run-off from heavy rainfall on the mountains creates a permanent freshwater layer on the surface of the saltwater that varies in depth from 5 cm to over 10 m. At the same time, tannins, washed out of the vegetation on land, stain the water the colour of weakly-brewed tea and create a dark layer on the surface. In turn, this cuts down the amount of light entering the seawater, restricting most of the marine life to the top 40m. This band (below the freshwater layer) is calm, clear and relatively warm and is home to sponges, corals (including one of the world's largest populations of black coral trees, some of which are up to 200 years old) and fish of sub-tropical, cool water and deep-water varieties. Amazingly the waters are also home to brachiopods, clam-like animals that have remained relatively unchanged for over 300 million years!

STEWART ISLAND
EATING AND DRINKING
Church Hill Café and Bar

If there's one place you eat on Stewart Island, do make it this one. To house their café, Deanne and Allan have restored the charming, wooden 19th-century cottage that sits high on the hill above Halfmoon Bay. There's a simple menu of local delicacies, carefully chosen wines, an open fireplace and great views to the harbour outside. Top of the tipples when I visited were their specialty Bloody Mary-style Bluff Oyster shooters, only available in season from April time.

Contact: *Deanne McPherson and Allan Booth, 36 Kamahi Road, Oban Town Centre, Stewart Island;* **Tel:** *03-219-1323;* **Fax:** *03-219-1323; churchhill@stewartisland.org*

STEWART ISLAND
NATURE AND ACTIVITIES
Ruggedy Range Wilderness Experience

Furhana has an encyclopaedic knowledge of the birdlife, marine life, flora, fauna and geology of her adopted home, Stewart Island, and anything she doesn't know is probably not worth knowing anyway. Squawked over by kaka and kakariki (that's parrots and parakeets to me), Ruggedy Range HQ is a little building in a big native forest and the base from which Furhana operates a huge variety of trips on Stewart Island, Rakiura National Park and predator-free Ulva Island. You can hike, sea-kayak, kiwi-spot and walk on this bird filled island amidst dunes, wetlands, alpine tops, primeval forests, wild beaches and crystal clear waters. Educational, fun and with conservation as the guiding principle, Ruggedy Range offers unbeatable 'off the beaten track' wilderness experiences.

Prices: *Ulva Island - Birds & Forest: 4 hrs $85, 8 hrs $135. Coastal Highlights: 1 day $155. Sea Kayaking: day trips $95 - $155. Kiwi Journey: overnight kiwi spotting $385. Wilderness Escape: 4 days $1,950. Island Culture 2hrs $45. Rakiura Great Walk: 3 days $850.*
Contact: *FurhanaBirds & Forest Booking Office, 170 Horseshoe Bay Road, Stewart Island;* **Tel:** *03-219-1066;* **Fax:** *03-219-1078; mail@ruggedyrange.com; www.ruggedyrange.com*

Ulva's Guided Walks

No one is more suited to the task of guiding people around the predator-free, open bird sanctuary of Ulva Island than Ulva Goodwillie herself. Not only does she bear its name but she's also a direct descendent of the first peoples to inhabit Rakiura (Stewart Island). She is passionate about the place and soon you will be too. Take a leisurely ramble under the luxuriant green mantle of podocarp forest whilst she introduces you to the history, scenery and spectacular birdlife and fauna that the island has to offer. On a recent guided tour with Ulva, NZ prime minister Helen Clark described the experience as 'eco-tourism at its very best'.

Prices: *$85 pp for a half-day guided walk (inclusive of 7-min water taxi to and from the island and Dept. of Cons concession fees).* **Contact:** *Ulva Goodwillie, Stewart Island;* **Tel:** *03-219-1216; ulva@ulva.co.nz; www.ulva.co.nz*

Kayaking in Doubtful Sound

Redcliffe Cafe in Te Anau

A walk with Ruggedy Range

A litany of (introduced) disasters

Many of the park's threatened species owe their demise to predators such as possums, deer and stoats and, in turn, to humans who first introduced these pests to these peaceful green isles.

Possums were introduced in the 1830s to establish a fur trade and have adapted to NZ conditions so well that they are now considered a major threat not just to the forest greenery but to the bird and insect life as well. They browse heavily (an estimated 22,000 tonnes (!) of leaves being devoured every couple of nights) in the forests and grasslands and have been seen to take insects, birds' eggs and chicks. The threat they pose to eco-systems explains why these creatures have the unenviable reputation as New Zealand's public enemy number one. Several initiatives to control possum numbers exist throughout the country and there are increasing numbers of commercial ventures into possum fur and even possum meat! The hope is to provide lovely natural products and to throw the rescue of their threatened forests and birds into the bargain as well.

Also introduced to the forests back in the 1800s were deer. By the 1940s their numbers were also so out of control that the government had to employ deer cullers, paid on a bounty system, to shoot deer for a living. While they were reasonably effective in some places, it wasn't until helicopters were used as aerial gun-ships from the late 1960s to the early 1980s that the forests were freed from the threat of over-grazing by deer.

And as if that's not enough, yet another introduced species, the stoat was introduced to New Zealand in a foiled bid to control rabbits (which were also introduced!). Instead, these natural-born survivors shifted their feeding habits to the country's native birds....

Tragically, in an island environment isolated from the rest of the world for more than 80 million years, and free of mammalian predators (the only mammals native to these shores are two species of bat), a number of birds developed flightlessness (simply because they didn't need to fly) and rather eccentric habits. Each of them evolved to fill different ecological functions, roles normally taken by mammals in other eco-systems. For example, takahe are grass eaters, and kiwi and wrens are ground insect-eaters. Stoats and possums simply couldn't believe their luck. Furthermore, many of the birds are unafraid of humans, a common characteristic resulting from the absence of predators, and which became a deadly one when human hunters arrived. Most famed amongst the birds that were driven to extinction by humans is the giant moa. This impressive creature was over 3m tall and weighed about 250kg – one of the biggest birds ever known to the world.

West Coast

North Island

South Island

West Coast

Highlights

- Drive the beautiful coastal route from Westport to Haast; it's quite rightly considered one of the world's most extraordinary drives. Stop off to stretch your legs at Punakaiki and walk to see the Pancake Rocks and its blowholes.
- Try black-water rafting in the glowworm grotto of Charleston caves near Westport.
- Visit the country's only white heron (*kotuku*) colony near Whataroa.
- Paddle or boat through the shallow, open water of Okarito's coastal lagoon past wading birds and magnificent kahikatea and rimu rainforest.
- Tramp in the lush lowland rainforest around 'mirrored' Lake Matheson and see the glistening and mighty mountains reflected on its surface.
- Don crampons and waterproof gloves to walk on Franz Josef and Fox glaciers. Alternatively hold off the shackles and peer at them from above on a flight-seeing trip over the spectacular Mt Aspiring peaks.

Fox/Franz Josef Heli-services

WESTPORT
EATING AND DRINKING
Jack's Gasthof

It is definitely worth venturing off the highway and down the track to this tiny rural eatery on the banks of the Little Totara River, even if German owners Jack and Petra occasionally forget to remove the 'closed' sign on the road! Utterly divine sourdough rye bread and organic wholemeal loaves are baked here daily. They also make the meanest pizzas you'll find on the wild west coast and serve a three-course meal each Thursday evening. Closed Mondays.

Contact: *Jack and Petra Zander, SH 6, 23 km south of Westport;* **Tel:** *03-789-6501.*

CHARLESTON
NATURE AND ACTIVITIES
Underworld Adventures

The west coast of the South Island may not be as internationally renowned for its caves as North Island's Waitomo Caves, but I can assure you (after unskilfully squeezing through a couple myself) that Charleston has more than its fair share of sub-terrarium landscapes. Charleston Underworld Adventures presents cave-rafting in style. Kitted-out in a designer wetsuit and bum planted firmly in an inflatable tube, you bob merrily along the Nile River through a calcitic wonderland of stalactites and stalagmites before drifting below a canvas of glowworms. For those averse to getting wet you can take the dry-footed eco-tour or jump on the rainforest train for a unique look at the pre-historic Nile Valley landscape.

Prices: *Underworld Rafting $135, Charleston GloWorm Cave Tour $80, Adventure Caving $270, Nile River Rainforest Train $20.* **Contact:** *Geoff Schurr, The Charleston Hotel, State Highway 6, Charleston, West Coast;* **Tel:** *03-788-8168 or freephone 0800-116-686 (within New Zealand); Fax: 03-789-5508; norwest@orcon.net.nz; www.caverafting.com*

Pancake Rocks of Punakaiki

Wander the track that's lined with native ferns, pongas and nikau palms until you reach Punakaiki's famous Pancake Rocks. Here, looking rather like a heaped pile of pancakes, corrugated limestone stacks and arches cluster by the shore weathering the thunderous attack of the sea. The ridges of rock evolved when alternate layers of softer mudstone eroded faster than the limestone.

On calm days water swills slowly through the many caves and chambers. However, on rough ones, geyser-like jets explode through blowholes forced by the hydraulic pressure of the ocean... this is noisy, exciting, and very, very wet!

GREYMOUTH
CULTURE AND HISTORY

Shantytown

This faithfully-restored replica of an 1860's West Coast gold mining town is a living monument to the hardy pioneers who forded the wildly exotic rivers and streams, and scrambled through the rugged sub-tropical rainforest in search of their fortunes. Shantytown provides a 'real' sense of what it was like to live in New Zealand both during and after the dynamic great rush. Share in the early New Zealanders' experiences - ride on a steam train, pan for gold (guaranteed strike!), quench your thirst in The Golden Nugget Saloon and visit the confectionary store to try its original boiled lollies.

Prices: *Adults entry with gold-panning $20 (without gold-panning $16), student (13 - 17 yrs) $12, children (5 - 12 yrs) $10.00. Concessions and family passes available. All tickets include a steam train-ride, student and children's tickets include gold-panning.* **Contact:** *11km south of Greymouth off SH 6, Rutherglen Road, Paroa, Greymouth;* **Tel:** *03-762-6634;* **Fax:** *03-762-6649; info@shantytown.co.nz; www.shantytown.co.nz*

HOKITIKA
EATING AND DRINKING

Wildfoods Festival

Wildfoods is a hugely popular celebration of the West Coast's unique lifestyle, food and hospitality and is an extravaganza of gourmet bush-tucker. Based on the region's natural food sources, from the land and sea, the emphasis is on novel, tasty and healthy foods presented in an innovative manner. Be at your palate-punishing best and try some old favourites such as gorse-flower scones and billy tea, possum pâté, ostrich pie and West Coast whitebait.

Prices: *Day ticket $30 and $15 for the evening dance.* **Contact:** *Mike Keenan, 36 Weld Street, Hokitika, Westland;* **Tel:** *03-756-9049;* **Fax:** *03-756-9045; wildfoods@westlanddc.govt.nz; www.wildfoods.co.nz*

The Tin Shed

This Tin Shed tardis may hint at bygone gold-rush days but step inside and a wealth of local art, craft and playful design waits. Dine in the creatively lit gallery to softly moody jazz and blues tunes (Ray is big on his music) or claim a sea-viewing garden perch out the back. Either way you'll be surrounded by rustic charm and treated to great food and service.

Prices: *Breakfast $14; lunch $4 - $16, large pizzas $20; dinner, entrées $7.50 - $14, mains $21 - $27, desserts $7.50 - $9.* **Contact:** *Ray and Karen, 89 Revell Street, Hokitika;* **Tel:** *03-755-8444;* **Fax:** *03-755-8447.*

Charleston Adventures

Courting Greebe

A Glacier Valley Eco Tour

Tree-ferns

One of the most noticeable features of the NZ bush is the proliferation of tree-ferns. These evergreen plants are amazingly diverse and grow in a variety of habitats, though most are found in damp, shady pockets beneath tree canopies, thriving in well-drained, rich and loamy soils up the sides of gullies. One of my favourites is the largest of them all, the black tree fern or mamaku, which can grow to a whopping height of twenty metres and their fronds can extend to seven. About 170 different species grow naturally here, 89 of which are endemic to New Zealand. Especially well known is the silver fern or ponga - the symbol of the nation. Growing to a height of up to ten metres they are hard to miss; the silvery underside of its leaves are most striking. Being the country's emblem you'll find it depicted on everything here from jewels to caps to cars to rugby shirts. They even called the national netball team after it.

HARI HARI
NATURE AND ACTIVITIES
Tamati Nature Tours

A pair of Australian crested grebes, some of NZ's rarest birds, cut quite a dashing silhouette as they glide together across Lake Ianthe. This beautiful aquatic bird is classified as 'vulnerable to extinction' by the International Union for the Conservation of Nature. With feathering paddle wheels the 100-year-old kauri launch, Tamati, cuts its path alongside them so quietly that they barely notice the watchful eyes aboard peering down at them. These great natural history tours are kept personal and educational with typically just 2-6 people on board.

Prices: *40-minute natural history tours departing hourly from Lake Ianthe jetty adult $20, children $10. Free coffee, tea & refreshments on board.* **Contact:** *Dave Hindman, Lake Ianthe, State Highway 6, South Westland;* **Tel:** *0800-11-94-94 for daily schedule updates;* **Fax:** *03-753-3014; lakeianthe@xtra.co.nz*

WHATAROA
NATURE AND ACTIVITIES
White Heron Sanctuary Tours

Ken and Shirley run the sole operation to offer tours in NZ's only white heron breeding colony. Jetboat along the river past spectacular views of Mts Cook and Tasman, then walk through native Westland rainforest before spying the birds from the hide. Royal spoonbills and little shags are just a couple of the herons' exotically named neighbours that you might see too.

Prices: *White Heron Tours: 2.5 hrs duration, adults $95, children under 12 $45.* **Contact:** *Ken and Shirley Arnold, SH6, Whataroa, South Westland;* **Tel:** *03-753-4120;* **Fax:** *03-753-4087; info@whiteherontours.co.nz; www.whiteherontours.co.nz*

Tamati Tours　　*A majestic White Heron*　　*Kayaking in the Okarito Lagoon*

OKARITO
NATURE AND ACTIVITIES

Okarito Nature Tours

Paddle into the primitive depths of lush Kahikatea and the rimu rainforest at Okarito Lagoon with this petite, friendly and family-run outfit. New Zealand's largest unmodified wetland area covers more than 3,240 hectares and houses a colossal number of birds. Here you will only talk in whispers, if you talk at all. The graceful presence of white herons and the staggering views of Mt. Cook will render you speechless.

Prices: *2-hr guided kayak trips from $65 pp. Kayak rental 2 hr $35 pp, half-day $45 pp, full day $55 pp, overnight $80 pp. No experience necessary.* **Contact:** *Richard Saunders and Edwina Clarke, The Strand, Okarito;* **Tel:** *03-753-4014;* **Fax:** *03-753-4014; kayaks@okarito.co.nz; www.okarito.co.nz*

Okarito Kiwi Tours

Think of New Zealand and you think of this squat little bird who, after the country's invasion by rats and other unsavoury vermin, is dangerously close to extinction. There are around 250 Okarito Brown Kiwis left in the Tai Poutini National Park, and if you're lucky you will hear them snuffling for food on one of Ian and Wendy's night time tours. Using the stars as navigational aids, the couple interpret the haunting nighttime birdsongs and share local Maori legends. The office is based in tiny Okarito, so it's harder to miss than find!

Prices: *$45 for adults.* **Contact:** *Ian Cooper and Wendy Godfrey, The Strand, Okarito;* **Tel:** *03-753-4330; okaritokiwitours@paradise.net.nz; www.okaritokiwitours.co.nz*

The Okarito Trig

I pulled off State Highway 6 into this sleepy village full of mini-baches (Kiwi for 'holiday home') and started walking. Making my way up through primeval forests of dripping Nikau Palms, I came to a 360 degree view which stretched from sea to sea, across virgin bush sprouting from paths cut by ancient glaciers, and onwards to a very distant Mount Cook. Spectacular.

Contact: *Off State Highway 6, Okarito.*

Mt Cook Ski Planes

Franz Josef and Fox Glaciers

These massive rivers of ice that tumble down valleys towards the sea are unique, both in the speed at which they move and in the exceptionally low and temperate climate levels to which they descend.

There are two main reasons for this phenomenon: the climate and the shape of the glaciers. The southern part of the West Coast lies in the path of a band of wind known as the 'roaring forties'. The weather that flows onto the coast from the Tasman Sea is forced to rise up and over the Southern Alps, causing most of its moisture to cool and then drop as rain and snow. Every year, this process results in huge amounts of snow falling on the catchment areas of the glaciers, called the neves. These neves lie across exceptionally large, elevated blocks of land and so are able to collect enormous amounts of snow, often in piles of up to 30m deep. When this snow is compacted, it forms blue glacier ice (due to the compression of water particles which forces out the oxygen) that is then funnelled down the glaciers' particularly steep and narrow valleys, ideally shaped for chanelling the ice down.

The sheer weight of all that snowfall, and the angle and size of the valleys, allow the ice to descend to the extremely low altitude of just 240m above sea level. Elsewhere in the world (except of course in the poles), glaciers barely reach the timberline; those in the European Alps for example do not run below 2000m. And, whereas these glaciers move very slowly, the rate of ice turnover for Fox and Franz Josef is about 10 times as fast, progressing up to 2.5 metres per day.

Unusually for glaciers, this makes Fox and Franz Josef particularly accessible. It's a terrific experience to walk upon the glassy snouts of these great blocks of ice or even just to stand up close and feel tiny and very weedy in their presence.

Many Maori stories are derived from the dramatic landscape that makes up New Zealand. The creation of the Franz Josef Glacier, traditionally known as Ka Roimata o Hine Huhatere, is one such tale:

Hine Hukatere, an adventurous Maori wahine (woman) who loved mountaineering above all other pastimes, frequently persuaded her lover Tawe to accompany her on her many journeys into the mountains. On one such expedition the unfortunate Tawe, who had never been as fond of climbing as his sweetheart, slipped near the top of what is now Franz Josef Glacier, and plunged to his death. Hine's tears, so great in their volume, were frozen by the gods as a memorial to her grief and formed the glacier that we see today.

Fox Glacier

🌳 FRANZ JOSEF
🏔 NATURE AND ACTIVITIES

Franz Josef Glacier Guides

Hands-down, my absolute favourite experience in New Zealand! I longed to be able to go up again the very next day (ice queen is clearly my calling in life). Utterly breathtaking views down the glacier valley, across Lake Mapourika and to the far sea. And the glacier itself: a winter-wonderland adventure playground of ice crevasses, tunnels and staircases. Our guide was knowledgeable and enthusiastic, and with a mean swing to that ice pick. I guarantee you a spectacular experience in the safest of hands.

Prices: *Full day: adult $140, child $120. 3/4 day: adult $130, child $120. 1/2 day: adult $90, child $80.* **Contact:** *SH6, Main Road, Franz Josef Glacier;* **Tel:** *03-752-0763 or 0800 GUIDES (within New Zealand);* **Fax:** *03-752-0102; walks@franzjosefglacier.com; www. franzjosefglacier.com*

Mt Cook Ski Planes

Forget the incessant whirl from a helicopter when it lands on a glacier, when these ski planes touch down, the engine is shut off entirely allowing you to experience the natural quiet of the mountain, broken only by sounds of the ice as it creeps slowly down its side. These are the only ski planes in the southern hemisphere and with over 50 years in operation, there are fewer scenic flights with more experience as these. To fully appreciate the unrivalled beauty of the Southern Alps, its glaciers and Mt Cook you absolutely must see it from the air, and this is surely the only way to do it.

Prices: *From Franz Josef: glacier landing, adult $300 - $375, child $225 - $285; over flight, adult $220 - $310, child $170 - $230. From Mt Cook: glacier landing, adult $325 - $430, child $240 - $325; over flight, adult $220 - $295, child $180 - $220.* **Contact:** *Alex Miller;* **Tel:** *03-752-0747; amiller@mtcookskiplanes.com; www.mtcookskiplanes.com*

A West Coast gem

Formed in alpine fault lines under intense heat and pressure, greenstone or pounamu boulders are eventually flushed from the eroding mountains into rivers all around the West Coast.

This hard, opaque, emerald-coloured stone holds great spiritual significance for the Maori people. Long before the Europeans arrived, tribes sent missions out to search for the precious rock that would later be bartered for food. As it was the hardest material known to Maoris, it was especially used for making tools, weapons and items of personal adornment.

On a visit to New Zealand, you'll see no end of brooches, earrings, ornaments and tiki carved from greenstone. The latter are the tiny, stylised Maori figures, usually depicted with their tongue stuck out in war-like defiance, worn on a thong around the neck. Watch out though, supposedly they have great mana, or power, and also serve as fertility symbols.

There are several operations in Hokitika where you can carve your very own piece of greenstone or even bone; notwithstanding artistic talent (I just call mine 'abstract'), these make great keepsakes of a trip to NZ.

Glacier Valley Eco Tours

There's no need for shackles, crampons, ice picks (or wobbly nerves) on Mike and Julie's more sedate tours of the impressive Fox and Franz glaciers. Walk through primeval, regenerated forest for your first glimpse of these incredible hunks of ice and learn all about the glaciation, geology and natural history of their dynamic environment. They also do trips out kayaking in lagoons and rainforest tramps around photo-friendly 'mirrored' Lake Matheson.

Prices: *Eco-tours at Franz Josef Glacier 3 hrs, adult $60, child $30; Fox Glacier, 3 hrs adult $65, child $32.50; Lake Matheson, 3.5 hrs, adult $65, child $32.50. Okarito Sea Kayaking, $300 for half day. Under 15's half price, under 5's go free.* **Contact:** *Julie and Mike Charles, Franz Josef;* **Tel:** *03-752-0699;* **Fax:** *03-752-0690; mike@glaciervalley.co.nz; www.glaciervalley.co.nz*

Fox Glacier & Franz Josef Heliservices

This is the only 100% locally-owned and -operated helicopter company licensed to land in all designated landing sites within the Westland National Park. Which basically means you get seriously good advice and are treated to the best 'off the beaten track' views 20 years of local knowledge and experience can muster. If you opt for a snow-landing glacier flight (from the wide selection) you also get to leap out and roll in the snow.

Prices: *Snow landing flights from 20 mins to 40 mins $180 - $340, overflights from $150 (2008 2009).* **Contact:** *Michael Nolan, Alpine Adventure Centre, Main Road, Franz Josef;* **Tel:** *0800-800-793;* **Fax:** *03-752-0764; fox_heli@xtra.co.nz; www.scenic-flights.co.nz*

FRANZ JOSEF
CULTURE AND HISTORY
Flowing West Movie

Need a wet day activity? Look no further... the Flowing West Movie is a 20-minute armchair ride through glacier country. This visual journey is the next best thing to a helicopter flight, so if you suffer from motion sickness, are a little strapped for cash, or you just want a good spurt of entertainment it's well worth the tiny entrance fee.

Prices: *Movie tickets $10 adult, $5 child.* **Contact:** *Michael Nolan, Alpine Adventure Centre, Main Road, Franz Josef;* **Tel:** *0800-800-793;* **Fax:** *03-752-0764; fox_heli@xtra.co.nz; www.scenic-flights.co.nz*

BRUCE BAY
NATURE AND ACTIVITIES
John's Tour

This is an informal tour, lead by GG owner John Birchfield. On a gin-clear day he took me walking through Bruce Bay pointing out the community hall, once the site of raucous black tie balls when the village was a road-building community. He's especially knowledgeable on local Maori culture as well. The bay was the original landing site of the legendary Maori explorer, Maui. The area was also a big focal point for last century's gold rush and the beach sand is still rich in this most precious of metals. Ask John to help you pan for riches on his very own gold concession, just be sure to buy him a Monteiths local beer afterwards.

Contact: *John Birchfield, Mahitahi Lodge, State Highway 6, Bruce Bay;* **Tel:** *03-751-0095;* **Fax:** *03-751-0195; stay@mahitahilodge.co.nz; www.mahitahilodge.co.nz*

Franz Josef
Glacier Guides

INDEX - accommodation

Index By House Name

INDEX - accommodation

Index By Nearest Town Name

INDEX

things to do and places to eat

Otago:	Dublin Bay Pottery p.231, Artisans' Co-operative Studio p.231
West Coast:	The Tin Shed p.242

BIRD-WATCHING

Coromandel:	Miranda Shorebird Centre p.137
Waikato and King Country:	Otorohanga Kiwi House p.131
Wairarapa:	Pukaha Mount Bruce p.158
Wellington:	Matiu/Somes Island p.161 Karori Wildlife Sanctuary p.161, Staglands Wildlife Reserve p.164, Kapiti Island p.164
Canterbury:	Graeme Williams Guiding p.202, Encounter Kaikoura p.214
Otago:	The birds of Otago Peninsula p.219
Southland:	Ruggedy Range Wilderness Experience p.238, Ulva's Guided Walks p.238
West Coast:	Tamati Nature Tours p.243, White Heron Sanctuary Tours p.243, Okarito Nature Tours p.244, Okarito Kiwi Tours p.244

BEACHES

Coromandel:	Hot Water Beach p.127
Otago:	St Clair Beach p.220

BOAT CHARTERS AND CRUISES

Northland:	Snow Cloud p.108, Gungha II, Bay of Islands Sailing p.104, Earl Grey Fishing Charters p.104
Central Plateau:	Windsor Charters p.144
Marlborough:	Myths and Legends Eco-Tours p.193
Otago:	Clutha River Cruises p.221
Southland:	Trips and Tramps p.233, Fiordland Ecology Holidays p.236
West Coast:	Tamati Nature Tours p.243

BUNGY JUMPS

Otago:	The Bungy p.222, Advenure Junkies p.227

CAVES AND CAVING

Auckland:	Nikau Cave p.121
Waikato and King Country:	Spellbound p.133, Absolute Adventures p.133
West Coast:	Charleston Underworld Adventures p.241

CHILD-FRIENDLY

Northland:	Tua Tua Tours p.111, Sheepworld p.99
Auckland:	Kelly Tarlton's Antarctic Encounter and Underwater World p.115, Auckland Zoo p.115, Auckland Museum p.117
Coromandel:	Waiau Waterworks p.125
Waikato and King Country:	Otorohanga Kiwi House p.131, Spellbound p.133,
Bay of Plenty:	Zorb Rotorua p.139, Agrodome p.139, Paradise Valley Springs Wildlife Park p.140
Hawke's Bay:	Tractor Trips at Gannet Beach Adventures p.155, Clearview Estate Winery and Restaurant p.155,

INDEX

things to do  and places to eat

INDEX

things to do and places to eat

Wellington:	Te Papa Museum of New Zealand p.162, Katherine Mansfield's Birthplace p.163, Museum of Wellington City and Sea p.163, Southward Car Museum p.164, Trinity Farm Living Rose Museum p.165
Wanganui and Manawatu:	Army Museum Waiouru p167, John Vickers Homestead Architecture Tours p.170, New Zealand Rugby Museum p.171
Taranaki:	Puke Ariki p.173, Tawhiti Museum p.175
Nelson:	World of WearableArt and Classic Car Museum p.186, Nelson Provincial Museum p.186
Marlborough:	The Edwin Fox p.194
Canterbury:	Akaroa Guided Walks p.200, Okains Bay Maori and Colonial Museum p.201, International Antarctic Centre p.208, Canterbury Museum p.207, Willowbank Wildlife Reserve p.206, Maori Tours Kaikoura p.212
Otago:	Olveston p.220, Larnach Castle p.220
West Coast:	Shantytown p.242, John's Tour p.247

NATURE RESERVES, CONSERVATION AREAS AND NATIONAL PARKS

Coromandel:	Driving Creek Railway p.138
Central Plateau:	Mt. Ruapehu and Tongariro National Park p.144
Hawke's Bay:	Cape Kidnappers, Gannet Beach Adventures p.155
Wairarapa:	Pukaha Mount Bruce p.158
Wellington:	Matiu/Somes Island p.172, Karori Wildlife Sanctuary p.172, Staglands Wildlife Reserve p.172, Kapiti Island p.175
Wanganui and Manawatu:	Whanganui National Park p.169
Taranaki:	Mt. Taranaki and Egmont National Park p.174
Nelson:	Farewell Spit p.182
Canterbury:	Willowbank Wildlife Reserve p.206
Southland:	Fiordland National Park p.237

OLIVE OIL

Canterbury:	Athena Olive Groves p.214

QUAD BIKING

Northland:	Bush 'n' Bike Adventure Company p.103, Tua Tua Tours p.111
Canterbury:	Glenstrae Farm 4-wheeler Adventures p.215

SAILING

Northland:	Gungha II p.120
Auckland:	The Pride of Auckland p.114, America's Cup Experience p.114
Canterbury:	Akaroa Fox Sail p.200

SAND-BOARDING

Northland:	Cape Reinga, 4x4 Paradise p.109
Nelson:	Farewell Spit p.190

INDEX

things to do and places to eat

WALKING TOURS, HIKES AND TREKS

Auckland:	Bush and Beach Eco-Tours p.121
Central Plateau:	Whirinaki Rainforest Guided Walks p.143, Mt. Ruapehu and Tongariro National Park p.144
East Coast:	Eastwoodhill Arboretum p.148
Wairarapa:	Tora Coastal Walk p.158
Wanganui and Manawatu:	River Valley Adventure Lodge p.168
Marlborough:	Wilderness Guides p.193, Marlborough Sounds Adventure Company p.193
Canterbury:	Banks Peninsula Track p.200, the Kaikoura Coast Track p.214
Otago:	Otago Central Rail Trail p.222, Siberia Experience p.230,
Southland:	Trips and Tramps p.233, Ulva's Guided Walks p.238
West Coast:	The Okarito Trig p.244, Franz Josef Glacier Guides p.246, Glacier Valley Eco-tours p.247

WHITE-WATER RAFTING AND WHITE-WATER SLEDGING

Bay of Plenty:	Raftabout p.140
Wanganui and Manawatu:	River Valley Adventure Lodge p.168
Nelson:	Ultimate Descents p.188
Otago:	Advenure Junkies p.227, Frogz p.230

WINERIES AND WINE-TASTING

Northland:	Ransom Wines p.99, Ascension Vineyard p.100, Karikari Estate Winery p.111
Auckland:	Mudbrick Vineyard and Restaurant p.120
Coromandel:	Purangi Estate Winery p.125, Ohinemuri Estate Winery and Restaurant p.127
Hawke's Bay:	Vince's Vineyard Tours p.150, C.J. Pask Winery p.150, Ngatarawa Winery p.153, Te Awa Winery p.153, Hatton Estate Vineyard and Winery p.153, Te Awa Winery p.153, Clearview Estate Winery and Restaurant p.155
Wairarapa:	Martinborough Vineyard p.157, Coney Wines Ltd. p.157
Nelson:	Woolaston Estate p.186, Te Mania and Richmond Plains Cellar Door p.195
Marlborough:	Seresin Estate p.190, Highfield Estate p.191, Herzog Winery and Restaurant p.191, Bladen Estate p.192, Gibbs Vineyard Restaurant p.191, Wine Tours by Bike p.191, Grove Mill Winery p.192
Canterbury:	French Farm Winery p.197, Pegasus Bay Winery p.210, Hurunui River Wines p.210
Otago:	The Big Picture p.223, Amisfield Winery and Bistro p.224, The Winehouse and Kitchen p.224, Wine Tastes Central Otago p.223, Queenstown Wine Trail p.224

ZORBING!

Bay of Plenty:	Zorb Rotorua p.139

THE GREENWOOD GUIDE TO
SOUTH AFRICA
WITH MOZAMBIQUE AND NAMIBIA
Hand-picked Accommodation

Now in 6th edition. Annual editions published in June each year.

This guide-book contains some 380 B&Bs, guest houses, game lodges, self-catering places and farms. Each place has been personally visited by the authors and chosen for its great charm, character and friendliness.

This book is designed for holiday-makers, both Southern African and from overseas, who want to travel independently, avoid mass tourism and meet friendly, humorous and hospitable people at every turn.

With 8 years' research and 5 previous editions already under our belt, and rigorous annual updates ensuring the standard goes up year by year, this has now become the flagship GG title.

The guide now includes Namibia (40 places) with a small section covering Mozambique, Botswana, Zambia and Zimbabwe.

SOUTH AFRICAN HIGHLIGHTS
Hand-picked Things to Do and Places to Eat

This is our latest addition to the Greenwood Guides series, a separate companion book for our accommodation guide (above). It contains some 550 entries covering restaurants, wineries, cafés, tour guides, outdoor activities (bird-watching, golf, garden visits, walks, whale-watching etc), things to do with your kids, culture and history and a host of miscellaneous others that do not fit easily into any category. These entries have been whittled down from thousands of possibilities and have all been tried, tested and come highly recommended.

The two books, Greenwood Guides to South African Highlights (i.e. this book) and the accommodation guide are designed to be used in tandem.

The Greenwood Guides also cover Australia. This guide is now an online title only. See www.greenwoodguides.com.

Order form

	copy(ies)	price (each)	subtotal
greenwood guides: south africa highlights Hand-picked things to do and places to eat (First edition)		£13.95	
the greenwood guide to south africa Hand-picked accommodation (SIXTH EDITION)		£13.95	
the greenwood guide to new zealand Hand-picked accommodation (FIFTH EDITION)		£13.95	

post and packing costs

£2 per order in the UK, NZ or South Africa
£3 per order within Europe   Total
£4 per order elsewhere

Name ....

Address to send the book to ....

....

....

Payment is by UK sterling cheque made out to 'Greenwood Guides Ltd'

or by VISA/Mastercard (only)

Card number

Expiry date

CCV number

Please send this coupon to:
12 Avalon Rd, Fulham, London, SW6 2EX, UK

picture credits

Greenwood Guides would like to thank the following for their kind permission to reproduce their photographs (t = top, b = bottom, c = centre, l = left, r = right).North Island Accommodation Intro page: Charlotte Turner South Island Accommodation Intro page: Fox/Franz Josef Heli-services. **North Island** main picture: Salt Air pp.94-95. Northland main picture - Charlotte Turner p.98, Pakiri Beach Horse Rides p.100 b, Ransom Wines p.101 b, Bush 'n' Bikes Adventure Co p.102 bl, Dive! Tutukaka p.102 bc, Culture North p.102 br, Pure Tastes p.103 bl, Bush'n'Bikes Adventure Co p.103 bc, Earl Grey Fishing Charters p.103 br, Salt Air p.105 ,Fernz Eco Tours p.107 bl, Going Kayaking p.107 bc, Kerikeri's Historic Stone Store p.107 br, Kerikeri Art and Craft Trail p.109 bl, Jerusalem Café p.109 bc, Salt Air p.109 br, Gumdigger's Park p.111 bl, Dive! Tutukaka p.111 bc, Carington Golf Resort p.111 br. Auckland main picture: Charlotte Turner p.112, Revive! P114 bl, Nikau Cave p.114 bc, The National Maritime Museum p.114 br, Sahaa p.117 bl, Charlotte Turner p.117 bc & br, Ananda Tours p.119 ,Lopdell House p.120, Nikau Cave p.121, Coromandel main picture: Chris Ogilvie p.122, Chris Ogilvie, Waiau Waterworks p.123, p124 bl, bc & br, p.125 bl, The Peppertree Restaurant p.125 bc, Chirs Ogilvie p125 br & p126 bl, The Fireplace p.126 bc, Ohinemuri Estate Winery p.126 br, Tourism Coromandel p127. Waikato and King Country main picture: Vicky Norman p.128, Spellbound p.129 bc & p.146 b, Absolute Adventures p.129 bl & br , Willowbank p.130, Absolute Adventures p.132, Vicky Norman p.133. Bay of Plenty main picture: Tina Hillier p.134. Tajo Ostrich Farm p.135, PeeJays White Island p.136 & p.139 bl, Sirocco's Café and Restaurant p.137 bl, Slowfish p.137 bc, Bistro 1284 p.137 br, Tina Hillier p.138, Zorb Rotorua p.139 t, Agrodome p.139 bc, Tina Hillier p.139 br, Rotorua Museum p.140 bl, Raftabout p.140 bc, Ohope Golf Club p.140 br, Tamatekapua p.141 t, Charlotte Turner p.141 c, Agrodome p.141 bl, The Mission House p.141 bc, Tajo Ostrich Farm p.141 br. Central Plateau main picture: Tina Hillier p.142, Whirinaki Rainforest Guided Walks p.143 b & p.145 b, Tina Hillier p.144. East Coast main picture: Charlotte Turner p.146, Dive Tatapouri p.147 bl, Vicky Norman p.147 bc, br & p.147. Hawke's Bay main picture: Charlotte Turner p.149, Woolshed Art p.152 bl, Gannet Beach Adventures p.152 bc, Vicky Norman p.152 br, Te Awa Winery p.155 bl, Ngatarawa Winery p.155 br. Wairarapa main picture: Martinborough Vineyard p.156, Coney Wines Ltd. p.157 bl, Martinborough Vineyard p.157 bc, Charlotte Turner p.157 br, Vicky Norman p.158. Wellington main picture: Charlotte Turner p.159, Stephan's p.160 bl, Logan Brown p.160 bc, Matterhorn p.160 br, Museum of Wellington p.163 bl & br, Te Papa Museum p.165 bl, Staglands Wildlife Reserve p.165 bc, Southward Car Museum p.165 br. Wanganui and Manawatu main picture: River Valley Adventures p.166, River Valley p.167 bl & p.169, Hansen's Café p.167 bc, New Zealand Rugby Museum p.171 bl, Ruahine Adventures p.171 bc, John Vickers' Architecture Tours p.171 br. Taranaki main picture: Charlotte Turner p.172. **South Island** main picture: Balloon Advenutures – Up Up and Away pp.176 – 177. Nelson Main picture: Charlotte Turner p.180, Monza Gallery p.181 bl, The Naked Possum! P.181 bc & br, Mapua Adventures p182 & p.184 tl, The Sea Kayak Adventure Company p.183 bl & br, Hopgoods Restaurant and Bar p.184 bc, The Boatshed Café p.184 br, The Nelson Provincial Museum p.186 & p.187, Ultimate descents p.188 bl, World of WearableArt and Classic Car Museum p.188 bc & br. Marlborough main picture: Vicky Norman p.189, Gibb's Vineyard Restaurant p.190 bl, Grove Mill Winery p.190 bc, Herzog Winery and Restaurant p.190 br, Steve Gibbons, Wilderness Guides p.192, Wine by Bike Tours p.93 bl, Marlborough Sounds Adventure Co p.193 bc, The Mussel Pot p,193 br, Marlborough Travel, Greenshell Mussel Cruise p.194. Canterbury main picture: Vicky Norman p.195. Tina Hillier p.196, Akaroa Dolphins p.198, Dolphin Experience p.199 bl, International Antarctic Centre p.199 bc, The Giant's House p.199 br, Akaroa Fox Sail p.200, The Banks Peninsula Track p.201 bl, Suky Thompson, Akaroa Guided Walks p.201 bc, Okains Bay Museum p.201 br, Horse Connection NZ p.203 bl, C'est La Vie p.203 bc, Simo's Moroccan Restaurant p.203 br, Pegasus Bay Winery p.204 bl. The Curator's House p.204 bc, Graeme Williams Guiding p.204 br, Up Up and Away Ballooning p.205, Chirstchurch Bike Tours p.206 br, Tranz Scenic Railways p.206 bc, Willowbank Wildlife Reserve p.206 br, Charlotte Turner p.207, Tina Hillier p. 208, Pohatu Penguin Habitat p.209, Hapuku Lodge Restaurant p.210 bl. Tina Hillier p.210 bc, French Farm Winery p.210 br, Hanmer Springs Thermal Pools and Spa p.211, Charlotte Turner p.213, Kaikoura Coastal Track p.215. Otago main picture: Charlotte Turner p.216. Otago: Charlotte Turner p.217, Wild South p.219, Larnach Castle p.220, Dux de Lux p.221 bl, Mediterranean Market p.221 bc, Olveston p.221 br, The Secrets of Bungy Tour p.223, Wine Tastes p.225 bl, Amisfield p.225 bc, The Winehouse and Kitchen p.225 br, Dart Stables p.226 bl, Queenstown Guided Walks p.226 bc, Air Milford p.226 br, Adventure Junkies p.227, The Postmaster's House Restaurant p.228 bl, Dublin Bay Pottery p.228 bc, Dart Wilderness Jet p.228 br, Te Tawara p.229 bl, Missy's Kitchen p.229 bc, Café Fe p.229 br. Frogz p231 bl, Southern Alps Air p.231 bc, Puzzling World p.231 br. Southland main picture: Trips 'n' Tramps p.232, Trips 'n' Tramps p.234, Fiordland Ecology Holidays p.236 bl, Ruggedy Range p.236 bc, Ulva's Guided Walks p.236 br, Tina Hillier p.237, Doubtful Sound Adventure Kayak and Cruises p.238 bl, Redcliff Café p.238 bc, Ruggedy Range p.238 br. A stewart robin, Ruggedy Range p.239. West Coast main picture: Fox/Franz Josef Heli-services p.240, Ian Smith p.241 & p.245, Charleston Underworld Adventures p.242 bl, Tamati Nature Tours p.242 bc & p.243 bl, Glacier Valley Eco-tours p.242 br, White Heron Sanctuary Tours p.243 bc, Christian Heeb, Okarito Nature Tours p.243 br, Mt. Cook Ski Planes p.244. Franz Josef Glacier Guides p.246. **Jacket** image courtesy of Up Up and Away Balloon Adventures, Christchurch. Small photos on the front of the cover from the left courtesy of the following: Gibbs Restaurant, Hahei Oceanfront, Whare Ora, Simo's Moroccan Restaurant and Herzog Winery and Restaurant. Smaill photos on the back of the cover from the left courtesy of the following: Hahei Oceanfront, Hapuku Lodge & Tree Houses and Doubtful Sound Adventure Kayak and Cruises. We have made every effort to ensure that all the images that we have used have been properly credited. Many thanks to all those who have provided them. Apologies if any errors have slipped through the net.